TOMORROW'S TANGLE

"THAT'S MY LIFE,—TO WORK IN WILD PLACES WITH MEN"

TOMORROW'S TANGLE

BY
GERALDINE BONNER

ILLUSTRATIONS BY
ARTHUR I. KELLAR

WILDSIDE PRESS

Copyright 1903
The Bobbs-Merrill Company

October

PRESS OF
BRAUNWORTH & CO.
BOOKBINDERS AND PRINTERS
BROOKLYN, N. Y.

TOMORROW'S TANGLE

CONTENTS

PROLOGUE

CHAPTER		PAGE
I	THE DESERT	1
II	STRIKING A BARGAIN	7
III	HE RIDES AWAY	28
IV	THE ENCHANTED WINTER	50

MARIPOSA LILY

I	HIS SPLENDID DAUGHTER	71
II	THE MILLIONAIRE	86
III	RETROSPECT	100
IV	A GALA NIGHT	119
V	TRIAL FLIGHTS	130
VI	THE VISION AND THE DREAM	147
VII	THE REVELATION	157
VIII	ITS EFFECT	172
IX	HOW COULD HE	181
X	THE PALE HORSE	194
XI	BREAKS IN THE RAIN	214
XII	DRIFT AND CROSSCUT	229
XIII	THE SEED OF BANQUO	245
XIV	VAIN PLEADINGS	260
XV	THROUGH A GLASS DARKLY	276
XVI	REBELLIOUS HEARTS	294
XVII	FRIEND AND BROTHER	311
XVIII	WITH ME TO HELP	331

CONTENTS

CHAPTER		PAGE
XIX	NOT MADE IN HEAVEN	350
XX	THE WOMAN TALKS	366
XXI	THE MEETING IN THE RAIN	382
XXII	A NIGHT'S WORK	398
XXIII	THE LOST VOICE	410
XXIV	A BROKEN TOOL	426
XXV	HAVE YOU COME AT LAST	435

EPILOGUE

I	THE PRIMA DONNA	451

PROLOGUE

TOMORROW'S TANGLE

CHAPTER I

THE DESERT

"To every man a damsel or two."
—JUDGES.

The vast, gray expanse of the desert lay still as a picture in the heat of the early afternoon. The silence of waste places held it. It was gaunt and sterile, clad with a drab growth of sage, flat as a table, and with the white scurf of the alkali breaking through its parched skin. It was the earth, lean, sapless, and marked with disease. A chain of purple hills looked down on its dead level, over which a wagon road passed like a scar across a haggard face. From the brazen arch of the sky heat poured down and was thrown back from the scorched surface of the land. It was August in the Utah Desert in the early fifties.

In the silence and deadness of the scene there was one point of life. The canvas top of an emigrant wagon made a white spot on the monotone of gray. At noon there had been but one shadow in the desert and this was that beneath the wagon which was stationary in the road. Now the sun was declining from the zenith and the shadow was broadening; first a mere edge, then a substantial margin of shade.

In it two women were crouched watching a child that lay gasping. Some distance away beside his two horses, a man sat on the ground, his hat over his eyes.

One of the thousand tragedies the desert had seen was being enacted. Crushed between that dead indifference of earth and sky, its participators seemed to feel the hopelessness of movement or plaint and sat dumb, all but the child, who was dying with that solemn aloofness to surroundings, of which only those who are passing know the secret. His loud breathing sounded like a defiance in the silence of that savagely unsympathizing nature. The man, the women, the horses, were like part of the picture in their mute immobility, only the dying child dared defy it.

He was a pretty boy of three, and had succumbed to one of the slight, juvenile ailments that during the rigors of the overland march developed tragic powers of death. His mother sat beside him staring at him. She was nineteen years of age and had been married four years before to the man who sat in the shadow of the horses. She looked forty, tanned, haggard, half clad. Dazed by hardship and the blow that had just fallen, she had the air of a stupefied animal. She said nothing and made no attempt to alleviate the sufferings of her first-born.

The other woman was some ten years older, and was a buxom, handsome creature, large-framed, capable, stalwart—a woman built for struggles and endurance—the mate of the pioneer. She, too, was the wife of the man who sat by the horses. He was of the Mormon faith, which he had joined a year before for the purpose of marrying her.

THE DESERT

The sun sloped its burning course across the pale sky. The edges of the desert shimmered through veils of heat. Far on the horizon the mirage of a blue lake, with little waves creeping up a crescent of sand, painted itself on the quivering air. The shadow of the wagon stealthily advanced. Suddenly the child moved, drew a fluttering breath or two, and died. The two women leaned forward, the mother helplessly; the other, with a certain prompt decision that marked all her movements, felt of the pulse and heart.

"It's all over, Lucy," she said bruskly, but not unkindly; "I guess you'd better get into the wagon; Jake and I'll do everything."

The girl rose slowly like a person accustomed to obey, moved to the back of the wagon, and climbed in.

The man, who had seen this sudden flutter of activity, pushed back his hat and looked at his wives, but did not move or speak. The second wife covered the dead child with her apron, and approached him.

"He's dead," she said.

"Oh!" he answered.

"We must bury him," was her next remark.

"Well, all right," he assented.

He went to the wagon and detached from beneath it a spade. Then he walked a few rods away and, clearing a space in the sage, began to dig. The woman prepared the child for burial. The silence that had been disturbed resettled, broken at intervals by the thud of the spade. The heat began to lessen and a still serenity to possess the barren landscape. The desert had received its tribute and was appeased.

The rites of the burial were nearly completed, when

a sound from the wagon attracted the attention of the man and the woman. They stopped, listened and exchanged a glance of alarmed intelligence. The woman walked to the wagon rapidly, and exchanged a few remarks with the other wife. Her voice came to the man low and broken. He did not hear what she said, but he thought he knew the purport of her words. As he shoveled the earth into the grave his brow was contracted. He looked angrily harassed. The second wife came toward him, her sunburnt face set in an expression of frowning anxiety.

"Yes," she said, in answer to his look, "she feels very bad. We got to stop here. We can't go on now."

He made no answer, but went on building up the mound over the grave. He was younger by a year or two than the woman with whom he spoke, but it was easy to be seen that of her, as of all pertaining to him, he was absolute master. She watched him for a moment as if waiting for an order, then, receiving none, said:

"I'd better go back to her. I wish a train'd come by with a doctor. She ain't got much strength."

He vouchsafed no answer, and she returned to the wagon, and this time climbed in.

He continued to build up and shape the mound with sedulous and evidently absent-minded care. The sweat poured off his forehead and his bare, brown throat and breast. He was a lean but powerful man, worn away by the journey to bone and muscle, but of an iron fiber. He had no patience with those who hampered his forward march by sickness or feebleness.

When he had finished the mound the sun was declin-

THE DESERT

ing toward the tops of the distant mountains. The first color of its setting was inflaming the sky and painting the desert in tones of strange, hot brilliancy. The vast, grim expanse took on a tropical aspect. Against the lurid background the chain of hills turned a transparent amethyst, and the livid earth, with its leprous eruption, was transformed into a pale lilac-blue. Presently the thin, clear red of the sunset was pricked by a white star-point. And in the midst of this vivid blending of limpid primary colors, the fire the man had kindled sent a fine line of smoke straight up into the air.

The second wife came out of the wagon to help him get the supper and to eat hers. They talked a little in low voices as they ate, drawn away from the heat of the fire. The man showed symptoms of fatigue; but the powerful woman was unconquered in her stubborn, splendid vigor. When she had left him, he lay down on the sand with his face on his arm and was soon asleep. The sounds of dole that came from the wagon did not wake him, nor disturb the deep dreamlessness of his exhausted rest. The night was half spent, when he was wakened by the woman shaking his shoulder. He looked up at her stupidly for a minute, seeing her head against the deep blue sky with its large white stars.

"It's over. It's a little girl. But Lucy's pretty bad."

He sat up, fully awake now, and in the stillness of the night heard the cat-like mew of the new-born. The canvas arch of the wagon glowed with a fiery effect from the lighted lanterns within.

"Is she dying?" he said hurriedly.

"No—not's bad as that. But she's terribly low. We'll have to stay here with her till she pulls up some. We can't move on with her this way."

He rose and, going to the wagon, looked in through the opened flap. His wife was lying with her eyes closed, waxen pale in the smoky lantern-light. The sight of her shocked him into a sudden spasm of feeling. She had been a fresh and pretty girl of fifteen when he had married her, four years before at St. Louis. He wondered if her father, who had given her to him then, would have known her now. In an excess of careless pity he laid his hand on her and said:

"Well, Lucy, how d'ye feel?"

She shrank from his touch and tried to draw a corner of the blanket, on which her head rested, over her face.

He turned away and walked back to the fire, saying to the second wife:

"I guess she'll be able to go on to-morrow. She can stay in the wagon all the time. I don't want to run no risks 'er gittin' caught in the snows on the Sierra. I guess she'll pull herself together all right in a few days. I've seen her worse 'n that."

CHAPTER II

STRIKING A BARGAIN

"How the world is made for each of us!
How all we perceive and know in it
Tends to some moments' product thus,
When a soul declares itself—to wit:
By its fruit, the thing it does!"
—BROWNING.

Where the foothills fold back upon one another in cool, blue shadows, and the tops of the Sierra, brushed with snow, look down on a rugged rampart of mountains falling away to a smiling plain, Dan Moreau and his partner had been working a stream-bed since June. Placerville—still Hangtown—though already past the feverish days of its first youth, was some twenty-five miles to the southwest. A few miles to the south the emigrant trail from Carson crawled over the shoulder of the Sierra. Small trails broke from the parent one and trickled down from the summit, by "the line of least resistance," to the outposts of civilization that were planted here and there on foothill and valley.

The cañon where Moreau and his "pard" were at work was California, virgin and unconquered. The forty-niners had passed it by in their eager rush for fortune. Yet the narrow gulch, that steamed at midday with heated airs and was steeped in the pungent fragrance which California exhales beneath the ardors of the sun, was yielding the two miners a good supply of gold. Their pits had honeycombed the stream's banks far up and down. Now, in September, the water had dwindled to a silver thread, and they had dammed it near the rocker into a miniature lake, into which Fletcher—Moreau's partner—plunged his dipper with untiring regularity, at the same time moving the rocker which filled the hot silence of the cañon with its lazy monotonous rattle.

They had been working with little cessation since early June. The richness of their claim and the prospect that the first snows would put an end to labors and profits had spurred them to unremitting exertion. In a box under Moreau's bunk there were six small buckskin sacks of dust, joint profits of the summer's toil.

Moreau, a muscular, fair-haired giant of a man, was that familiar figure of the early days—the gentleman miner. He was a New Englander of birth and education, who had come to California in the first rush, with a little fortune wherewith to make a great one. Luck had not been with him. This was his first taste of success. Five months before he had picked up a "pard" in Sacramento, and after the careless fashion of the time, when no one sought to inquire too closely into another's antecedents, joined forces with him and spent a wandering spring, prospecting from bar to bar and camp to camp. The casual words of an Indian had directed them to the cañon where now the creak of their rocker filled the hot, drowsy days.

Of Harney Fletcher, Moreau knew nothing. He

had met him in a lodging-house in Sacramento, and the partnership proved to be a successful one. What the New Englander furnished in money, the other made up in practical experience and general handiness. It was Fletcher who had constructed the rocker on an improved model of his own. His had been the directing brain as well as the assisting hand which had built the cabin of logs that surveyed the stream-bed from a knoll above. The last remnants of Moreau's fortune had stocked it well, and there were two good horses in the brush shed behind it.

It was now September, and the leaves of the aspens that grew along the stream-bed were yellowing. But the air was warm and golden with sunshine. Above, in the high places of the Sierra, where the emigrant trail crept along the edges of ravines and crawled up the mighty flank of the wall that shuts the garden of California from the desert beyond, the snow was already deep. Fletcher, who had gone into Hangtown the week before for provisions, had come back full of stories of the swarms of emigrants pouring down the main road and its branching trails, higgledy-piggledy, pell-mell, hungry, gaunt, half clad, in their wild rush to enter the land of promise.

There was no suggestion of winter here. The hot air was steeped in the aromatic scents that the sun draws from the mighty pines which clothe the foothills. At midday the little gulley where the men worked was heavy with them. All about them was strangely silent. The pines rising rank on rank stirred to no passing breezes. There was no bird note, and the stream had shrunk so that its spring-time song had become a whisper. Heat and silence held the long days, when the red dust lay motionless on the trail above, and the noise made by the rocker sounded strangely intrusive and loud in the enchanted stillness that held the landscape.

On an afternoon like this the men were working in the stream-bed—Moreau in the pit, Fletcher at his place by the rocker. There was no conversation between them. The picture-like dumbness of their surroundings seemed to have communicated itself to them. Far above, glittering against the blue, the white peaks of the Sierra looked down on them from remote, aërial heights. The tiny thread of water gleamed in its wide, unoccupied bed. Save the men, the only moving thing in sight was a hawk that hung poised in the sky above, its winged shadow floating forward and pausing on the slopes of the gulch.

Into this spellbound silence a sound suddenly broke—a sound unexpected and unwished for—that of a human voice. It was a man's, harsh and loud, evidently addressing cattle. With it came the creak of wheels. The two partners listened, amazed and irresolute. The trail that passed their cabin was an almost unknown offshoot from the main highway. Then, the sounds growing clearer, they scrambled up the bank. Coming down the road they saw the curved top of a prairie schooner that formed a background for the forms of two skeleton horses, beside which walked a man who urged them on with shouts and blows. Wagon and horses were enveloped in a cloud of red dust.

At the moment that the miners saw this unwelcome

sight, one of the wretched beasts stumbled, and pitching forward, fell with what sounded like a human groan. The man, with an oath, went to it and gave it a kick. But it was too far spent to rally, and settling on its side, lay gasping. A woman, stout and sunburned, ran round from the back of the cart, with a face of angry consternation. As Moreau approached, he heard her say to the man who, with oaths and blows, was attempting to drag the horse to its feet:

"Oh, it ain't no use doing that. Don't you see it's dying?"

Moreau saw that she was right. The animal was in its death throes. As he came up he said, without preliminaries:

"Take off its harness, the poor brute's done for," and began to unbuckle the rags of harness which held it to the wagon.

The man and woman turned, startled, and saw him. Looking back they saw Fletcher, who was coming slowly, and evidently not very willingly, forward. The sight of the exhausted pioneers was a too familiar one to interest him. The dying horse claimed a lazy cast of his indifferent eye. Moreau and the man loosed the harness, lifted the pole, and let the creature lie free from encumbrance. The other horse, freed, too, stood drooping, too spent to move from where it had stopped. If other testimony were needed of the terrible journey they were ending, one saw it in the gaunt face of the man, scorched by sun, seamed with lines, with a fringe of ragged beard, and long locks of unkempt hair hanging from beneath his miserable hat.

This stoppage of his journey with the promised land in sight seemed to exasperate him to a point where he evidently feared to speak. With eyes full of savage despair he stood looking at the horse. Both he and the woman seemed so overpowered by the calamity that they had no attention to give to the two strangers, but stood side by side, staring morosely at the animal.

"What'll we do?" she said hopelessly. "Spotty," indicating the other horse, "ain't no use alone."

Moreau spoke up encouragingly.

"Why don't you leave the wagon and the other horse here? You can walk into Hangtown by easy stages. The Porter ranch is only twelve miles from here and you can stay there all night. The poor beast can't do much more, and we'll feed it and take care of your other things while you're gone."

"Oh, damn it, we can't!" said the man furiously.

As if in explanation of this remark, a woman suddenly appeared at the open front of the wagon. She had evidently been lying within it, and had not risen until now.

When Moreau looked at her he experienced a violent thrill of pity, that the evident sufferings of the others had not evoked. He was a man of a deeply tender and sympathetic nature toward all that was helpless and weak. As his glance met the face of this woman, he thought she was the most piteous object he had ever seen.

"You'd better come into the cabin," he said, "and see what you can do. You can't go on now, and you look pretty well used up."

The man gave a grunt of assent, and taking the other horse by the head began to lead it toward the cabin, being noticeably careful to steer it out of the way of all stumbling-blocks. The woman in the sunbonnet called to her companion in the wagon:

"Come, Lucy, get a move on! We're going to stop and rest."

Thus addressed, the woman moved to the back of the cart, drew the flap aside and slipped out. She came behind the others, and Moreau, looking back, saw that she walked slowly, as if feeble, or in pain.

Advancing to the sunbonneted figure in front of him he said, with a backward jerk of his head: "What's the matter with her? Is she sick?"

The woman gave an indifferent glance backward. Like the man, she seemed completely preoccupied by their disaster.

"Not now," she answered, "but she has been. But good Lord!"—with a sudden burst of angry bitterness—"women like her ain't meant to take them sort of journeys. If it weren't for her, Jake and I could go on all right."

She relapsed into silence as the cabin revealed itself through the trees. It appeared to interest her, and she went to the door and looked in.

It was the typical miner's cabin of the period, consisting of a single room with two bunks. Opposite the doorway was the wide-mouthed chimney, a slab of rock before it doing duty as hearthstone. There was an armchair formed of a barrel, cushioned with red flannel and mounted on rockers. Moreau's bunk was covered with a miner's blanket, and the ineradicable habits of the gentleman spoke in the very simple but sufficient toilet accessories that stood on a shelf under a tiny square of looking-glass. Over the roof a great pine spread its boughs, and in passing through these the slightest breaths of air made soft eolian murmurings. To the pioneers, the wild, rough place looked the ideal of comfort and luxury.

A small spring bubbled up near the roots of the pine and trickled across the space in front of the cabin. To this, by common consent, the party made its way. The exhausted horse plunged its nose in the cool current and drank and snorted and drank again. The elder woman knelt down and laved her face and neck and even the top of her head in the water. The man stood looking with a moody eye at his broken animal, and joined by Fletcher, they talked over its condition. The miner, versed in this as in all practical matters, deemed the beast incapacitated for journeys of any length for some time to come. Both animals had been driven to the limit of their strength.

The pioneer asserted:

"I had to get acrost before the snows blocked us, and they're heavy up there now," with a nod of his head toward the mountains above; "then I wanted to get down into the settlements as soon's I could. I knew there weren't two more days work in 'em, but I calk'lated they'd get me in. After that it didn't matter."

"The only thing for you to do is to walk into Hangtown, buy a mule there, and come back."

The man made a despairing gesture.

"How the hell can I, with her?" he said, indicating the younger woman.

Fletcher turned round and surveyed her with a cold, exploring eye where she had sunk down on the roots of the pine, with her back against its trunk.

"She looks pretty well tuckered out," he said. "Your wife?"

"Yes."

"And the other one's your sister?" he continued with glib curiosity.

"She's my wife, too."

The inquirer, who was used to such plurality on the part of the Utah emigrants, gave a whistle and said:

"Mormons, eh?"

The man nodded.

Meantime Moreau had entered the cabin to get some food and drink to offer the sick woman. In a few moments he reappeared carrying a tin cup containing whisky diluted with water from the spring, and approached the woman sitting by the tree trunk. Her eyes were closed and she presented a deathlike appearance. The shawl she had worn round her shoulders had fallen back and disclosed a small bundle that she held with a loose carefulness. The man noticed the way her arms were disposed about it and wondered. Coming to a standstill before her, he said:

"I've brought you something that'll brace you up. Would you like to try it?"

She raised her lids and looked at him, and then at the cup. As he met her glance he noticed that her eyes were a clear brown like a dog's, and for the first time he realized that she might be young. She stretched out her hand obediently and taking the cup drank a little, then silently gave it back.

"You've had a pretty rough time I guess," he said, holding the cup which he intended to give her again in a minute.

She nodded. Then suddenly the tears began to well out of her eyes, quantities of tears that ran in a flood over her cheeks. She did not sob or attempt to hide her face, but leaning her head against the tree, let the tears flow as though lost to everything but her sense of misery.

"Oh, poor thing! poor thing!" he exclaimed in a burst of sympathy, "you're half dead. Here take some more of this," and he pressed the cup into her hand, not knowing what else to do for her.

She took it, and then, through the tears, he saw her cast a look of furtive alarm toward her husband. She was within his line of vision and tried to shift herself behind Moreau.

With a sensation of angry disgust he understood that she feared this unkempt and haggard creature to whom she belonged. He moved so that he sheltered her and watched her try to drink again. But her tears blinded her and she handed the cup back with a shaking hand.

"It's been too much," she gasped. "If I could only have died! My boy did. Out there on them awful plains where there ain't a tree and it's hot like a furnace. And they buried him there—Bessie and he."

"Bessie and he?" he repeated vaguely, his pity entirely preoccupying his mind for the moment.

STRIKING A BARGAIN 17

"Yes, Bessie,—the second wife. I'm the first."

"Oh," he said, comprehending, "you're from Utah?"

"Not me," she answered quickly, "I'm from Indiana. I'm no Mormon. He wasn't neither till he married Bessie. He wanted her and he did it."

Here she was suddenly interrupted by a weak whining cry from the bundle that one arm still curved about. She bent her head and drew back the covering, and Moreau saw a strange wizened face and a tiny, claw-like hand feeling feebly about. He had never seen a very young infant before and it seemed to him a weirdly hideous thing.

"Is it yours?" he said, amazed.

"Yes," she answered, "it was born in the desert three weeks ago."

Her tears were dry, and she bent over the feeble thing that squirmed weakly and made small, cat-like noises, with something in her attitude that changed her and made her still a woman who had a life above her miseries.

"Wouldn't you like to go into the cabin?" said the man, feeling suddenly abashed by his ignorance of all pertaining to this infinitesimal bit of life. "You might want to wash it or put it to sleep or give it something to eat. There's a basin and soap and—er—some flour and bacon in there."

The woman responded to the invitation with a slight show of alacrity. She stumbled as she rose, and he took her arm and guided her. At the cabin door he left her and as he passed to the back where the rest of the party had gone, the baby's feeble cry, weak, but insistent, followed him.

The emigrant, Bessie and Fletcher, had repaired to the brush shed where Moreau's horses were stabled and had put the half-dead Spotty under its shelter. Here the exhausted beast had lain down. The trio had then betaken themselves to a bare spot on the shaded slope of the knoll and were eating ship's biscuits and drinking whisky and water from a tin cup, that circulated from hand to hand. As Moreau approached he could hear his partner volubly expatiating on the barrenness of the stream-beds in the vicinity. The stranger was listening to him with a cogitating eye, his seamed, weather-worn face set in an expression of frowning attention. Her hunger appeased, Bessie had curled up on her side, and with her sunbonnet still on, had fallen into a deep, healthy sleep.

Moreau joined them, and listened with mingled surprise and amusement to Fletcher's glib lies. Then, when his partner's fluency was exhausted, he questioned the emigrant on his trip. The man's answers were short and non-committal. He seemed in a morose, savage state at his ill luck, his mind still engrossed by the question of moving on.

"If I'd money," he said, "I'd give you anything you'd ask for them two horses 'er your'n in the shed. But I ain't a thing to give—not a red."

"Your wife, your other wife," said Moreau, "doesn't seem to me fit to go on. She's dead beat."

The man gave an angry snort.

"She's been like that pretty near the whole way," he said. "Everything's been put back because of her."

He relapsed into moody silence and then said suddenly: "We're goin' if she's got to walk."

STRIKING A BARGAIN

Moreau went back to the cabin. They had half killed the woman already; now if they insisted on her walking the wretched creature might collapse altogether. Would they leave her on the mountain roads, he wondered?

He reached the cabin door, knocked and heard her answering "come in." She was sitting on an upturned box beside the bunk on which the baby slept. Her sunbonnet was off, and he noticed that she had bright hair, rippled and thick, and of the same reddish-brown color as her eyes. She had washed away the traces of her tears, but her clothes, hardly sufficient covering for her lean, toil-worn body, were dirty and ragged. No beggar he had ever seen in the distant New England town where he had spent his boyhood, had presented a more miserable appearance. She looked timidly at him and rose from the box, pushing it toward him.

"I put the baby on the bunk," she said apologetically, "but I can hold her."

"Oh, don't disturb her," he said quickly. "It's the only place you could have put her." Then, seeing her standing, he said, "Why don't you sit down?"

She sat charily and evidently ill at ease.

"They've been eating out there," he said, "and I thought you might like something, too. There's some stuff over there in the corner if you'll wait a moment."

He went to the corner where the supplies were stored and rifled them for more ship's biscuit and a wedge of cheese, a delicacy which Fletcher had brought from Hangtown on his last visit, and which he carefully refrained from offering to the hungry emigrants. Coming back with these he drew out another box and spread them on it before her. She looked on in heavy, silent surprise. When he had finished he said:

"Now—fall to. You want food as much as anything."

She made no effort to eat, and he said, disappointed: "Don't you want it? Oh, make a try."

She "made a try," and bit off a piece of cracker, while he again retired to the supply corner for the tin cup and the whisky. He tried to step softly so as not to wake the child, and there was something ludicrous in the sight of this vast, bearded man, with his mighty, half-bared arms and muscular throat, trying to be noiseless, with as much success as one might expect of a bear.

Suddenly, in the midst of her repast, the woman broke down completely; and, with bowed head, she was shaken by a tempest of some violent emotion. It was not like her tears of an hour before, which seemed merely an indication of physical exhaustion. This was an expression of spiritual tumult. Sobs rent her and she rocked back and forth struggling with some fierce paroxysm.

Moreau, cup in hand, gazed at her in distracted helplessness.

"Come now, eat a little," he said coaxingly, not knowing what else to suggest, and then getting no response: "Suppose you lie down on the bunk? Rest is what you want."

"Oh, I can't go on," she groaned. "I can't. How can I? Oh, it's too much! I can't go on."

He was silent before this ill for which he had no

remedy, and she wailed again in the agony of her spirit:

"I can't, I can't. If I could only die! But now there's the baby, and I can't even die."

He got up feeling sick at heart at sight of this hopeless despair. What could he suggest to the unfortunate creature? He felt that anything he could say would be an insult in the face of such a position.

"Oh God, why can't we die?" she groaned—"why can't we die?"

As she said the words the sound of approaching voices came through the open door. Her husband's struck through her agony and froze it. She stiffened and lifted her face full of an animal look of listening. Moreau noticed her blunt and knotted hands, pitiful in their record of toil, as she held them up in the transfixed attitude of strained attention.

"What now?" she said to herself.

The pioneer, Fletcher and Bessie came slowly round the corner of the cabin. Bessie looked sleepily anxious, Fletcher lazily amused. As Moreau stepped out of the doorway toward them he realized that they had come to some decision.

"Well," said the man, "we got to travel."

"You're going on?" said Moreau. "How about the wagon?"

"We're goin' to leave the wagon, and I'll come back for it from Hangtown. It's the only thing to do."

"And the horse?".

"He calk'lates," said Fletcher, "to mount his wife— the peaked one—on the horse and take her along till one or other of 'em drops."

"Take your wife on that horse?" exclaimed Moreau. "Why, it can't go two miles."

"Well, maybe it can't," returned the man with an immovable face.

There was a pause. Moreau was conscious that the woman was standing behind him in the doorway. He could hear her breathing.

"Come on, Lucy," said the husband. "We got to move on sometime."

Here the second wife spoke up:

"I don't see how the horse is goin' to get Lucy twelve miles, and this man says the first place we can stop is twelve miles farther along."

"Don't you begin with your everlasting objections," said the husband, furiously. "Get the horse."

The woman evidently knew the time had passed for trifling and turned away toward the brush shed. Fletcher followed her with a grin. The situation appealed to his sense of humor, and he was curious as to the outcome.

Moreau and the emigrant were left facing each other, with the first wife in the doorway.

"Your wife's not able to go on," said the miner—his manner becoming suddenly authoritative; "no more than your horse is."

"Maybe not," said the other, "but they're both goin' to try."

"But can't you see the horse can't carry her? She certainly can't walk into Hangtown, or even to Porter's Ranch."

"No, I can't see. And how's it come to be your business—what they can do or what they can't?"

"YOUR WIFE'S NOT ABLE TO GO ON, NO MORE THAN YOUR HORSE IS"

"It's any one's business to prevent a woman from being half killed."

"Since you seem to think so much about her, why don't you keep her here yourself?"

The man spoke with a savage sneer, his eyes full of steely defiance.

Before he had realized the full import of his words, burning with rage against the brutal tyrant to whom the wife was of no more moment than the horse, Moreau answered:

"I will—let her stay!"

There was a moment's pause. The emigrant's face, dark with rage, was suddenly lightened by a curiously alert expression of intelligence. He looked at the woman in the background and then at the miner.

"I'm not giving anything away just now," he answered. "When she's well she's of use. But I'll swap her for your two horses."

In the heat of his indignation and disgust Moreau turned and looked at the woman. She was leaning against the door frame, chalk-white, and staring at him. She made no sound, but her dog-like eyes seemed to speak for his mercy more eloquently than her tongue ever could.

"All right," he said quietly. "It's a bargain."

"Done," said the emigrant. "You'll find her a good worker when she pulls herself together. You stay on here, Lucy. Bessie," he sang out, "bring around them horses."

Under the phlegm of his manner there was a sudden expanding heat of shame that he strove to hide. The woman neither stirred nor spoke, and Moreau stood with his back to her, struggling with his passion against the man who had been her owner. The impulse under which he had spoken had full possession of him, and his main feeling was his desire to rid himself of the emigrant and his other wife.

"Here," he said, "go on and tell them that you'll take the horses. Hurry up!"

The man needed no second bidding and made off rapidly round the corner of the cabin.

Moreau and the woman were silent. For the moment he had forgotten her presence, engrossed by the rage that filled his warmly generous nature. Instinctively he followed the man to the angle of the cabin whence he could command the brush shed. The trio were standing there, Fletcher and the woman listening amazed to the emigrant's explanation. Moreau turned back to the cabin and his eye fell on the woman in the doorway.

"Well," he said—trying to speak easily—"you don't mind staying on here for a while, do you? I guess we can make you comfortable."

She made no answer, and after waiting a moment he said:

"When you get stronger I'll be able to find you something to do in Hangtown. You know you couldn't go on, feeling so bad. And this air round here"— with a wave of his hand to the surrounding pines— "will brace you up finely."

She gave a murmured sound of assent, but more than this made no reply. Only her dog-like eyes again seemed to speak. Their miserable look of gratitude made Moreau uncomfortable and he could think of nothing more to say.

The sound of the trio advancing from the shed came as a welcome interruption. They appeared round the corner of the cabin, leading the miner's two powerful and well-fed horses. Evidently the situation had been explained. Fletcher's face was enigmatical. The humorousness of the novel exchange had come a little too close to his own comfort to be quite as full of zest as it had been earlier in the afternoon. He had insisted that the emigrant leave his horse, which the man had no objection to doing. Bessie looked flushed and excited. Moreau thought he detected shame and disapproval under her agitated demeanor. But to her work was a matter of second nature. She put the horses to the tongue of the wagon and buckled the rags of harness together before she turned for a last word to her companion. This was characteristically brief:

"So long, Lucy," she said, "let's see the baby again."

It was shown her and she kissed it on the forehead with some tenderness. Then she climbed on the wheel of the wagon and took from the interior a bundle tied up in printed calico and laid it on the ground. It contained all the personal belongings and wardrobe of the first wife. There were a few murmured sentences between them and then she turned to ascend to her seat. But before she had fairly mounted a sudden impulse seized her and whirled her back to give Lucy a good-by kiss.

There was more feeling in this action than in anything that had passed between the trio during the afternoon. The two wives had been women who had mutually suffered. There were tears in Bessie's eyes as she climbed to her place. The husband never turned his head in the direction of his first wife. But as he took the reins and prepared to start the team, he called:

"Good by, Lucy."

He clucked at the horses, and the wagon moved forward amid a stir of red dust. The woman on the front seat drew her sunbonnet over her face. The man beside her looked neither to the right nor the left, but stared out over his newly-acquired team with an impassively set visage. His long whip curled out with a hiss, the spirited animals gave a forward bound, and the wagon went clattering and jolting down the trail.

Moreau stood watching its canvas arch go swinging downward under the dark boughs of the pines and the flickering foliage of the aspens. He watched until a bend in the road hid it. Then he turned toward the cabin. Fletcher was standing behind him, surveying him with a cold and sardonic eye:

"Well, you've done it!"

"I guess I have."

"What the devil are you going to do with her?"

"Don't know."

"And the horses gone; nothin' but that busted cayuse left!"

They stood looking at each other, Fletcher angrily incredulous, Moreau smilingly deprecating and apologetic.

As they stood thus, neither knowing what to say,

the emigrant's wife appeared at the doorway of the cabin.

"I'll get your supper now if it's the right time," she said timidly.

CHAPTER III

HE RIDES AWAY

"Alas, my Lord, my life is not a thing
Worthy your noble thoughts! 'Tis not a life,
'Tis but a piece of childhood thrown away."
—BEAUMONT AND FLETCHER.

That night the two miners rolled themselves in their blankets and lay down on the expanse of slippery grass under the pine. Moreau did not sleep soon. The day's incidents were the first interruption to the monotony of their uneventful summer.

Now, the strong man, lying on his back, looking at the large white stars between the pine boughs, thought of what he had done with perplexity, but without regret. In the still peacefulness of the night he turned over in his mind what he should do when the woman grew stronger. Women were rare in the mining districts, and he knew that the emigrant wife could earn high wages as a servant either in Hangtown or the growing metropolis of Sacramento. The child might hamper her, but he could help her to take care of the child until she got fairly on her feet. He had nothing much to do with his "dust." Strong and young and in California, that always meant money enough.

So he thought, pushing uneasiness from his mind.

Turning on his hard bed he could see the dark bulk of the cabin with a glint of starlight on its window. Above, the black boughs of the pine made a network against the sky sown with stars of an extraordinary size and luster. He could hear the river sleepily murmuring to itself. Once, far off, in the higher mountains, the shrill, weird cry of a California lion tore the silence. He rose on his elbow, looking toward the cabin. The sound was a terrifying one, and he was prepared to see the woman come out, frightened, and had the words of reassurance ready to call to her. But there was no movement from the little hut. She was evidently wrapped in the sleep of utter fatigue.

In the morning he was down at a basin scooped in the stream bed making a hasty toilet, when Fletcher, sleepy-eyed and yawning, came slipping over the bank.

"What are we goin' to do for breakfast?" he said. "Is that purchase o' yourn goin' to git it? She'd oughter do something to show she's worth the two best horses this side er Hangtown."

Moreau, with his hair and beard bedewed with his ducking, was about to answer when a sound from above attracted them.

Lucy was standing on the bank. In the clear morning light she looked white and pinched. Her wretched clothes of yesterday, a calico sack and skirt, were augmented by a clean apron of blue check. Her skirt was short and showed her feet in a pair of rusty shoes that were so large they might have been her husband's.

"Are you comin' to breakfast?" she said; "it's ready." Then she disappeared. The men looked at each other and Moreau shook the drops from his beard and began to try to pat his hair into order. The civilizing influence of woman—even such an unlovely woman as the emigrant's wife—was beginning its work.

Lucy had evidently been busy. The litter that had disfigured the ground in front of the cabin was cleared away. Through the open door and window a current of resinous mountain air passed which counteracted the effect of the fire. Nevertheless she had evidently feared its heat would be oppressive, and had brought two of the boxes to the rude bench outside the doorway, and on these the breakfast was laid. It was of the simplest—fried bacon, coffee and hot biscuits—but the scent of these, hot and appetizing, was sweet in the nostrils of the hungry men.

Sitting on the bench, they fell to and were not disappointed. The emigrant's wife had evidently great skill in the preparation of the simple food of the pioneer. With the scanty means at her hand she had concocted a meal that to the men, used to their own primitive cooking, seemed the most toothsome they had eaten since they left San Francisco.

As she retired into the cabin, Fletcher—his mouth full of biscuit—said:

"Well, she can cook anyway. I wonder how she gets her biscuits so all-fired light? They ain't all saleratus, neither."

Here she reappeared, carrying the coffee-pot, and, leaning over Fletcher's shoulder, prepared to refill his tin cup.

"Put it down on the table. He can do it himself," commanded Moreau suddenly.

She set it down instantly, with her invariable frightened obedience.

"We're not used to being waited on," he continued. "Now you sit down here,"—he rose from his end of the bench and pointed to it,—"and next thing we want I'll go in and get it. You've had your own breakfast, of course?"

"No—I ain't had mine yet," she answered meekly.

"Well, why ain't you?" he almost shouted. "What d'ye mean by giving us ours first?"

She looked terrified and shrank a little on the bench. Moreau had a dreadful idea that for a moment she was afraid of being struck.

"Here, take this cup," he said, giving her his,—"and this bacon," picking from the pan, which stood in the middle of the table, the choicest pieces, and a biscuit. "There—now eat. I'm done."

She tried to eat, but it was evidently difficult. Her hands, bent and disfigured with work, shook. At intervals she cast a furtive, questioning look at him where he sat on an overturned box, eying her with good-humored interest. As he met the frightened dog-eyes he smiled encouragingly, but she was grave and returned to her breakfast with nervous haste.

As the men descended the bank to the stream-bed, Fletcher said:

"Well, she's some use in the world. That's the first decent meal we've had since we left Sacramento."

"She didn't eat much of it herself," returned his pard as he began the morning's work.

"She is the gol-darnedest lookin' woman I ever seen. Looks as if she'd been fed on shavings. I'll lay ten to one that emigrant cuss she b'longs to has 'most beat the life out er her."

Ascending to the cabin an hour later, Moreau came upon the woman, washing the breakfast dishes in the stream that trickled from the spring. She did not hear him approach, and, watching her, he saw that she was slow and feeble in her movements. The sun spattered down through the pine boughs on her thick, brilliant-colored hair, and on the nape of her neck, where the skin was tanned to a coarse, russet brown.

"What are you doing that for?" he said, coming to a standstill in front of her. "You needn't bother about the pans."

"They'd oughter be cleaned," she answered.

"You don't want to feel," he said, "that you've got to work all the time. I wanted you to rest up a bit. It's a good place to rest here."

She made no answer, drying the tin cups on a piece of flour sack.

"I ain't so awful tired," she said presently in a low voice.

"Well, don't you worry about having everything so clean; they'll do anyway. And the cabin's pretty clean,—isn't it?" he asked, somewhat anxiously.

"Yes—awful clean," she said. Then, after a moment, she continued: "I hadn't oughter have stayed in the cabin. It's your'n. Me and the baby'll be all right in the brush shed with Spotty."

"What nonsense!" retorted Moreau. "Do you suppose I'd let you and that baby stay in the brush shed, the place where the horses have been kept all summer? You're going to keep the cabin, and if there's anything you want—anything that's short, or that you might need for the baby—why, Fletcher'll go to Hangtown and get it. Just say what you want. Not having women around, we're probably short of all sorts of little fixings."

"I don't want nothing," she said with her head down—"I ain't never been so comfortable sence I was married."

"Have you been married long?" he asked, less from curiosity than from the desire to make her talk.

"Four years," she replied; "I was married in St. Louis, just before dad and I was startin' to cross the plains. Dad was taken sick. He was consumpted, and some one tol' him to go to California, so we was goin' to start along with a heap of other folks. We was all waitin' 'round St. Louis for the weather to settle and that's how I met Jake."

"Jake?" said Moreau, interrogatively; "who was Jake?"

"My husband—Jake Shackleton. He was one o' the drivers of the train. He drove McGinnes' teams. He was there in camp with us, and up and asked me, and dad was glad to get any one to take care of me, bein' as he was so consumpted. We was married a week afore the train started. I didn't favor it much, but dad thought it was a good thing. My father was a Methodist preacher, and knowin' as how he couldn't last long, he was powerful glad to get some one to look after me. I was pretty young to be left—just fifteen."

"Fifteen!" echoed Moreau—then piecing together her scant bits of biography—"Then you're only *nineteen* now?"

"That's my age," she said with her laconic dryness.

He looked at her in incredulous amaze. Nineteen! A girl, almost a child! A gush of pity and horror welled up in him, and for the moment he could find no words. She went on, evidently desirous of telling him of herself as in duty bound to her new master.

"Dad died before we got to Salt Lake. Then Jake and I settled there and Willie was born, and for two years it wern't so bad. Jake liked me and was good to me. But he got to know the Mormons and kep' sayin' all the time it weren't no good doin' anything not bein' a Mormon. He said they had no use for him, bein' a Gentile. And then he seen Bessie,—she was a waitress in the Sunset Hotel,—and got powerful set on her. She was a big, strong woman, and could work. Not like me. I couldn't never work except in the house. I was no good for outdoor work. I was always a sort er drag, he said. So he turned Mormon and married Bessie, and she came to live with us." She stopped and began rubbing a pan with a piece of flour sack.

"Don't tell any more if you don't want to," said the man, hearing his voice slightly husky.

"Oh, I don't mind," she answered with her colorless, unemotional intonation; "I couldn't ever come to feel she was his wife, too. I hadn't them notions. My father was a preacher. I hated it all, but I couldn't seem to think of anything else to do. I had to stay. There was no one to go to. Dad was dead and he didn't have no relations. Then we started to come here, and on the way my little boy died. That was all I had, and I didn't care then what happened. And only for the other baby I'd er crep' out er the wagon some night and run away and got lost on them plains. But—"

She stopped and made a gesture of extending her hands outward and then letting them fall at her sides. It was tragic in its complete hopelessness. Of gratitude to Moreau she seemed to have little. She had been so beaten down by misfortune that nothing was left in her but acquiescence. Her very service to him seemed an instinctive thing, the result of rigorous training.

"Well," he said after a pause, "you've had a hard time. But it's over now. Don't you think about it any more. You're going to rest up here, and when you're strong and well again we'll think about something for you to do. Time enough for that then. But you can always get work and high pay in Hangtown or Sacramento. Or if you don't fancy it at any of those places I'll see to it that you go down to San Francisco. Don't bother any more anyhow. You'd about got to the bottom of things and now you're coming up."

She gathered up her pans and said dully: "Thank you, sir."

The cry of the baby struck on her ear and she scrambled to her feet, and without more words turned and walked to the cabin.

At dinner she again made her appearance on the bank and called the two men. Again they were greeted by a meal that was singularly appetizing, considering the limited resources. Obeying Moreau's order, she sat down with them, but ate nothing, at intervals starting to her feet to return to the cabin, then restraining the impulse and sitting rigid and uncomfortable on the upturned box. To wait on the men seemed the only thing she knew how to do, or that gave her ease in the doing.

The child cried once or twice during dinner, and, in the afternoon, working in the pit which was in the stream bed just below the cabin window, Moreau heard it crying again. It seemed a louder and more imperious cry than it had given previously. The miner, whose knowledge of infancy and its ills was of the most limited, wondered if it could be sick.

At sunset, the day's work over, both men mounted the bank, their takings of dust in two tin cups, from which it was transferred to the buckskin sacks in the box under the bunk. Moreau entered the cabin to get the sacks and found Lucy there curled on the end of the bunk where the baby slept. As his great bulk darkened the door she started up, with her invariable frightened look of apology.

"Don't move—don't move," he said, kneeling by her; "I want to get the box under the bunk."

She started up, and being nearer the box than he, thrust her hand under and tried to pull it out. It was heavy with the sacks of dust and required a wrench. She rose from the effort, gave a gasp, and, reeling, fell against him. He caught her in his arms, and as her head fell back against his shoulder saw that she was death-white and unconscious.

HE RIDES AWAY

With terrified care he laid her on Fletcher's bunk, and, seizing a pan of water, sprinkled her face and hands, then tore one of the tin cups off its nail, and, pouring whisky into it, tried to force it between her lips. A little entered her mouth, though most of it ran down her chin. As he stood staring at her, Fletcher appeared in the doorway.

"Hullo!" he said; "what's the matter with her? By gum, but she looks bad!" And then, with a quick and practised hand, he pulled her up to a sitting posture, and, prying her mouth open with a fork, poured some of the whisky down. It revived her quickly. She sat up, felt for her sunbonnet, and then said:

"I hadn't oughter have done that, but it came so quick."

She tried to get up, but Moreau pushed her back.

"Oh, I ain't sick," she said, trying to speak bravely; "I've been took like that before. It's just tiredness. I'm all right now."

She again tried to rise, stood on her feet for a moment, then reeled back on the bunk, with white lips.

"It's such a weakness," she whispered; "such a weakness!"

At this moment the baby woke up, and, lifting up its voice, began a loud, violent wail. The woman looked in terror from one man to the other.

"Oh, my poor baby!" she cried; "what'll I do? Is that one goin' to go, too?"

"The baby's all right," said Moreau. "Don't begin to worry about that. All babies cry, don't they?"

"Oh, my poor baby!" she wailed, unheeding, and

suddenly beginning to wring her hands. "It'll die like Willie. It'll die, too."

"Why should it die? What's the matter with it? It was all right this morning, wasn't it?" he answered, feeling that there were mysteries here he did not grasp.

"It'll die because it don't get nothing to eat," she cried desperately. "I've nothing for it. I'm too sick! I'm too sick! And it'll starve. Oh, my poor baby!"

She burst into the wild, weak tears of exhaustion, her sobs mingling with the now strident yells of the hungry baby.

The two men looked at each other, sheepishly, beginning to understand the situation. The enfeebled condition of the mother made it impossible for her to nourish the child. It was a predicament for which even the resourceful mind of Fletcher had no remedy. He pushed back his cap, and, scratching slowly at the front of his head, looked at his mate with solemn perplexity, while the cabin echoed to sounds of misery unlike any that had ever before resounded within its peaceful walls.

"Can—can—we get anything?" said Moreau at length—"any—any—sort of food, meat, eggs—er—er any sort of stuff for it to eat?"

"Eat?" exclaimed Fletcher scornfully; "how can it eat? It hasn't a tooth."

"How would it do if Fletcher went into Hangtown and brought the doctor?" suggested Moreau, soothingly. "It'll take twenty-four hours, but he's a good doctor."

The woman shook her head.

"A goat," she sobbed, the menace to her offspring having given her a fictitious courage. "If you could get a goat."

"A goat!"

The two men looked at each other, horror-stricken at the magnitude of the suggestion.

"She might as well ask us to get an elephant," muttered Fletcher morosely. "There's not a goat nearer than San Francisco."

"And it would take us two weeks anyway to get one up from there and across the mountains from Sacramento," said Moreau.

"By the time you got it here it'd be the most expensive goat you ever bucked up against," said his partner disdainfully.

"A cow!" exclaimed Moreau. "Say, Lucy, would a cow do?"

"A cow!" came the muffled answer; "oh, it don't need a whole cow."

"But a cow would do? If I could get a cow the baby could be fed on the milk, couldn't it?"

"Oh, yes; it 'ud do first rate."

"Very well, I'll get a cow. Don't you bother any more; I'll have a cow here by to-morrow noon. The baby'll have to hold out till then, for, not having a decent horse, I can't get it here any sooner."

"And where do you calk'late to get a cow?" demanded Fletcher; "cows ain't much more common than goats round these parts."

"On the Porter ranch. It's twelve miles off. I can go in to-night, rest there a bit, and by noon be here with the cow."

"And is that baby goin' to yell like this from now till to-morrow noon? You might's well have a mountain lion tied up in the bunk."

The difficulty was indeed only half solved. The infant's lusty cries were unabated. The miserable mother, with tear-drenched face and quivering chin, sat up in the bunk and tried to rise and go to it, but was restrained by Moreau's hand on her shoulder.

"You stay here and I'll get it," he said, then crossed to the other bunk, and gingerly lifted with his huge, hairy hands the shrieking bundle, from which protruded two tiny, red fists, jerking and clawing about, and carried it to its mother. Her practised hand hushed it for a moment, but its pangs were beyond temporary alleviation, and its cries soon broke forth.

"If I could git up and mix it some flour and water," she said, feebly attempting to rise.

"What's the matter with us doing that?" queried Moreau. "How do you do it? Just give us the proportions and we'll dish it up as if we were born to it."

Under her direction he put flour in one of the dippers, and handed Fletcher a tin cup with the order to fill it with water at the spring. Both men were deeply interested, and Fletcher rushed back from the spring with a dripping cup, as if fearful that the infant would die unless the work of feeding was promptly begun.

"Now go on," said Moreau, armed with the dipper and a tin teaspoon; "what's next?"

"Sugar," she said; "if you put a touch of sugar in it tastes better to them."

"Here, sugar. Hand it over quick. Now, there we are. How do you mix 'em, Lucy?"

She gave the directions, which the men carefully followed, compounding a white, milky-looking liquid. The crucial moment came when they had to feed this to the crimson and convulsively screaming baby.

To forward matters better they moved two boxes to the doorway, where the glow of sunset streamed in, and seated themselves, Fletcher with the dipper and spoon, Moreau with the baby. Both heads were lowered, both faces eagerly earnest when the first spoonful was administered. It was a tense moment till the tip of the spoon was inserted between the infant's lips. Her puckered face took on a look of rather annoyed surprise; she caught at it, and then, with an audible smack, slowly drew in the counterfeit. The men looked at each other with heated triumph.

"Takes it like a little man, doesn't she?" said Moreau proudly.

"She wasn't hungry," said Fletcher. "Oh-h, no! Listen to her smack."

"Here, hold up the dipper. Don't keep her waiting when she's so blamed hungry."

"You're spilling half of it. You're getting it on her clothes."

"Well, she don't want to eat any faster. That's the way she likes to eat—just slowly suck it out of the spoon. Take your time, old girl, even if you don't swallow it all."

"My! don't she take it down nice! Look alive there, it's running outer the corner of her mouth."

"Give us that bit of flour sack behind you. We ought to have put something round her neck."

The baby, its round eyes intent, one small red fist

still fanning the air, sucked noisily at the tip of the spoon. The mother, sitting up on the bunk in the background, watched it with craned neck and jealous eye.

Finally, when the meal was over, it was triumphantly handed back to her, sticky from end to end, but sleepy and satisfied.

A few hours later, in the star-sown darkness of the early night, Moreau started on his twelve-mile walk to the Porter ranch. The next morning, some time before midday, he reappeared, red and perspiring, but proudly leading by a rope a lean and dejected-looking cow.

The problem of the baby's nutriment was now satisfactorily solved. The cow proved eminently fitted for the purpose of its purchase, and though the two miners had several unsuccessful bouts in learning to milk it, the handy Fletcher soon overcame this difficulty, and the stock of the cabin was augmented by fresh milk.

The baby throve upon this nourishment. Its cries no longer disturbed the serenity of the cañon. It slept and ate most of the time, but kindly consented to keep awake in the late afternoon and be gentle and patient when the men charily passed it from hand to hand during the rest before supper. Fletcher regarded it tolerantly as an object of amusement. But Moreau, especially since the feeding episode, had developed a deep, delighted affection for it. Its helplessness appealed to all that was tender in him, and the first faint indications of a tiny formed character were miraculous to his fascinated and wondering observation. He was secretly ashamed of letting the sneeringly indifferent Fletcher guess his sudden attachment, and made foolish excuses to account for the trips to the cabin which frequently interrupted his morning's work in the stream bed.

Lucy's recovery was slow. The collapse from which she suffered was as much mental as physical. The anguish of the last two years had preyed on the bruised spirit as the hardships of the journey had broken the feeble body. No particular form of ailment developed in her, but she lay for days silent and almost motionless on the bunk, too feeble to move or to speak beyond short sentences. The men watched and tended her, Moreau with clumsy solicitude, Fletcher dutifully, but more through fear of his powerful mate than especial interest in Lucy as a woman or a human being.

In his heart he still violently resented Moreau's action in acquiring her and parting with the valuable horses. Had she possessed any of the attractions of the human female, he could have understood and probably condoned. But as she now was, plain, helpless, sick, unable even to cook for them, demanding care which took from their work and lessened their profits, his resentment grew instead of diminishing. Moreau saw nothing of this, for Fletcher had long ago read the simple secrets of that generous but impractical nature, and knew too much to bring down on himself wrath which, once aroused, he felt would be implacable.

At the end of two weeks Lucy began to show signs of improvement. The fragrant air that blew through the cabin, the soothing silence of the foothills, broken only by the drowsy prattle of the river or the sad murmuring of the great pine, began its work of healing. The autumn was late that year. The days were still warm and dreamily brilliant, especially in the little cañon, where the sun drew the aromatic odors from the pines till at midday they exhaled a heavy, pungent fragrance like incense rising to the worship of some sylvan god.

Sometimes now, on warm afternoons, Lucy crept out and sat at the root of the pine where she had found her first place of refuge. There her dulled eyes began to note the beauties that surrounded her, the pines mounting in dark rows on the slopes, the blue distances where the cañon folded on itself, the glimpses of chaste, white summits far above against the blue. Her lungs breathed deep of the revivifying air, clean and untainted as the water in the little spring at her feet. The peace of it all entered her soul. Something in her forbade her to look back on the terrible past. A new life was here, and her youth rose up and whispered that it was not yet dead.

During the period of her illness Moreau had begun to see both himself and the cabin through feminine eyes. Discrepancies revealed themselves. He wanted many things heretofore regarded as luxuries. From the tin cups of the table service to the towels made of ripped flour sacks, his domestic arrangements seemed mean and inadequate. They were all right for two prospectors, but not fitting for a woman and child. Lucy's illness also revealed wants in her equipment that struck him as piteous. Her only boots were the ones he had seen her in on the morning after her arrival. She had no shawl or covering for cold weather. The baby's clothes were a few torn pieces of calico and flannel. Moreau had washed these many times himself, doing them up in an old flour sack, which was attached to an aspen on the stream's bank, and then placed in one of the deepest parts of the current. Here it remained for two days, the percolating water cleansing its contents as no washboard could.

One evening, smoking under the pine, he acquainted Fletcher with a design he had been some days formulating. This was that Fletcher should ride into Hangtown the next day and not only replenish the commissariat, but buy all things needful for Lucy and the baby. Spotty was now also recovered, and, though hardly a mettlesome steed, was at least a useful pack horse. But the numerous list of articles suggested by Moreau would have weighted Spotty to the ground. So Fletcher was commissioned to buy a pack burro, and upon it to bring all needful food stuffs for the cabin and the habiliments for Lucy and the baby.

"She's got no shoes. You want to buy her some shoes, one useful pair and one fancy pair with heels."

"What size do I git? I ain't never bought shoes for a woman before."

This was a poser, and both men cogitated till Moreau suggested leaving it to the shoe dealer, who should be told that Lucy was a woman of average size.

"But her feet ain't," said Fletcher spitefully, never having been able to forgive Lucy her lack of beauty.

"Never mind; you'll have to make a bluff at it. Get the best you can. Then I want a shawl for her. It'll be cold soon, and she's got nothing to keep her warm."

"What kind of a shawl? I don't know no more about shawls than I do about shoes."

"A pink crochet shawl," said Moreau slowly, and with evident sheepish reluctance at having to make this exhibition of unexpected knowledge.

"And what's that? I dunno what crochet is."

"I don't, either"—and then, with desperate courage—"well, anyway, that's what she said she'd like. I asked her yesterday and she said that. You go into the store and ask for it. That'll be enough."

Fletcher grunted.

"And then I want some toys for the kid. Anything you can get that seems the right kind. She's a girl, so you don't want a drum, or soldiers, or guns, or things of that kind. Get a doll if you can, and a musical box, or anything tasty and that's likely to catch a baby's eye."

"Why, she can't hardly see yet. She's like a blind kitten. Lucy told me herself yesterday she were only six weeks old."

"Never you mind. She's a smart kid; knows more now than most babies at six months. You might get a rattle—a nice one with bells; she might fancy that."

"Silver or gold?" sneered Fletcher, whom this conversation was making meditative.

"The best you can get. Don't stint yourself for money; everything of the best. Then clothes for her; she is going to be as well dressed as any baby in California. I take it you'd better go to Mrs. Wingate, at the Eldorado Hotel, and get her to make you out a list; then go to the store and buy the list right down."

"Seems to me you'll want a pack train, not a burro, to carry it all."

"Well, if you can't get everything on Spotty and one burro, buy two. I'll give you a sack of dust and you can spend it all."

Fletcher was silent after this, and as he lay rolled in his blanket that night he looked at the stars for many hours, thinking.

Early in the morning he departed on the now brisk and rejuvenated Spotty. Besides his instructions he carried one of Moreau's buckskin sacks, roughly estimated to contain twelve hundred dollars' worth of dust, and, he told Moreau, one of his own. He was due to return the next morning. With a short word of farewell, he touched Spotty with the single Mexican spur he wore, and darted away down the rough trail. Moreau watched him out of sight.

The day passed as quietly as its predecessors. The main events that marked their course had been the men's clean-up, Lucy's gain in strength and the evidences of increasing intelligence in the child.

To-day Lucy had walked to a point a little distance up the cañon, rested there, and in the afternoon came creeping back with the flush of returning health on her face. It was still there when Moreau ascended from the stream bed with his cup. He had had a good day's work and was joyful, showing the fine yellow grains in the bottom of the rusty tin. Then he noticed her improved appearance and cried:

"Why, you look blooming. A fellow'd think you'd panned a good day's work, too."

To himself he said with a sudden inward wonder:

"She looks almost pretty. And she *is* only nineteen, I believe."

The next morning he awaited the coming of Fletcher with impatience. He had wanted to surprise Lucy, having only told her Fletcher had gone to buy a burro and some supplies. But the morning passed away and he had not returned. Then the afternoon slipped by, and Lucy and Moreau took their supper without him, the latter rather taciturn. The delay wore on his patience. His knowledge of Fletcher was limited. He had seen him drunk once in Sacramento, and he wondered if he had gone on a spree and was now lying senseless somewhere, the contents of the sacks squandered.

When the next morning had passed and Fletcher had still not come, his suspicions strengthened and he began to think uneasily of his dust. One sack full was a good deal to lose, now that he had a woman and child on his hands. Lucy, he could see, was also uneasy. Twice he surprised her standing by the trail, evidently listening. When evening drew in and there were still no signs of him, both were frankly anxious and oppressed. Suddenly, as they sat by the box that answered as dinner table, she said:

"Did he have much dust?"

"Yes—one sack of mine and one of his own. They're equal to about twelve hundred dollars each."

She gave a startled look at him and sat with her mouth a little open, fear and amaze on her face.

"Where's the rest?" she asked.

Moreau indicated the box under the bunk. At the

same moment her suspicion seized him and he pulled it out and threw up the lid. It was empty of all save a few clothes. Every sack was gone.

Moreau shut down the lid quietly, a little pale. He was not a man of quick mind, and he hardly could realize what had happened. It was Lucy's voice that explained it as she said:

"He did it while I was out in the morning. I went up the stream to that pool to wash some things at sunup. He took it then."

CHAPTER IV

THE ENCHANTED WINTER

> "I choose to be yours for my proper part,
> Yours, leave me or take, or mar or make;
> If I acquiesce, why should you be teased
> With the conscience prick and the memory smart?"
> —BROWNING.

Fletcher had gone silently and without leaving a trace, and with him the money. It was a startling situation for Moreau. From comparative affluence he suddenly found himself without a cent or an ounce of dust. This, had he had only himself to look after, would not have affected his free and jovial spirit, but now the woman and the child he had so carelessly come into possession of loomed before him in their true light of a heavy responsibility. Lucy, as far as supporting herself went, was still a long way off from the state of health where that would be possible. And at the thought of sending her forth, even though she were cured of her infirmities, Moreau experienced a sensation of depression. He felt that the cabin would be unbearably lonely when she and the baby were gone.

That night under the pine he turned over the situation in his mind. The conclusion he arrived at was that there was nothing better to be done than stay by

THE ENCHANTED WINTER 51

the stream bed and work it for all it was worth. Lucy would continue to improve in the fine air and the child was thriving. If the snows would hold off till late, as they had done in the open winter of '50, he could amass a fair share of dust before it would be necessary to move Lucy and the baby to the superior accommodations of Hangtown or Sacramento. It was now October. In November one might expect the first snows.

He must do a good deal in the next six weeks. This he started to do. The next day he spent in raising a brush shed against the back of the cabin where the chimney would offer warmth on cold nights. Into this he moved such few belongings as he had retained after Lucy and the baby had taken possession of the cabin. Then the working of the stream bed went on with renewed vigor. The water was low, hardly more than a thread, rendering the washing of the dirt harder labor than during the earlier summer when the watercourses were still full. But he toiled mightily, rejoicing in the splendor of his man's work, not with the same knightly freedom that he felt when he had been that king of men, the miner with his pick on his shoulder and all the world before him, but with the soberer joy of the man into whose life others have entered to lay hold upon it with light, clinging hands.

Against the complete and perfect lonelinesss of his life the woman and child, who had started up from nowhere, stood out as figures of vital significance. They had grown closer to him in that one month's isolation than they would have done in a year of city life. The child became the object of his secret but deep devotion. He had been ashamed to let Fletcher see it. Now that Fletcher was gone, Moreau often stole up from his work in the creek to look at it as it slept in a box by the open door. It was as fresh as a rosebud, its skin clean and satiny, its tiny hands, crumpled, white and pink, like the petals of flowers. The big man leaned on his shovel to watch it adoringly. The miracle of its growth in beauty never lost its wonder for him.

Lucy, too, grew and bloomed in these quiet autumn days. Never talkative, she became less laconic after the departure of Fletcher. She seemed relieved by his absence. Moreau began to understand, as he saw her daily increase in freshness and youthful charm, that she was as young in nature as she was in years. Points of character that were touchingly childish appeared in her. Her casting of all responsibility on him was as absolute as if she had been ten years of age. She obeyed him with trustful obedience and waited on him silently, her eyes always on him to try to read his unexpressed wish. Sometimes he caught these watching eyes and read in them something that vaguely disturbed him.

One day, coming up from the creek for one of his surreptitious views of the baby, he found its cradle empty, and was about to return to his work, when he heard a laugh rising from a small knoll among the aspens. It was a laugh of the most infectious, fresh sweetness, and made Moreau's own lips part. He stole in its direction, and as he advanced it sounded again, rippling deliciously on the crystal air. He brushed through the aspens and came on Lucy and her baby. She was holding it in her lap, one hand on the back of its head. Something had touched its unknown sense of the ludicrous, and its lips were parting in a slow but intensely amused smile over its toothless gums. Each smile was answered by its mother with a run of the laughter Moreau had heard.

He looked at them for a moment, and then, advancing, his foot cracked a dry branch, and Lucy turned. Her face was flushed, her eyes still full of their past merriment, her smiling lips looked a coral red against the whiteness of her small, even teeth. Her sunbonnet was off and her rich hair glowed like copper in the sun. He had never seen her look like this, and stopped, regarding her with a curious, sudden gravity. The thought was in his heart:

"She's only a girl, and—and—almost beautiful."

Lucy looked confused.

"Oh, I was just laughing at the baby," she said apologetically; "she looked so sorter cute smiling that way."

"I never heard you laugh like that before. Why don't you do it oftener?"

She seemed embarrassed and murmured:

"I didn't think you'd like to hear me."

"I think you're sometimes afraid of me," he said; "is that true?"

She bent her face over the baby and said very low:

"I'm afraid as how you might get mad at me. I don't know much and—I'm different, and you've been more good to me than—"

She stopped, her face hidden over the child. Moreau felt a sudden sense of embarrassed discomfort.

"Oh, don't talk that way," he said, hastily, "or I may get mad. That's the sort of talk that annoys me. Laugh and be happy—that's the way I want you to be. Enjoy yourself; that's the way to please me."

He swung himself down from the knoll into the creek bed and went back to his rocker. He found it hard to collect his thoughts. The music of Lucy's laugh haunted him.

A week, and then two, passed away. The golden days slipped by, still warm, still scented with the healing pine balsam. The nights were white with great stars, which Moreau could see between the pine boughs, for it was still warm enough to sleep on the knoll. His nights' rests were now often disturbed. A change had come over the situation in the cabin. The peace and serenity of the first days after Fletcher's departure had gone, leaving a sense of constraint and uneasiness in their stead. Moreau now looked up at the stars not with the calm content of the days when Lucy had first come, but with the trouble of a man who begins to realize menace in what he thought were harmless things.

Nearly a month had passed since Fletcher's departure when one day, walking down the stream with an idea of trying diggings farther down, he came upon Lucy washing in a pool of water enlarged by a rough dam she herself had constructed. She was kneeling on a flat stone on the bank, her sunbonnet off, her sleeves rolled up, laving in the water the few articles of dress that made up the baby's wardrobe. Her arms above the sunburned wrists shone snow-white, her roughened hair lay low on her forehead in damp, curly strands. The sight of her engaged in this menial toil irritated Moreau and he called:

"What are you doing there, Lucy? Get up."

She started with one of her old nervous movements and sat back on the stone. Then, seeing who it was, smiled confidently, and brushed the hair back from her forehead with one wet hand.

"I was washing the baby's things. That's the dam I made."

Moreau stood looking, not at the dam, but at the woman, flushed, breathless and smiling, a blooming girl.

"No one would ever think you were the same woman who came here two months ago," he said, more to himself than to her.

"I don't feel like the same," she answered, beginning to wring her clothes. "I don't feel now as if that was me."

"I thought you were quite an old woman then. Do you know that? I'd no idea you were young."

"I felt old. Oh, God—!" she said, suddenly dropping her hands and looking across the pool with darkly reminiscent eyes—"how awful I felt!"

"But you're quite well now? You're really well, aren't you?" he asked.

"Oh, I'm all right," she said, returning to her tone of gaiety. "I ain't never been like this before. Not sence I was married, anyway."

The allusion to her marriage made Moreau wince. Of late the subject had become hateful to him. Standing, leaning on his shovel, he said:

"You know it'll be winter here soon, so it's a good thing we've got you well and nicely rested up."

"Yes, I guess 'twill be winter soon," she said, looking vaguely round; "does it snow?"

"Sometimes tons of it, if it's a hard winter. But we've got to get out before that. Or you have, anyhow. Can't run any risks with the baby. Got to get her out and into some decent shelter before the snow falls."

For a moment Lucy made no answer. She had stopped wringing the clothes and was kneeling on the stone, her eyes on the water, a faint line drawn between her brows.

"Where to—? What sort o' place?" she said slowly.

Moreau shifted his eyes from her face to the earth in which the point of his shovel had imbedded itself.

"I told you as soon as you got well I'd take you to Hangtown or Sacramento, or even 'Frisco if they didn't suit. Now I haven't got dust enough to do that. Fletcher put that spoke in my wheel. But I'll take you and the baby into Hangtown."

"Hangtown?" she repeated faintly.

"Yes; it's quite a ways off. I'll have to go in myself and get a horse first, and then I'll take you both in on that. I thought I'd go to Mrs. Wingate. Her husband runs the Eldorado Hotel, and she isn't strong, and told me last time I was there she'd give a fancy salary if she could get a housekeeper. How'd you like to try that? It would be a first-class home for you and the baby."

Lucy had bent her face over the wet clothes.

THE ENCHANTED WINTER

"Ain't it all right here?" she said in a scarcely audible voice.

"No," said Moreau irritably; "I just told you there was danger of being snowed in after the first of November. You don't want to be snowed in here with the baby, do you?"

"I don't care," said Lucy.

"If you don't feel strong enough to do work like that," he continued, "you can stay on in the hotel. I can make the dust for that easily. Then in the spring, when the streams are full, I'll have enough to send you to Sacramento or San Francisco, and you can look about you and see how you'd like it there."

"Why can't I stay here?" she said suddenly, her voice quavering, but full of protest.

Its note thrilled Moreau.

"I've just told you why," he said quietly.

"Well, I'm not afraid. I don't mind snow. You can get things to eat from Hangtown. Oh, let me stay."

She turned toward him, still kneeling on the stone. Her face was quivering with the most violent emotions he had ever seen on it. The dead apathy was gone forever, at least as far as he was concerned.

"Oh, let me stay," she implored; "don't send me away from you."

"Oh, Lucy," he almost groaned, "don't you see that won't do?"

"Let me stay," she reiterated, and stretched out her hands toward him. The tears began to pour down her cheeks, and suddenly with the outstretched hands she seized him, and burst forth into a stream of impassioned words:

"Let me stay. Let me be with you. Don't send me away. There ain't no use in anything if I'm not with you. Let me work for you. Let me be where I can see you—that's all I want. I don't want no money nor clothes. If you'll just let me be near by! And I kin always work and cook, and you know you like things clean, and I kin keep 'em clean. Oh, you can't mean to send me off. I ain't never been happy before. I ain't never had no one treat me so kind before. I ain't never known what it was like to be treated decent. I can't leave you—I can't—I can't—"

She sank down at his feet in a quivering heap.

Moreau raised her and held her in his arms, pressed against his breast, his cheek against her hair. He had no thought for the moment but an ecstasy of pity and joy. Clinging close to him, she reiterated between broken breaths:

"I kin stay? Oh! I kin stay?"

"Lucy," he said, "how can you? Do you know what you're asking?"

"But I kin stay?" she repeated.

She slid one arm round his neck, and he felt her wet cheek against his.

"Let me just stay and work," she whispered, "just where I can see you."

"Do you forget that you're married?" he said huskily.

"I'll not be in your way. I'll not ask for anything or be any trouble," was her whispered answer, "so long's you let me be near you."

THE ENCHANTED WINTER 59

They walked back to the cabin silently. Lucy knew that she had gained her point and would stay. Her childish nature invaded and possessed by a great passion built on gratitude and reverence, asked no more than to be allowed to work for and worship the man who was to her a god. She did not look into the future, nor demand its secrets. The perfect joy of the present filled her. In the days that followed she grew in beauty, and in some subtle way acquired a new girlishness. Her past seemed wiped out. The blighting effects of the four previous years fell away from her and she seemed to revert to the sweet and simple youthfulness that had been hers when Jake Shackleton had married her at St. Louis. Silent and gentle as ever, it was plain to be seen that whatever Moreau asked for—service, friendship, love—she would unquestioningly give.

Early in November a cold evening came with a red sunset and a sharpening of every outline. For the first time they were driven into the cabin for supper. A fire of boughs and dried cones burned in the chimney and before this, supper being over, they sat, Lucy in the rocker made of a barrel, Moreau on the end of an upturned box, staring at the flames.

Finally the man broke the silence by telling her that he was going to take his dust and walk into Hangtown the next day, remaining there over night and returning in the morning with fresh supplies and a burro.

"Lucy," he said, drawing his box nearer to her, "I want to talk to you of something."

She looked up, saw that the moment both had been dreading had come, and paled.

"Lucy, the winter's coming. The snow may be here now at any moment. Have you thought of what we're to do?"

She shook her head and began to tremble. His words called up the specter of separation—what she feared most in the world.

"You know we can't live on this way. Will you, if I go into Hangtown and bring back a mule, ride there with me the day after to-morrow and marry me? There are two or three preachers there who will do it."

She looked at him with surprised eyes.

"I'm married already to Jake," she said. "How kin I get married again?"

"I know it, and it's no good trying to break that marriage. But in your eyes and mine that was none. You and your baby are mine to take care of and support and love for the rest of our lives. Though you can't be my lawful wife, I can protect you from scandal and insult by making you what all the world will think is my lawful wife. Only you, and I and Jake and his second wife will know that there has been a previous marriage and not one of that four will ever tell."

She put her rough hand out and felt his great fist close over it, like a symbol of the protection he was offering her.

"We can be married in Hangtown by your maiden name. If any one asks I can say I am marrying a young widow whose husband died on the Sierra. Your husband *did* die there when he sold you to me for a pair of horses."

She nodded, not quite understanding his meaning.

"Kin Jake ever come and claim me?" she asked in a frightened voice.

"How could he? How could he dare tell the world how he left you and his child sick, almost dying, in the hut of an unknown miner in the foothills? This is California, where men don't forgive that sort of thing."

She was silent, and then said: "Yes, let's go to Hangtown and be married."

"Was your first marriage perfectly legal? Have you got the marriage certificate?"

She rose, dragged out the bundle she had brought with her, and from it drew a long dirty envelope which she handed to him.

He opened it and found the certificate. It was accurate in every detail. His eye ran over the ages and names of the contracting parties—Lucy Fraser, fifteen, to Jacob Shackleton, twenty-four, at St. Louis.

Twisting the paper in his hands he sat moodily eying the fire. The second marriage was the only way he could think of by which he could lend a semblance of right to the impossible position in which his generous action had placed him. Divorce, in that remote locality and at that early day of laws, half administered and chaotic, was impossible, and even had it been easily obtained he shrank from dragging into publicity the piteous story of how the woman he loved had been sold to him.

That a marriage with Jake Shackleton's wife was a legal offense he knew, but with one of those strange whimsies of character which mark mankind, he felt that the reading of the marriage service over Lucy and himself would in some way sanctify what could never be a lawful tie.

In a spasm of rage and disgust he held out the paper to the flames, when Lucy, with a smothered cry sprang forward and seized it. It was the first violent action into which he had ever seen her betrayed. He looked in surprise into her flushed and alarmed face.

"Why not? Why not destroy everything that could connect you with such a past?" he said, almost angrily.

She hesitated, smoothing out the paper with trembling hands. Then she said falteringly:

"I don't know—but—but—he was her father," indicating the sleeping baby. "I was married to him all right."

He understood the instinct that made her wish to keep the paper as a record of her child's legitimacy, and made no further comment.

The next morning at dawn he started for his long walk into Hangtown, taking with him all the dust he had accumulated since Fletcher's departure. He was absent till the afternoon of the following day, when he reappeared leading a small pack-mule, laden with supplies, among which were several articles of dress for Lucy and the baby, so that they might make a fitting appearance when they rode into camp for the wedding. Lucy was overjoyed at her finery, and arrayed in it looked so pretty and so girlish that Moreau, for the first time since the scene by the creek, took her in his arms and kissed her. It was the kiss of the bridegroom and the master.

The next morning when she woke the cabin was

THE ENCHANTED WINTER 63

curiously dark. Going to the door to open it, she found it resisted, and went to the window. The world was wrapped in a blinding fall of snow. When Moreau came in for breakfast, he reported a blizzard outside. The cold was intense, the wind high, and the snow so fine and so torn by the gale that it was like a mist of whiteness enveloping the cabin. Already it was piled high about the walls and had to be shoveled from the door to permit of its opening. Fortunately they had collected a large amount of fire wood which was piled in the brush shed in which the man lived. During the morning Moreau took the animals from their shelter and stabled them in his. There was fodder for them and a bed of leaves, and the heat of the chimney warmed the fragile hut.

All day the storm raged, and in the evening, as he and Lucy sat before the fire, they could hear the turmoil of the tempest outside, moaning through the ranks of the sentinel pines. They were silent, listening to this shouting of the unloosed elements, and feeling an indescribably sweet sense of home and shelter in their rugged cabin and each other's society.

The storm was one of those unexpected blizzards which sometimes visit the Sierras in the early winter. With brief intervals of sunshine, the snow fell off and on for nearly a month. Moreau had to exercise almost superhuman effort to keep the cabin from being buried, and, as it was, the drifts nearly covered the window. It was impossible to travel any distance, as the snow was of a fine, feathery texture which did not pack tight, and into which the wanderer sank to the arm-pits. Fortunately the last trip into Hangtown had stocked the cabin well with provisions. No cares menaced its inmates, who, warm and happy in the vast snow-buried solitudes of the mountains, led an enchanted existence, forgetting and forgotten by the world.

When the storm ended the miner attempted to get into the settlements with the mule. But the beast, exhausted by the insufficient food, as the best part of the fodder had to be given to the cow, fell by the way, dying in one of the drifts. This seemed to sever their last link with the world. Nature had drawn an unbroken circle of loneliness around them. Under its spell they were drawn closer together till their lives merged—the primitive man and woman living for and by love in the primitive wilderness.

So the enchanted winter passed. The man, at intervals, making his way into the settlements for food and the few articles of clothing that they needed. It was a terrible winter, nearly as fierce as that of '46, but between the storms Moreau fitfully worked the stream, obtaining enough dust to pay for their provisions. The outside world seemed to fade from their lives, which were bounded by the walls of the cabin. Here, in the long fire-lit evenings, Moreau read to Lucy, taught her from his few books, strove to develop the mind that misfortune had almost crushed. She responded to his teachings with the quickness of love. Without much mental ability she improved because she lived only for what he desired. She smoothed the roughness of her speech and studied to correct her grammatical errors. She made him set her little tasks such as a child studies, and in the evenings he watched her with surreptitious amusement, as she conned over her spelling, or traced letters in her copy-book. She was passionately desirous of being worthy of him, and of leaving her old chrysalis behind her when she issued from the cabin.

This was not to be until the early spring. It was nearly six months from the time the emigrant wagon had stopped at his door, that Moreau, having accumulated enough dust to buy another mule and another outfit—took Lucy and the child into Hangtown for the marriage. This ceremony, about which in the beginning she had been somewhat apathetic, she now earnestly desired. It was accomplished without publicity or difficulty, Lucy assuming her maiden name of Fraser, and passing as a young widow. In the afternoon they started back for the cabin, Moreau on foot, with his wife and baby on the mule. They had decided to stay by their claim during the spring and early summer when the streams were high.

Thus the spring passed and the summer came. During this season Lucy, for the first time, saw that most lovely of Californian wild-flowers, the mariposa lily, and called her baby after it. As time went on and no other child was born, Moreau came to regard the little Mariposa as more and more his own. His affection for her became a paternal passion. It was decided between himself and Lucy that she should never know the secret of her parentage, but be called by his name and be brought up as his child. As the happiness of the union grew in depth and strength both the man and woman desired more ardently to forget beyond all recall the terrible past from which she had entered his life. It grew to be a subject to which Moreau could bear no allusion, and their life was purposely quiet and secluded, for fear of a chance encounter with some disturbing reminder.

So the time passed. In the course of the next few years Moreau moved from the smaller camps into Sacramento. Though a man of little commercial ability, he was always able, in those halcyon days, to make a good living for the woman and child to whom he had given his life. Years of prosperity made it possible to give to Mariposa every educational advantage the period and town offered. The child showed musical talent, and for the development of this he was keenly ambitious.

Across their tranquil life, now and then, came a lurid gleam from the career of the man who was Lucy Moreau's lawful husband. Jake Shackleton was soon a marked figure in the new state. But his rise to sensational fortune began with the booming days of the Comstock. Then his star rose blazing above the horizon. He was one of the original exploiters of the great lode and was one of those who owned that solid cone of silver which has gone down to history as the Reydel Monte. Ten years from his entrance into the state he was a rich man. In twenty, he was one of that group of millionaires, whose names were sounded from end to end of an astonished country.

A quarter of a century from the time when he had crossed the desert in an emigrant wagon, with his two wives, he read in the paper he had recently bought as an occupation and investment, a notice of the death of Daniel Moreau in Santa Barbara. It was brief, as befitted a pioneer who had sunk so completely out of sight and memory, leaving neither vast wealth nor picturesque record. The paragraph stated that "the pioneer's devoted wife and daughter attended his last hours, which were tranquil and free from pain. It is understood that the deceased leaves but little fortune, having during the last two or three years been incapacitated for work by enfeebled health."

MARIPOSA LILY

CHAPTER I

HIS SPLENDID DAUGHTER

"Hast thou found me, O mine enemy?"
—Kings.

Four months after the death of Dan Moreau his adopted daughter, Mariposa, sat at the piano, in a small cottage on Pine Street, in San Francisco, singing. Her performance was less melodious than remarkable, for she was engaged in "trying her voice." This was Mariposa's greatest claim to distinction, and, she hoped, to fortune. With it she dreamed of conquering fame and bringing riches to her mother and herself.

She was so far from either of these goals that she permitted herself to speculate on them as one does on impossible glories. The merits of her voice were as unknown in San Francisco as she was. Its cultivation had been a short and exciting episode, relinquished for lack of means. Now it was not only given up, but Mariposa was teaching piano herself, and was feverishly exalted when, the week before, her three pupils had been augmented by a fourth. Four pupils, at fifty cents a lesson, brought in four dollars a week—sixteen a month.

"If I make sixteen dollars a week after four months' work," Mariposa had said to her mother, on the acquisition of this fourth pupil, "then in one year I ought to make thirty-two dollars a month. Don't you think that's a reasonable way of reckoning?"

From which it will be seen that Mariposa was not only young in years, but a novice at the work of wage-earning.

She was in reality twenty-five years of age, but passed as, and believed herself to be, twenty-four. She had developed into one of those lordly women, stately of carriage, wide of shoulder and deep of breast, that California grows so triumphantly. She had her mother's thick, red-brown hair, with its flat loose ripple and the dog's brown eyes to match, a skin as white as a blanched almond with a slight powdering of freckles over her nose, and lips that were freshly red and delicately defined against the warm pallor surrounding them. She was, in fact, a beautified likeness of the Lucy that Moreau saw come gropingly back to youth and desirableness in the cabin on the flank of the Sierra. Only happiness and refinement and a youth passed in an atmosphere of love, had given her all that richness of girlhood, that effervescent confidence and joy of youth that poor Lucy had never known.

Despite her air of a young princess, her proudly-held head, her almost Spanish dignity, where only her brown eyes looked full of alertness and laughter, she was in character and knowledge of life foolishly young —in reality, a little girl masquerading in the guise of a triumphantly maturing womanhood. Her life had been one of quietude and seclusion. Her parents had been agreed in their desire for this; the father in the fear of a reëncounter with some phantom from the past. Lucy's ostensible reason was her own delicate health; but her dread was that Shackleton might see his child and claim her. It seemed impossible to the adoring mother that any father could see this splendid daughter and not rise up and call her his before all men.

The afternoon was cold and Mariposa wore a jacket as she sang. The cottage in Pine Street was all that a cottage ought not to be,—on the wrong side of the street, "too far out," cold, badly built, and with only one window to catch the western sun. It had one advantage which went a long way with the widow and her daughter—the rent was twenty dollars a month. Mariposa had paid ten dollars of this with her earnings, and kept the other six for pocket-money. But the happy day was dawning, so she thought, when she could pay the whole twenty. She cogitated on this and the affluence it would indicate, as her real father might have cogitated when he and the inner ring of his associates began to realize that the Reydel Monte was not a pocket, but a solid mound of mineral.

On this gray afternoon the cold little parlor, with its bulge of bay window looking out on the dreariness of the street, seemed impregnated with an air of dejection. In common with many poor dwellings in that city of extravagant reverses, it was full of the costly relics of better days. San Francisco has more of such parlors than any city in the country. The pieces of buhl and marquetry hiding their shame in twenty-dollar cottages and eighteen-dollar flats furnish pathetic commentary on many a story of fallen fortunes. The furniture looks abashed and humbled. Sometimes its rich designs have found a grateful seclusion under the dust of a quarter century, which finally will be removed by the restoring processes of the second-hand dealer, who will eventually become its owner.

There was a beautiful marquetry sideboard in the gray front parlor and a fine scarlet lacquer Chinese cabinet facing it. Moreau had had the tall, gilt-framed mirror and console brought round The Horn from New York when he had been in the flush of good times in Sacramento. The piano Mariposa was playing dated from a second period of prosperity, and had cost what would have now kept them for a year. It had been considered cheap at the time, and had been bought when the little Mariposa began to show musical tastes. She had played her first "pieces" on it, and in that halcyon period when she had had the singing lessons, had heard the big voice in her chest slowly shaking itself loose to the accompaniment of its encouraging notes.

Now she was singing in single tones, from note to note, higher and higher, then lower and lower. Her voice was a mezzo, with a "break" in the middle, below which it had a haunting, bell-like depth. As it went down it gained a peculiar emotional quality which seemed to thrill with passion and tears. As it began to ascend it was noticeable that her upper tones, though full, were harsh. There was astounding volume in them. It was evidently a big voice, a thing of noble promise, but now crude and unmanageable.

She emitted a loud vibrant note that rolled restlessly between the four walls, as if in an effort to find more space wherein to expand, and her hands fell upon the keys. In the room opening off the parlor there was an uncertain play of light from an unseen fire, and a muffled shape lying on the sofa. To this she now addressed a query in a voice in which dejection was veiled by uneasy inquiry:

"Well, does it seem to improve? Or is it still like a cow when she's lost her calf?"

"It's wonderfully improved," came the answer from the room beyond; "I don't think any one sings like you. Anyway, no one has such a powerful voice."

"No one howls so, you mean! Oh, mother, do you suppose I *ever* shall be able to take any more lessons?"

"Oh, yes, of course. We are in a large city now. Even if you don't make enough money yourself, there are often people who become interested in fine voices and educate them. Perhaps you'll meet one of them some day. And anyway—" with cheerfulness caught on the upward breath of a sigh—"you'll make money enough soon yourself."

Mariposa's head bent over the keys. When she came to view it this way, her sixteen dollars a month did not seem so big with promise as it did when ten dollars for rent was all it had to yield up.

"I've heard about those rich people who are looking for prima donnas to develop, but I don't know where to find them, and I don't see how they're to find me. The only way I can ever attract their notice is to sing on the street corner with a guitar, like Rachel. And then I'd have to have a license, and I've got no money for that."

She rose, and swept with the gait of a queen into

the next room. Her mother was lying on a sofa drawn closely to a tiny grate, in which a handful of fire flickered.

Lucy was still a pretty woman, with a thin, faded delicacy of aspect. Her skin was singularly white, especially on her hands, which were waxen. Though love and happiness had given her back her youth, her health had never recovered her child's rude birth in the desert and the subsequent journey across the Sierra. She had twined round and clung to the man whom she had called her husband, and with his loss she was slowly sinking out of the world his presence had made sweet for her. Her daughter—next in adoration to the hero who had succored her in her hour of extremity—had no power to hold her. Lucy was slowly fading out of life. The girl had no knowledge of this. Her mother had been a semi-invalid for several years, and her own youth was so rich in its superb vigor, that she did not notice the elder woman's gradual decline of vitality. But the mother knew, and her nights were wakeful and agonized with the thought of her child, left alone, poor and unfriended.

Mariposa sat down on the end of the sofa at the invalid's feet and took one of her hands. She had loved both parents deeply, but the fragile mother, so simple and unworldly, so dependent on affection for her being, was the object of her special devotion. They were silent, the girl with an abstracted glance fixed on the fire, meditating on the future of her voice; the mother regarding her with pensive admiration.

As they sat thus, a footfall on the steps outside broke upon their thoughts. The cottage was so built that one of its conveniences was, that one could always hear the caller or the man with the bill mounting the steps before he rang. The former were rarer than the latter, and Mariposa, in whose eventless life a visit from any one was a thing of value, pricked up her ears expectantly.

The bell pealed stridently and the servant could be heard rattling pans in the kitchen, evidently preparatory to emerging. Presently she came creaking down the hall, the door opened and a female voice was heard asking for the ladies. It *was* a visitor. Mariposa was glad she had stayed in that afternoon, and with her hand still clasping her mother's, craned her neck toward the door.

The visitor was a tall, thin woman of forty years, her cheaply fashionable dress telling of many a wrestle between love of personal adornment and a lean purse. She was one of those slightly known and unquestioningly accepted people that women, in the friendless and unknown condition of the Moreaus, constantly meet in the free and easy social life of western cities.

She was a Mrs. Willers, long divorced from a worthless husband, and supporting, with a desperate and gallant courage, herself and her child, who was one of Mariposa's piano pupils. Her appearance gave no clue to the real force and indomitable bravery of the woman, who, against blows and rebuffs, had fought her way with a smile on her lips. Her appearance and manner, especially in this, her society pose, were against her. The former was flashy and overdressed, the latter loud-voiced and effusive. A large hat, flaunting with funeral plumes, was set jauntily on one side of her head, and a spotted veil was drawn over a complexion that was carelessly made up. Her corsets were so long and so tight that she could hardly bend, and when she did they emitted protesting creaks. No one would have thought from her flamboyantly stylish get-up that she was a reporter and "special" writer on Jake Shackleton's newly acquired paper, *The Morning Trumpet!* But in reality she was an energetic and able journalist. It was only when adorned with her best clothes and her "society" manners that she affected a sort of gushing silliness.

"Well," she said, rustling in, "here's the lady! How's everybody? Just as cozy and cute as a doll's house."

She pressed Mrs. Moreau's hand and then sent an eagle glance—the glance of the reporter that is trained to take in every salient object in one sweep—about the room. She could have written a good description of it from that moment's survey.

"Better? Of course you're better," she interrupted Lucy, who had been speaking of improved health. "Don't San Francisco cure everybody? And daughter there?" her bright tired eye rested on Mariposa for one inspecting moment. "She looks nice enough to eat."

"Mariposa's always well," said Lucy, pressing the hand she still held. "She was always a prize child ever since she was a baby."

Mrs. Willers leaned back and folded her white gloved hands over her creaking waist.

"You know she's the handsomest thing I've seen in a

coon's age," she said, nodding her head at Mariposa. "There ain't a girl in society that compares to her."

Lucy smiled indulgently at her daughter. Mariposa, though embarrassed, was not displeased by these sledge-hammer compliments. They were a novelty to her, and she regarded Mrs. Willers—despite a few peculiarities of style—as a woman of vast knowledge and experience in that wonderful world of gaiety and fashion, of which she herself knew so little.

"I go to most of the big balls here," continued the visitor. "It's always the same thing on *The Trumpet*—'Send up Mrs. Willers to the Cotillion Club to-night; we don't want any other reporter but her. If you send up any of those other jay women we'll turn 'em down.' So up I have to hop. The other night at the Lorley's big blow-out, when Genevieve Lorley had her début, it was the same old war-cry—'We want Mrs. Willers tonight to do the Society, and don't try and work off any incompetents on us. Send her up early so's Mrs. Lorley can give her the dresses herself.' So up I went, and was in the dressing-room for an hour and saw 'em all, black and white and brown, heiresses and beggars, and not one of 'em, Mrs. Moreau, to touch daughter here—not one."

"But there are so many beautiful girls in San Francisco. Mariposa has seen them on the cars and down town. She often tells me of them."

"Beauties—yes, lots of 'em; dead loads of 'em. But there's a lot that get their beauty out of boxes and bottles. There's a lot—I don't say who, I'm not one to mention names—but there's a lot that when they go to bed the beauty all comes off and lies in layers on the floor. Not that I blame them—make yourself as good-looking as you can, that's my motto. It's every woman's duty. But you don't want to begin so young. I rouge myself," said Mrs. Willers, with the careless truthfulness of one whose reputation is beyond attack, "but I don't like it in a young girl."

"Who was the prettiest girl at the ball?" said Mariposa, deeply interested. She had the curiosity of seventeen on such subjects—subjects of which her girlhood had been unusually barren.

"My dear, I'll tell you all that later—talk for an hour if you can stand it. But that's not what I came to say to-day. It's business to-day—real business, and I don't know but what all your future hangs on it."

She gave a triumphant look at the startled mother and daughter. With the introduction of serious matter her worn face took on a certain sharp intelligence and her language grew more masculine and less slovenly.

"It's this," she said, leaning forward impressively: "I'm not sure that I haven't found Mariposa's backer."

"Backer," said Lucy, faintly, finding the word objectionable. "What's that?"

"The person who's to hear her sing and offer to educate the finest voice he's likely to hear in the next ten years."

Mariposa gave a suppressed exclamation and looked at her mother. Lucy had paled. She was trembling at what she felt she was to hear.

"It's Jake Shackleton," said Mrs. Willers, proudly launching her bombshell.

"Jake Shackleton," breathed Mariposa, to whom the name meant only vaguely fabulous wealth. "The Bonanza Man?"

Lucy was sitting up, deadly pale, but she said nothing.

"The Bonanza Man," said Mrs. Willers. "My chief."

"But what does he know of me?" said Mariposa. "He's never even heard of me."

"That's where you're off, my dear. Jake Shackleton's heard of everybody. He has every one ticketed and put away in some little cell in his brain. He never forgets a face. Some people say that's one of the secrets of his success; that, and the way he knows the man or woman who's going to get on and the one who's going to fall out of the procession and quit at the first obstacle. He's got no use for those people. Get up and hustle, or get out—that's his motto."

"But about me?" Mariposa entreated. "Go on."

"Well, it's a queer story, anyhow. The other morning I was sent for to the sanctum. There was a little talk about work and then he says to me, 'Didn't you tell me your daughter was taking piano lessons, Mrs. Willers?' Never forgets a word you say. I told him yes; and he says: 'Isn't her teacher that Miss Moreau, whose father died a few months ago in Santa Barbara?' I told him yes again, and then he wheels round on the swivel chair, looks at me so, from under his eyebrows, and says: 'I knew her father once; a fine man!'"

"Oh, how odd," breathed Mariposa, quivering with interest. "I never heard father speak of him."

"It was a long time ago. He knew your father up in the mines some time in the fifties, and he said he admired him considerably. Then he went on and asked me a lot of questions about you, your circumstances, where you lived and if you were as good-looking as your father. He said he'd heard you were an accomplished young lady. Then I saw my cue and I said, as carelessly as you please, that Miss Moreau had a fine voice and plenty of musical ability, but unfortunately was not able to cultivate either, because her means were small, and it was a great pity some one with money didn't help her. I says—just as casual as could be—it's a great shame to see a voice like that lying idle for want of tuition."

"What did he say then?" said Mariposa.

"Well, that's the point I'm working up to. He thought a while, asked a few more questions, and then said: 'I'd like to meet the young lady and hear her sing. It goes against me to have Dan Moreau's daughter lack for anything. Her father'd have left a fortune if he hadn't been a man that thought of every one else before himself.'"

"That was father exactly. He must have known him well. Mother, isn't it odd he never spoke of him? What did you say then?"

"I? Why, of course, I saw my opening and jumped in. I said, 'Well, I guess I can arrange for you to meet Miss Moreau at my rooms. I see her twice a week when she comes to give Edna her piano lesson. I'll ask her when she can come, and let you know and then she'll sing for you.' He was pleased, he was real pleased, and said he'd come whenever I said. And now, young woman," laying a large white-gloved hand on

Mariposa's knee, "that ought to be the beginning of a career for you!"

"Good gracious!" said Mariposa, whose cheeks were crimson, "I never heard anything so exciting in my life, and we were just talking about it. I'll probably sing like a dog baying the moon."

"Don't you talk that way. You'll sing your best. And he's not a man that you wouldn't like Mariposa to meet"—turning to the pale and silent Lucy. "Whatever other faults he's had he's always been a straight man with women. There's never been that sort of scandal about Jake Shackleton. There's a story you've probably heard, that he was originally a Mormon. I don't believe much in that myself. He had, anyway, only one wife when he entered California, and she's been his wife ever since, and she ain't the kind to have stood any nonsense of the Mormon sort."

Lucy gave a sudden gasping breath and sat up. The light of the gray afternoon was dying outside, and by the glow of the fire her unusual pallor was not noticeable.

"It was very good of you," she said. "Mariposa will be glad to go."

"And you'll come, too?" said Mrs. Willers. "He asked about you."

"Did he say he'd ever known me?" said Lucy, quietly.

"No—not exactly that. No, I don't believe he said that. But he was interested in you as the wife of the man he'd known so long ago."

"Of course it would be only in that way," murmured

Lucy, sinking back. "No, I can't come. It wouldn't be possible. I'm not well enough."

"Oh, mother, do. You know you go out on the cars sometimes, and the Sutter Street line is only two blocks from here. I know you'd enjoy it when you got there."

"No, dearest. No, Mrs. Willers. Don't, please, urge me. I am not able to meet new people. No— Oh, please don't talk any more about my going.".

Something of pain and protest in her voice made them desist. She was silent again, while Mariposa and Mrs. Willers arranged the details of the party. This was to be small and choice. Only one other person, a man referred to as Essex, was to come. At the name of Essex, Mrs. Willers shot a side look of inspection at Mariposa, who did what was expected of her in displaying a fine blush.

It was decided that Mrs. Willers' hospitality should take the form of wine and cake. There was a consultation about other and lesser viands, and finally an animated discussion as to the proper garb in which Mariposa should present herself to the first truly distinguished person she had ever met. During the conversation over these varied questions Lucy lay back among her cushions, sunk in the same pale silence.

Darkness had fallen when the guest, having threshed out the subject to the last grain, took herself off. Mariposa looked from the opened doorway into a black street, dotted with the yellow blurs of lighted lamps. The air was cold with that penetrating, marrow-searching coldness of a foggy evening in San Francisco. As the night swallowed Mrs. Willers, Mariposa shut the door and came rushing back.

"Mother!" she cried, before she got into her room, "isn't that the most thrilling thing? Oh, did you ever know of anything so unexpected and wonderful and exciting. *Do* you think he'll like my voice? *Do* you think he really could be interested in me because he knew father? And he can't have known him so very well, or father would have said more of him. Did *you* ever hear father speak about him?"

The mother gave no answer, and the girl bent over her. Lucy, motionless and white, was lying among her cushions, unconscious.

CHAPTER II

THE MILLIONAIRE

"And one man in his time plays many parts."
—SHAKESPEARE.

At two o'clock on the afternoon of her party Mrs. Willers was giving the finishing touches to her rooms. These were a sitting and bed-room in one of the large boarding-houses that already had begun to make their appearance along Sutter Street. "To reside" on Sutter Street, as she would have expressed it, was a step in fashion for Mrs. Willers, who previously had lived in such ignominious localities as North Beach and upper Market Street, renting the surplus rooms in dingy "private families." Her rise to fairer fortunes was signalized by the move to Sutter Street. Her parlor announced it in its over-furnished brilliancy. All the best furniture of the poor lady's many migrations had been squeezed into the little room. The Japanese fans and umbrellas, flattened against the walls with pins, were accumulated at some cost, for they represented one of those strange and unaccountable vagaries of popular taste that from time to time seize a community with blighting force. Silk scarfs were twisted about everything whereon they could twist.

THE MILLIONAIRE 87

The "lunch," as the hostess called it, had already been prepared and stood on a side table. Edna, Mrs. Willers' daughter, had made many trips up and down the street that morning collecting its component parts and bringing them home in paper bags. The ladies in the lower windows of the house had been aware of these goings and comings, and so were partly prepared when, at luncheon, Mrs. Willers casually told them of the distinguished guest she expected. The newspaper woman had not lived her life with her eyes shut and her ears closed, and she knew the value to the fraction of a hair of this information, and just how much it would add to her prestige.

She was now fluttering about in a wrapper, and with a piece of black net tied tight over her forehead. Through this the forms of dark circular curls outlined themselves like silhouettes. Mrs. Willers had no warpaint on, and though she looked a trifle worn, was much more attractive in appearance than when decorated with her pink and white complexion and her spotted veil. Edna, who was already dressed, was a beautiful, fair-haired child of twelve. The struggles she had seen her mother pass through, with her eyes bright and her head high, had developed in her a precocity of mind that had not spoiled the sweet childishness of a charming nature. It would be many years yet before Edna would understand that she had been the sheet-anchor of the mother who was to her so clever and so brave; the mother, who, in her moments of weakness and temptation, had found her child the one rock to cling to in the welter of life.

Mrs. Willers retired to the bedroom to dress, occasionally coming to the doorway in various stages of déshabille to give instructions to the child. Her toilet was accomplished with mutilated rites, and by the time the sacrificial moment came of laying on the rouge her cheeks were too flushed with excitement to need it. When she did appear it would have been difficult to recognize her as the woman of an hour earlier. Even the black silhouettes had passed through a metamorphosis and appeared as a fluff of careless curls.

The first guest to arrive was the man she had spoken of as Essex. The ladies at the windows below had been struck into whispering surprise by his appearance. San Francisco was still enjoying its original reputation as a land of picturesque millionaires, who lived lives of lawlessness and splendor. Men of position still wore soft felt hats and buttoned themselves tight into prince-albert coats when they went down to business in the morning. Perhaps in the traveled circles, where the Bonanza kings and their associates lived after European models, there were men who bore the stamp of metropolitan finish, as Barry Essex did. But they did not visit Sutter Street boarding-houses nor wear silk hats when they paid afternoon calls. San Francisco was still in that stage when this form of headgear was principally associated in its mind with the men who drew teeth and sold patent medicines on the sand lots behind the city hall.

Barry Essex, anywhere, would have been a striking figure. He was a handsome man of some thirty years, tall and spare, and with a dark, smooth-shaven face where the nose was high and the eyes veiled and cold. He looked like a person of high birth, and there were stories that he was, though by the left hand. He spoke with an English accent, and, when asked his nationality, shrugged his shoulders and said it was hard to say what it was—his father had been a Spaniard, his mother an Englishwoman, and he had been born and reared in France.

That he was a man of ability and education, superior to the work he was doing as special writer on Jake Shackleton's paper, *The Trumpet,* was obvious. But San Francisco had become so used to mysteriously interesting strangers, that come from no one knows where, and suggest an attractively unconventional history, that the particular curiosity excited by Essex soon died, and he was merely of moment as the author of some excellent articles on art, literature and music in *The Sunday Trumpet.*

He greeted Mrs. Willers with a friendly fellowship, then let a quick, surreptitious glance sweep the room. She saw it, knew what he was looking for, but affected unconsciousness. His manner was touched by the slightest suggestion of something elaborate and theatrical, which, in Mrs. Willers' mind, seemed to have some esoteric connection with the silk hat. This he now—after slowly looking about for a safe place of deposit—handed to Edna with the careless remark: "Will you put this down somewhere, Edna?"

The child took it, flushing slightly. She was accustomed to being made much of by her mother's guests, and Essex's manner stung her little girl's pride. But she put the hat on the piano and retired to her corner, behind the refreshment table.

A few moments later she opened the door to Jake

Shackleton. Mrs. Willers, red-cheeked and triumphant, felt that this was indeed a proud moment for her. She said as much, drawing an amused laugh from her second guest. He, too, had swept the room with a quick, investigating glance. This time Mrs. Willers did not affect unconsciousness, and said briskly:

"No, our young lady hasn't come yet. You'll have to try and put up with me for a while."

It would have been difficult for the eye of the deepest affection to see in the Comstock millionaire the emigrant of twenty-five years before. A mother might have been deceived. The lean figure had grown chunky and heavy. The drawn face was now not full—it was the type of face that would never be full—but was lacking in the seams that had then furrowed it. The hair was gray, worn thin on the temples, and the beard, trimmed and well-tended, was gray, too. Perhaps the strongest tie with the past was that the man suggested the same hard, fine-drawn, wiry energy. It still shone in his narrow, light-colored eyes, and still was to be seen in his lean, muscular hand, that was frequently used in gesticulation.

In manner the change was equally apparent. Though colloquial, his speech showed none of the coarse illiterateness of the past. His manner was quiet, abruptly natural, and not lacking in a sort of easy dignity, the dignity of the man who has won his place among men. He was dressed with the utmost simplicity. His soft felt wide-awake was not new, his black prince-albert coat did not fit him with anything like the elegance with which Barry Essex's outlined his fine shape. A little purple cravat tied in a bow appeared from beneath his turned-down collar. It was somewhat shiny from the brushing of his beard.

"You must suppose I'm anxious to see this young lady," he said, "after what you've told me about her."

"Well, ask Mr. Essex if I've exaggerated," said Mrs. Willers. "He knows her, too."

"I don't know what you've said," he returned, "but I don't think anything could be too complimentary that was said of Miss Moreau."

"Eh!—better and better," said the elder man. "I didn't know you knew her, Essex?"

He turned his gray eyes, absolutely cold and noncommittal on Essex, who answered them with an equally expressionless gaze.

"I've known Miss Moreau for three months," he replied. "I met her here."

Shackleton turned back to Mrs. Willers.

"I understand from you, Mrs. Willers, that these ladies are left extremely badly off. Are they absolutely without means?"

"No-o," she answered, "not exactly that. Mr. Moreau left a life insurance policy of five thousand dollars. Mariposa tells me that three thousand of that went to pay his doctors' bills and funeral expenses. He was sick a long time. They are now living on their capital, and they've been here four months, and Mrs. Moreau has constant medical attendance."

The millionaire gave a little click of his tongue significant of annoyance.

"Moreau had a dozen chances of making his pile, as every man did in those days," he said. "He was the sort of man who is predestined to leave his family poor."

"Yet they worship his memory," said Mrs. Willers. "He must have been very good to them."

Shackleton made no answer. She was used to reading his expression, and the odd thought crossed her mind that this remark of hers was unpleasant to him.

Before she had time to reply a knock at the door announced the arrival of Mariposa. As she entered the two men stood up, both looking at her with veiled eagerness. To Essex his feeling for her was making her every appearance an event. To Shackleton it was a moment of quivering interest in a career full of tumultuous moments.

A slight flush mounted to his face as he met her eyes. She instinctively looked at him first, with a charming look, girlish, shy, and deprecating. Her likeness to her mother struck him like a blow, but she was an Amazonian Lucy, with all that Lucy had lacked. He saw himself in the stronger jaw and the firm lips. Physically she was molded of them both. His heart swelled with a passionate pride. This, indeed, was his own child, bone of his bone, and flesh of his flesh.

The introductions over, they resettled themselves, and Mariposa found herself beside this quiet, gray-haired man, talking quite volubly. She was not shy nor nervous, as she had expected to be, but felt peculiarly at her ease. Looking at her with intent eyes, he spoke to her of the early days in California, when he and her parents had come across.

"You know, I knew your father in the Sierra, long ago," he said.

"TO SHACKLETON IT WAS A MOMENT OF QUIVERING INTEREST"

"Yes," she answered rather hurriedly, fearful lest he should ask her if her father had not spoken of him, "so Mrs. Willers said. It must have been a long time ago. Was I there?" she added with a little smile.

He was taken aback by the question and said, stammeringly:

"Well, really now, I—I—don't quite remember."

"I guess I wasn't," she said laughing. "You must have known father before that. *He* came over in forty-nine, you know. I was born twenty-four years ago up in the mountains, in Eldorado County, in a little cabin miles above Placerville. Mother's often described the place to me. They left soon after."

He lowered his eyes. He was a man of no sentiment or tenderness, yet something in this false statement, uttered so innocently by these fresh young lips, and taught with all the solicitude of love to this simple nature, pierced like an arrow to the live spot in his deadened conscience.

"It was more than twenty-five years ago that I was there," he said. "You evidently were not born then."

"But my mother was there then. Do you think I look like her? My father thought I was wonderfully like her."

He looked into the candid face. Memories of Lucy before his own harsh treatment and the hardships of her life had broken her, stirred in him.

"Yes," he said slowly, "you're very like her. But you're like your father, too."

"Am I?" she cried, evidently delighted. "Do you really think so? I do want to look like my father."

"Why?" he could not help asking.

She stared at him surprised.

"Wouldn't you like to look like both your parents, if they were the two finest people in the world?"

Here Mrs. Willers cut short the conversation by asking Mariposa to sing. The girl rose and went directly to the piano. For days this moment had been looming before her in nightmare proportions. She was feverishly anxious to do her best and sickeningly fearful of failure. Now her confidence was unshaken. Something—impossible to say just what—had reassured her. Her hands were trembling a little as she struck the keys, and her first notes showed the oscillation of nervousness, but soon the powerful voice began to come more under her control, and she poured it out exultantly. She never sang better. Her voice, much too large for the small space, was almost painful in its resonant force.

Of the two men the elder was without musical knowledge of any kind. He was amazed and delighted at what seemed to him an astonishing performance. But Essex knew that with the proper training and guidance there were possibilities of a brilliant future for this handsome and penniless young woman. He had lived much among professional singers, and he knew that Mariposa Moreau possessed an unusual voice. For reasons of his own he did not desire her to know her own power, and he was secretly irritated that she had sung so well.

She continued, Shackleton requesting another, and yet another song. Only the clock chiming four roused him to the fact that he must go. He was living at his country place at Menlo Park and had to catch a train.

He left them with assurances of his delight in the performance. To Mariposa, as he pressed her hand in farewell, he said:

"I'll see you again. You've a wonderful voice, there's no mistake about that. It's a gift, a great gift, and it must have its chance."

The girl, carried away with the triumph of the afternoon, said gaily:

"I'll sing for you whenever you like. Could you never come up to our cottage on Pine Street and meet my mother? I know she would like to see you."

The slightest possible look of surprise passed over his face, gone almost as soon as it had come. Mariposa saw it, however, and felt embarrassed. She evidently had been too forward, and looked down, blushing and uncomfortable. He recovered himself immediately, and said:

"Not now, much as I should like to, Miss Moreau. I am living at Menlo Park, and all my spare time when business is over is spent in catching trains. But give your mother my compliments on the possession of such a daughter."

Mariposa and Essex stayed chatting with Mrs. Willers for some time after Shackleton's departure. The clock had chimed more than once, when finally they left, and their hostess, exhausted, but exultant, threw herself back in a chair and watched Edna gather up the remains of the lunch.

"Put the cakes in the tin, dearie. They'll do for to-morrow, and be sure and cork the bottle tight. There's enough for another time."

"Several other times," said Edna, holding the bottle

of port wine up to the light and squinting at it with her head on one side. "It was a cheap party—they hardly drank anything."

Mariposa and her companion walked up Sutter Street with the lagging step of people who find each other excellent company.

It was the end of a warm afternoon in September, one of those still, deeply flushed evenings when the air is tepid and smells of distant fires, and the winged ants come out of the rotting sidewalks by the thousand. The west was a clear, thin red smudged with brown smoke. The houses grew dark and ever darker, and seemed to loom more solidly black every moment. They looked dreamlike and mysterious against the fiery background.

"How did you like it?" said Mariposa, as they loitered on, "my singing, I mean?"

"It was excellent, of course. You've got a voice. But the room was too small—and such a room to sing in, all crowded with ridiculous things."

Mariposa felt hurt. She thought Essex was the finest, the most elegant and finished person she had ever met. He seemed to her to breathe the atmosphere of those great sophisticated cities she had never seen. In his talks with her he now and then chilled her by his suggestion of belonging to another and a wiser world, to which she was a provincial outsider.

This quality was in his manner now, and she began to feel how raw her poor performance must have seemed to the man who had heard the great prima donnas of London and Paris.

"It was a small room, of course," she assented, "but I had to sing somewhere, and I couldn't hire a place."

"Shackleton wanted to hear you, as I understand it. Mrs. Willers said something about his knowing your father."

There was no question about the coldness of his voice now. Had Mariposa known more about men she would have seen he was irritated.

She repeated the fable of her father's early acquaintance with Jake Shackleton, and of the latter's desire expressed to Mrs. Willers, of hearing her sing.

"Mrs. Willers is such an ass!" he said suddenly and vindictively.

Mariposa was this time hurt for her friend and spoke up:

"I don't see why you say that. I don't think a woman's an ass who can support herself and a child as she does,"—she thought of her sixteen dollars and added: "It's very hard for a woman to make money."

"Oh, she's not an ass that way," he answered. "She's an ass to try and work Shackleton up to the point of becoming a patron of the arts—as represented by you."

He turned on her with a slight smile, that brought no suggestion of amusement to his somewhat saturnine face.

"Isn't that her idea?" he asked.

Mariposa felt her hopes as to the training of her voice becoming mean and vulgar.

"He said he wanted to hear me," she said stumblingly, "and she said it would be a good thing. And I have no money to educate my voice, and it's all I have. Why do you seem to disapprove of it?"

"I?—disapprove? That would hardly do. Why even if I wanted to, I have not the right to, have I?"

Mariposa's face flushed. She felt now, that she had presupposed an intimacy between them which he wanted politely to suggest did not exist. This was not by any means the first time Essex had baffled and embarrassed her. It amused him to do it, but to-day he was in a bad temper and did it from spleen.

"Somehow Jake Shackleton doesn't suggest himself to me as a patron of the arts," he said. "I don't think he knows Yankee Doodle from God Save the Queen."

Mariposa thought of the brilliant article on the Italian opera, from Bellini to Verdi, that the man beside her had contributed to last Sunday's *Trumpet,* and Jake Shackleton's enthusiastic admiration of her singing immediately seemed the worthless praise of sodden ignorance.

"Then," she said desperately, "you wouldn't attach any importance, if you were I, to his liking my singing? It was just the way some people like a street organ simply because it plays tunes."

"Oh, I wouldn't think that. There's no reason why he shouldn't know a good voice when he hears it."

"Do *you* think I've got a good voice?" said Mariposa, stopping in the street and staring morosely at him.

"Of course I do, dear lady."

"Do you, really?"

"Yes, really."

She smiled, and tried to hide it by looking down. It was hardly in man to continue bad-humored before this naïve display of pleasure at his commending word.

"You really think I might some day become a singer, a professional singer?"

"I really do."

The smile broadened and lit her face.

"You always make me feel so stupid—and—and—as if I didn't amount to anything," she murmured.

It was so sweet, so childishly candid, that it melted the last remnant of his bad temper.

"You little goose," he said softly, "don't you know I think more of you than I do of any one in San Francisco? It's getting dark; take my arm till we get to the car."

She did so and they moved forward.

"Or anywhere else," he murmured.

CHAPTER III

RETROSPECT

"Your young men shall see visions, and your old men shall dream dreams."—THE ACTS.

After he had put Mariposa on her car, Essex went down town to the paper with some copy. He was making a fair living on *The Trumpet,* and the work he was doing suited him. He thought it might last the winter and he had no objections to passing the winter in San Francisco. Like many of his kind, he felt the lazy Bohemian charm of the diverse, many-colored, cosmopolitan city sprawled on its sand dunes. The restaurants alone made life more worth while than anywhere else in the country except New York.

To-night he went to one, for dinner, that stood in Clay Street, a short distance below Kearney. He had a word to say to the white-clothed chef, who cooked the dinner in plain sight, on a small oven and grill, beneath which the charcoal gleamed redly. He stopped for a moment's badinage with the buxom, fresh-faced French woman who sat at the desk. She was the chef's wife, Madame Bertrand, and liked "Monsieur Esseex," who spoke her natal tongue as well as she did. There was evidently truth in one piece of Essex's autobiography. Only a childhood spent in France could teach the kind of French he spoke with Madame Bertrand.

He sat long over his dinner, smoking and reading the evening papers. It was so late when he left that Bertrand himself came out of his cooking corner and talked with him about Paris. "Monsieur Esseex" knew Paris as well as Bertrand, some parts of it better. He had been educated there at one of the large *lycées,* and had gone back many times, living now on one side of the river, now on the other. Bertrand, in his white cap and apron, conversing with his guest, retained a curious manner of deference unusual in California.

"Monsieur is a gentleman of some kind or other," he told madame.

"There are many different kinds of gentlemen in California," returned that lady, oracularly.

It was nearly nine when Essex left the restaurant, and passing down Kearney Street for a few blocks, turned to his right and began to mount the ascending sidewalk that led to his lodgings. These were in an humble and unfashionable neighborhood in Bush Street. The house was of a kind whence gentility has departed. It stood back on the top of two small terraces, up which mounted two wooden flights of stairs, one with a list to starboard so pronounced that Essex had, once or twice, while ascending, thought the city in the throes of an earthquake.

The darkness of night wrapped it now. As it was early a light within shone out dimly through two narrow panes of glass flanking the hall door. He let himself in and mounted a dirtily carpeted stairway. The place smelled evilly of old cooking and the smoke of many and various cigarettes, cigars and pipes. It was a man's rooming-house, and the men evidently smoked where and what they listed. Essex had no idea who they were and had seen only one of them: a man on the same floor with him who, he surmised, by the occasional boisterousness of his entrances, frequently came home drunk.

His room was one of the best in the house, on the front, and with a large bay window commanding the street. It was fairly comfortable and well furnished, and the draft of soft, chill air that crossed it from the opened window kept it fresh. Essex, after lighting the gases in the pendent chandelier, bent and kindled the fire laid in the grate. Like many foreigners he found San Francisco cold, and after the manner of his bringing up would no more have denied himself a fire when he was chilly, than a glass of wine when he was thirsty. Different nations have their different extravagances, and Essex's French boyhood had stamped him with respect for the little comforts of that intelligent race.

He pulled up an easy chair and sat down in front of the small blaze, with his hands out. Its warmth was pleasant, and he stayed thus, thinking. Presently he smiled slightly, his ear having caught the sounds of his fellow lodger's stumbling ascent of the stairs. The man was evidently drunk again, and he wondered vaguely how he ever managed to mount the terrace steps with the list to starboard.

The lodger's door opened, shut, and there was silence. Essex—an earnest reader—was soon deep in his book. From this he was interrupted by a step in the passage and a light knock on the door. In response to his "Come in," the door opened hesitantly, and the man from across the hall thrust in his head. It was a head of wild gray hair, with an old yellow face, seamed and shriveled beneath it. The eyes, which were beadily dark and set close to the nose, were bloodshot, the lips slack and uncertain. A very dirty hand was curled round the edge of the door.

"Well, what is it?" said Essex.

"I've lost my matches agin," said the man, in a whiningly apologetic tone.

"There are some," said Essex, designating his box on the mantelpiece. "Take what you want."

The stranger shambled in, and after scratching about the box with a tremulous hand, secured a bunch. Essex looked at him with cynical interest. He was miserably dressed, dirty and ragged. He walked with an apologetic slouch, as if continually expecting a kick in the rear. He was evidently very drunk, and the odor of the liquids he had imbibed compassed him in an ambulating reek.

"Thanks to you, Doc," he said, as he went out. "So long."

A few minutes later Essex heard a crash from his neighbor's room, and then exclamations of anger and dole. These continuing with an increased volume, Essex rose and went to the source of sound. The room was pitch dark, and from it, as from the entrance to the cave of the damned, imprecations and lamentations were issuing in a strenuous flood. With the match he had brought he lit the gas, and turning, saw his late visitor holding by the foot-board of the bed, having overturned a small stand, which had evidently been surmounted by a nickel clock.

"What the devil do you mean by making such a noise?" he said angrily.

"Pardon, pardon!" said the other humbly, "but I couldn't find the gas this time, Doc. This is a small room, but things do get away somehow."

He looked stupidly about with his bleared eyes. The room was small and miserably dirty and uninviting.

"There's a room," he said suddenly in a loud, dramatic tone and with a sweep of his arm, "for a man who might er been a bonanza king!"

Essex turned to go.

"If you make any more of this row to-night I'll see that you're turned out to-morrow," he said haughtily.

He wheeled about on the drunkard as he spoke. The man's sodden face was lit with a flash of malevolent intelligence, to be superseded immediately by a wheedling smile.

"I seen you before to-day," he said.

"Well, you'll see me again to-night if you don't keep quiet, and this time you won't like it."

"You was with a lady, a fine-looking lady."

"Here—no more of that talk," said Essex threateningly.

The man stopped, looking furtively at him as if half expecting to be struck. Essex turned toward the door and passed out. As he did so he heard him mutter: "And I'd seen her before, too."

Back in his room the young man took up his book again, but the thread of his interest was broken. His mind refused to return to the prescribed channels before it, but began to drift here and there on the wayward currents of memory.

The house was now perfectly quiet. The little fire had fallen together into a pleasant core of warmth that genially diffused its heat through the room. Essex, sprawling in his chair, his long arms following its arms, his finely-formed, loose-jointed hands depending over the rounded ends, let his dreaming gaze rest on this red heart of living coal, while his pipe smoke lay between it and his face in delicate layers.

His thoughts slipped back over childish memories to his first ones, when he had lived a French boy's life with his mother in Paris.

He remembered her far back in the days when he sat on her knee and was read to out of fairy books. She had been very pretty then and very happy, and had always talked English with him while every one else spoke French. She had been an Englishwoman, an actress of beauty and promise, who in the zenith of her popularity had made what the world called a fine marriage with a rich Venezuelan, who lived in Paris. The stories of Essex's doubtful paternity were false. Rose Barry—Rose Essex, on the stage—had been the lawful wife of Antonio Perez, and for ten years was the happy wife as well.

They were very prosperous in those days. Barry had gone to the *lycée* all week and come back every Friday to the beautiful apartment in the Rue de Ponthieu. There were lovely spring Sundays when they drove in the Bois and sometimes got out of the carriage and walked down the sun-flecked *allées* under the budding trees. And there were even lovelier winter Sundays when they loitered along the boulevards in the crisp, clear cold, with the sky showing leaden gray through the barring of black boughs, and when they came home to a parlor lit with fire and lamplight and had oranges and hard green grapes after dinner.

He had loved his pretty mother devotedly in those happy days, but for his saturnine, dark-visaged father he had only a sentiment of uneasy fear. He was twelve, when at his mother's request he was sent to England to school. He could remember, looking back afterward, that his mother had not been so pretty or so happy then.

When he came home from school for vacations she was living at Versailles in a little house that presented a secret, non-committal front to the stony street, but that in the back had a delightful garden full of miniature fountains and summer-houses and grottoes. From the wall he could see the mossy trees and stretches of sun-bathed sward of the Trianon. His father was not always there when he came. One Easter vacation he was not there at all, and when he had asked his mother why, she had burst into sudden, terrible tears that frightened him.

During the long summer holidays after that Antonio Perez was only there once over a Sunday. Then he did not come again, and Barry was glad, for he had never cared for his father. He passed delightful days in the Trianon Park with his mother, who was very silent and had gray hair on her temples. She walked beside him with a slow step, dragging her rich lace skirts and with her parasol hanging indolently over her shoulder. It pleased him to see that many people looked at her, but she took no notice of them.

When Barry went back to England to school that year he began to feel that he knew what was coming. It came the next vacation. His mother had not dared to tell him by letter. Her husband had deserted her and disappeared, leaving her with a few thousand francs in the bank, and not a friend.

After that there were three miserable years when they lived in a little apartment on the Rue de Sèvres, up four flights of stairs with a *bonne à tout faire*. His mother had had to conquer the extravagant habits of a lifetime, and she did it ill. During the last year of her life the sale of her jewels kept them. Barry was eighteen when she died, and those long last days when she lay on the sofa in the remnants of the rich and splendid clothes she found it so hard to do without were burned into his memory forever.

Their furniture—some of which was rare and handsome—brought them in a few hundred francs, and on this he lived for another year, eking out his substance with his first tentative attempts at journalism. When he was twenty-one he received a legal notice that his father had died in Venezuela, leaving him all he possessed, which, debts paid and the estate settled, amounted to about ten thousand dollars.

This might have been a fortune to the youth, but the bitter bread he had eaten had soured the best in him. He took his legacy and resolved to taste of the joy of life. For several years he lived on the crest of the wave, now and then diverting himself with journalism, the only profession that attracted him and one in which his talents were readily recognized. He saw much of the world and its ways, living in many cities and among many peoples. He tried to cut himself off from the past, adopting, after his mother's death, her old stage name of Essex.

Then, his money spent, there had been a dark interval of bad luck and despondency, when Barry Essex, the brilliant amateur journalist, had fallen out of the ranks of people that are seen and talked about. Without means, he sank to the level of a battered and out-at-elbows Bohemian. There was a year or two when he swung between London and Paris, making money as he could and not always frequenting creditable company. Then the tide of change struck him and he went to New York, worked there successfully till once again the *Wanderlust* carried him farther afield.

He had now arrived at the crucial point of his career. In his vagabond past there were many episodes best left in darkness, but nothing that stamped him as an outcast by individual selection. Shady things were behind him in that dark, morose year when he found disreputable company to his taste. But he had never stepped quite outside the pale. There had always been a margin.

Now he stood on that margin. He was thirty years old with shame and bitterness behind him, and before him the dead monotony of a lifetime of work. He hated it all. No memory sustained him. The past was as sore to dwell on as the future was sterile. It was the parting of the ways. And where they parted he saw Mariposa standing drawing him by the hand one way, while he gently but persistently drew her the other.

In his softly lit library in his great house at Menlo Park another man was at that time also thinking of Mariposa. He had been thinking of her off and on ever since he had bidden her good by that afternoon at Mrs. Willers'.

As the train had whirled him over the parched, thirsty country, burnt to a leathern dryness by the summer's drouth, he had no thought for anything but his newly discovered daughter. His glance dwelt unseeing on the tanned fields with their belts of olive eucalyptus woods, and the turquoise blue of the bay beyond the painted marsh. Men descending at way stations raised their hats to him as they mounted into the handsome carriages drawn up by the platform. His return to their salutes was a preoccupied nod. His mind was full of his child—his splendid daughter.

Jake Shackleton had not forgotten his first wife and child, as Dan Moreau and Lucy had always hoped. He was a man of many and secret interests, pulling many wires, following many trails. He knew their movements and fortunes from the period of their marriage in Hangtown. At first this secret espionage was due to fear of their betraying him. He had begun to prosper shortly after his entrance into the state, and with prosperity and the slackening of the strain of the trip across the desert came a realization of what he had done. He saw quickly how the selling of his wife would appeal to the California mind in those days fantastically chivalrous to women. He would be undone.

With stealthy persistence he followed the steps of the peaceful couple who had it in their power to ruin him. Serenity began to come to him as he heard that the union was singularly happy; that Moreau, confident no one would molest them, had gone through a ceremony of marriage with Lucy, and that the child was being brought up as their own.

As wealth came to Shackleton he thought of them with a sort of jealous triumph. With his remarkable insight into men he knew that Dan Moreau would never make money; that he was one of the world's predestined poor men. Then as riches grew and grew, and the emigrant of the fifties became the bonanza king of the seventies, he wondered if the time might not come when they would turn to him.

He would have liked it, for under the cold indifference of his manner the transaction at the cabin in the Sierra forever haunted him with its savage shamelessness. It was the one debasing blot on a career which, hard, selfish, often unprincipled, had yet never, before or after, sunk to the level of that base action.

When Moreau died at Santa Barbara Shackleton heard it with a sense of relief. He was secretly becoming very anxious to see his child. Bessie had borne him two children, a boy and a girl, and it was partly the disappointment in these that made him desirous of seeing Mariposa. He knew and Bessie knew that she was his only legitimate child. Though he had virtually entered California with but one wife, and the blot of Mormonism had been wiped from his record before he had been two days in the state, the rumor that he had once been a Mormon still carelessly passed from mouth to mouth. Should it ever become known that there had been a former wife, Bessie and her children would have no lawful claim on him, though the children, as acknowledged and brought up by him, would inherit part of his estate.

With his great wealth the pride that was one of the dominant characteristics of his hard and driving nature grew apace. He had money by millions, but no one to do it credit. It would have been the crowning delight of his tumultuous career to have a beautiful daughter or talented son to grace the luxury that surrounded him. But Bessie's children were neither of these things. They were dull and commonplace. Maud was fat and heavy both in mind and body, while Winslow was, to his father, a slow-witted, characterless youth, without the will, energy or initiative of either of his parents. Affection not grounded on admiration was impossible to Shackleton, who sometimes in his exasperation,—for the successful man bore disappointment ill,—would say to himself:

"But they are not my real children; I have only one child—Dan Moreau's daughter."

After the death of Moreau he learned that Lucy and Mariposa were in San Francisco. There he lost trace of them and was forced to consult a private detective who had done work for him before. It was an easy matter to find them, and only a few letters passed between him and the detective. In these the man gave the address and financial condition of the ladies and added that the daughter was said to be "a beautiful, estimable and accomplished young woman." This fired still further the father's desire to see her. He learned, too, of their crippled means and it pleased him to think that now they might be dependent on him. But he shrank with an unspeakable repugnance from the thought of seeing Lucy again, and he was for weeks trying to find some way of meeting Mariposa and not meeting her mother. It was at this stage that, purely by accident, he learned that Mrs. Willers' daughter was one of Mariposa's pupils. A day or two after he summoned Mrs. Willers to the interview that finally brought about the meeting.

Satisfied pride was still seething in him when he alighted from the train and entered the waiting carriage. This magnificent girl was worthy of him, worthy of the millions that were really hers. She had everything the others lacked—beauty, charm, talents. Her whole air, that regalness of aspect which sometimes curiously distinguishes the simple women of the West, appealed passionately to his ambition and love of success. She was born to conquer, to be a queen of men. The image of Maud rose beside her, and seemed clumsier and commoner than ever. The father felt a slight movement of distaste and irritation against his second daughter, who had supplanted in his home and in the world's regard his elder and fairer child.

The carriage turned in through a lofty gate and rolled at a slackened pace up a long winding drive. Jacob Shackleton's Menlo Park estate was one of the showy ones of that gathering-place of rich men's mansions.

The road wound for some half mile through a stretch of uncultivated land, dotted with the forms of huge live-oaks. The grass beneath them was burnt gray and was brittle and slippery. The massive trees, some round and compact and so densely leaved that they were as impervious to rain as an umbrella, others throwing out long, gnarled arms as if spellbound in some giant throe of pain, cast vast slanting shadows upon the parched ground. Some seemed, like trees in Doré's drawings, to be endowed with a grotesque, weird humanness of aspect, as though an imprisoned dryad or gnome were struggling to escape, causing the mighty trunk to bow and writhe, and sending tremors of life along each convulsed limb. A mellow hoariness marked them all, due to their own richly subdued coloring and the long garlands of silvery moss that hung from their boughs like an eldrich growth of hair.

A sudden greenness in the sward and brilliant glimpses of flower-beds pieced in between dark tree-trunks, told of the proximity of the house. It was a massive structure, architecturally ugly, but gaining a sort of majesty from its own ponderous bulk and from the splendor of lawns and trees about it. The last level rays of the sun were now flooding grass and garden, piercing bosky thickets where greens melted into greens, and sleeping on stretches of close-cropped emerald turf. From among the smaller trees the lordly blue pines—that with the oaks were once the only denizens of the long rich valley—soared up, lonely and somber. Their crests, stirred by passing airs, emitted eolian murmurings, infinitely mournful, as if repining for the days when they had ruled alone.

At the bend in the drive where the road turned off to the stables Shackleton alighted and walked over the grass toward the house. The curious silence that is so marked a characteristic of the California landscape wrapped the place and made it seem like an enchanted palace held in a spell of sleep. Not a leaf nor pendent flower-bell stirred. In this hour of warmth and stillness evanescent breaths of fragrance rose from the carpets of violets that were beginning to bloom about the roots of the live-oaks.

As he reached the house Maud and a young man came round the corner and approached him. The girl was dressed in a delicate and elaborate gown of pale pink frilled with much lace, and with the glint of falling ribbons gleaming here and there. She carried a pink parasol over her shoulder, and against the background of variegated greens her figure looked modish as a fashion-plate. It was a very becoming and elegant costume, and one in which most young girls would have looked their best.

Maud, who was not pretty, was the type of woman who looks least well in handsome habiliments. Her irremediable commonness seemed thrown into higher prominence by adornment. The softly-tinted dress robbed her pale skin of all glow and made her lifeless brown hair look duller. She had a round, expressionless face, prominent pale blue eyes, and a chin that receded slightly. She was not so plain as she was without vivacity, interest, or sparkle of youth. With her matter-of-fact manner, heavy figure, and large, unanimated face she might have been forty instead of twenty-one.

She was somewhat laboriously coquetting with her companion, a tall, handsome young Southerner, some six or seven years her senior, whom her father recognized as one of his superior clerks and shrewdly suspected of matrimonial designs. At sight of her parent a slight change passed over her face. She smiled, but not so spontaneously; her speech faltered, and she said, coming awkwardly forward:

"Oh, Popper! you're late to-day; were you delayed?"

"Evidently, considering I'm an hour later than usual. Howdy, Latimer; glad to see you down."

He stopped and looked at them with the slightest inquiring smile. Though he said nothing to indicate it, both, knowing him in different aspects, felt he was not pleased. His whole personality seemed to radiate a cold antagonism.

"It's good you got down anyhow," said Maud constrainedly; "this is much nicer than town, isn't it, Mr. Latimer?"

All the joy had been taken out of Latimer by his chief's obvious and somewhat terrifying displeasure. Had he been alone with Maud, he would have known well how to respond to her remark with Southern fervency of phrase. But now he only said with stiff politeness:

"Oh, this is quite ideal!" and lapsed into uncomfortable silence.

"Was it some one interesting that made you late?" queried Maud, as her father made no attempt to continue the conversation.

"Very," he responded; "handsome and interesting."

"Won't you tell us about them?" the girl asked, feeling that the word "handsome" contained a covert allusion to her own lack of beauty of which she was extremely sensitive.

"Not now, and I don't think it would interest you much, anyway. Is your mother indoors?"

The girl nodded and he turned away and disappeared round the corner of the house. She and Latimer sauntered on.

"The handsome and interesting person doesn't seem to have made your paternal any fuller than usual of the milk of human kindness," said the young man, whose suit had progressed further than people guessed.

"Popper's often like that," said Maud slowly,—and in a prettier and more attractive girl the tone and manner of the remark would have been charmingly plaintive,—"I don't know what makes him so."

"He can be more like a patent congealing ice-box when he wants to be than anybody I ever saw. But I don't see why he should be so to you."

"I don't, either, but he is often. He never says anything exactly disagreeable, but he makes me feel sort of—of—mean. Sometimes I think he doesn't like me at all."

"Oh, bosh!" said Latimer gallantly; "if that's the case he's ripe for a commission of lunacy."

Shackleton meantime had entered the house and ascended to his dressing-room. He was in there making the small change which marked his dinner from his business toilet when his wife entered.

The years had turned Bessie into a buxom, fine-looking matron, fashionably dressed, but inclined to be very stout. Her eye and its glance were sharp and keen-edged, still alight with vigor and alertness. It was easy to see why Jake Shackleton, the reader of character, had set aside his feeble first wife for this dominating and forceful partner. He had been faithful to her; after a fashion had loved her, and certainly admired her, for she had the characteristics he most respected.

In his success she had been the same assistance that she had been in his poverty. She had climbed the social heights and conquered the impregnable position they now occupied. Her rich dress, her handsome appearance, her agreeably modulated voice, all were in keeping with the position and great wealth that were theirs. The house of which she was the mistress was admirably ordered and sumptuously furnished. She had only disappointed him in one way—her children.

"What made you late?" she, too, asked; "several people came down this afternoon."

"I was detained—a girl Mrs. Willers wanted me to see; who's here?"

"Latimer, and Count de Lamolle, and George Herron and the Thurston girls; and the Delanceys are coming over to dinner."

He nodded at the names—Bessie knew well how to arrange her parties. The Thurstons were two impoverished sisters of great beauty and that proud Southern stock of which early California thought so highly and rewarded in most cases with poverty. Count de Lamolle was a distinguished foreigner that she was considering for Maud. The other two young men filled in nicely. The Delanceys were a brother and sister, claimants of the great Delancey Grant, which was now in litigation. It had come into their possession by the marriage of their grandmother, the Senorita Concepcion de Briones, in '36, to the Yankee skipper, Jeremiah Delancey.

"Who was the girl Mrs. Willers wanted you to see?" Bessie asked.

"Oh, I'll tell you about her to-morrow. It's a long story, and I don't want to be hurried over it."

He had made up his mind that he would tell Bessie he had seen and intended to assist his eldest child. He had always been frank with her and he was not going to dissemble now. He knew that with all her faults she was a generous woman.

CHAPTER IV

A GALA NIGHT

"He looked at her as a lover can;
She looked at him as one who awakes."
—Browning.

From his first meeting with her, Barry Essex had conceived a deep interest in Mariposa. He had known women of many and divers sorts, and loved a few after the manner of his kind, which was to foster indolently a selfish caprice. Marriage was out of the question for him unless with money, and some instinct, perhaps inherited from his romantic and deeply-loving mother, made this singularly repugnant to his nature, which was neither sensitive nor scrupulous. The mystery and hazard of life appealed passionately to him, and to exchange this for the dull monotony of a rich marriage was an unbearably irksome thought to his unrestrained and adventurous spirit.

Mariposa's charm had struck him deep. He had never before met that combination of extreme simplicity of character with the unconscious majesty of appearance which marked the child of the far West. He saw her in that Europe, which was his home, as a conquering queen; and he thought proudly of himself as the owner of such a woman. Moreover he was certain that her voice, properly trained and directed, would be a source of wealth. She seemed to him the real vocal artist, stupid in all but one great gift; in that, preëminent.

Mariposa was trembling on the verge of a first love. She had never seen any one like Essex and regarded him as the most distinguished and brilliant of beings. His attentions flattered her as she had never been flattered before, and she found herself constantly wondering what he saw in a girl who must appear to him so raw.

Her experience of men was small. Once in Sacramento, when she was eighteen, she had received an offer from a young lawyer, and two years ago, in Santa Barbara, she had been the recipient of a second, from a prosperous rancher. Both had been refused without hesitation, and had left no mark on imagination or heart. Then, at a critical period of her life—lonely, poor, a stranger in a strange city—she had fallen in with Essex, and for the first time felt the thrill at the sound of a footstep, the quickening pulse and flushing cheek at the touch of a hand, that she had read of in novels. She thought that nobody had seen this; but the eyes of the dangerous man under whose spell she had fallen were watching her with wary yet ardent interest.

He had known her now for three months and had seen her frequently. His visits at the Pine Street cottage were augmented by occasional meetings at Mrs. Willers, when that lady was at home and receiving company, and by walks together. Of late, too, he had asked her to go to the theater with him. Lucy was always included in these invitations, but was unable to go. The theater was an untarnished delight to Mariposa, and to refuse her the joy of an evening spent there was not in the mother's heart. Moreover, Lucy, in her agony at the thought of leaving the girl alone in the world, watched Essex with a desperate anxiety trying to fathom his feelings. It seemed to the unworldly woman, that this attractive gentleman might have been sent by fate to be the husband who was to love and guard the child when the mother was gone.

A few days after the party at Mrs. Willers' rooms Essex had invited Mariposa to go with him to a performance of "Il Trovatore," to be given at Wade's opera-house. The company, managed by a Frenchman called Lepine, was one of those small foreign ones that in those days toured the West to their own profit and the pleasure of their audiences. The star was advertised as a French diva of European renown. Essex had heard her on the continent, and pronounced her well worth hearing, if rather too fat to be satisfying to the esthetic demands of the part of Leonora. Grand opera was still something of a rarity in San Francisco and it promised to be an occasion. The papers printed the names of those who had bought boxes. Mariposa had read that evening that Jacob Shackleton would occupy the left-hand proscenium box with his wife and family.

"His daughter," said Mariposa, standing in front of the glass as she put on finishing touches, "is ugly, Mrs. Willers says. I think that's the way it ought to be. It wouldn't be fair to be an heiress and handsome."

"It wouldn't be fair for you to be an heiress, certainly," commented the mother from her armchair.

"You don't think I abuse the privilege a penniless girl has of being good-looking?" said Mariposa, turning from the glass with a twinkling eye.

She looked her best and knew it. Relics of better days lingered in the bureau drawers and jewel boxes of these ladies as they did in the small parlor. That night they had been mustered in their might for Mariposa's decking. She was proud in the consciousness that the dress of fine black lace she wore, through the meshes of which her statuesque arms and neck gleamed like ivory, was made from a shawl that in its day had been a costly possession. Her throat was bare, the lace leaving it free and closing below it. Where the black edges came together over the white skin a small brooch of diamonds was fastened. Below the rim of her hat, her hair glowed like copper, and the coloring of her lips and cheeks was deepened by excitement into varying shades of coral.

As they entered the theater, Essex was aware that many heads were turned in their direction. But Mariposa was too imbued with the joyous unusualness of the moment to notice it. She had forgotten herself entirely, and sitting a little forward, her lips parted, surveyed the rustling and fast-filling house.

The glow of the days of Comstock glory was still in the air. San Francisco was still the city of gold and silver. The bonanza kings had not left it, but were trying to accommodate themselves to the palaces they were rearing with their loose millions. Society yet retained its cosmopolitan tone, careless, brilliant, and unconventional. There were figures in it that had made it famous—men who began life with a pick and shovel and ended it in an orgy of luxury; women, whose habits of early poverty dropped from them like a garment, and who, carried away by their power, displayed the barbaric caprices of Roman empresses.

The sudden possession of vast wealth had intoxicated this people, lifting them from the level of the commonplace into a saturnalia of extravagance. Poverty, the only restraint many of them had ever felt, was gone. Money had made them lawless, whimsical, bizarre. It had developed all-conquering personalities, potent individualities. They were still playing with it, wondering at it, throwing it about.

Essex let his glance roam over the audience, that filled the parquet, and the three horseshoes above it. It struck him as being more Latin than American. That foreignness which has always clung to California was curiously pronounced in this gathering of varied classes. He saw many faces with the ebon hair and olive skins of the Spanish Californians, lovely women, languid and fawn-eyed, badly dressed—for they were almost all poor now, who once were lords of the soil.

The great Southern element which, in its day, set the tone of the city and contributed much to its traditions of birth and breeding, was already falling into the background. Many of its women had only their beauty left, and this they had adorned, as Mariposa had hers, with such remnants of the days when Plancus was consul, as remained—bits of jewelry, old and unmodish but cumbrously handsome, edgings of lace, a pale-colored feather in an old hat, a crape shawl worn with an air, a string of beads carried bravely, though beads were no longer in the mode.

An arrogant air of triumph marked the Irish Californians. With the opening up of the Comstock they had stuck their flag on the summit of the heights. They had always found California kindly, but by the discovery of that mountain of silver they had become kings where they were once content to serve. The Irish face, sometimes in its primeval, monkey-like ugliness, sometimes showing the fresh colored, blowsy prettiness of the colleens by their native bogs, repeated itself on every side. Now and then one of them shone out like a painting by Titian—the Hibernian of the red-gold hair and milk-white skin, refined by luxury and delicate surroundings into a sumptuous and arresting beauty. Many showed the metal that had carried their fathers on to victory. Others were only sleek, smooth-skinned animals, lazy, sensuous, and sly. And these women, whose mothers had run barefoot, were dressed with the careless splendor of those to whom a diamond is a detail.

Essex raised his glass from the perusal of the sea of faces, to the box which the Shackleton party had just entered. There was no question about the Americanism of this group, the young man thought, as he stared at Jake Shackleton. Square-set and unadorned, in the evening dress which Bessie made him wear, he sat back from the velvet railing, an uncompromising figure of dynamic force, unbeautiful, shrewd, the most puissant presence in that brilliant assemblage.

A GALA NIGHT

The two ladies in the front of the box were Mrs. and Miss Shackleton. The former was floridly handsome, almost aristocratic, the gazer thought, looking at her firmly-modeled, composed face under its roll of gray hair. The daughter was very like her father, but ugly. Even in the costly French costume she wore, with the gleam of diamonds in her hair, about her neck, in the lace on her bosom, she was ugly. Essex, with that thought of marrying money in the background of his mind, scrutinized her. To rectify his fortune in such a way became more repugnant than ever. If Mariposa had only been Jake Shackleton's daughter instead!

He turned and looked at her. She met his glance with eyes darkened by excitement.

"There's Mr. Shackleton in the box," she said eagerly, in a half-whisper. "Did you see?"

"Yes, I've been looking, and that's his daughter, Maud Shackleton, in the white with diamonds."

"Is it? Oh, what a beautiful dress! and quantities of diamonds. Almost too many; they twinkle like water, as if some one had squeezed a sponge over her."

"What can you do when you're a bonanza king's daughter and as ugly as that? You've got to keep up your end of the line some way. She evidently thinks diamonds are the best way."

Essex took the glass and looked at the bedecked heiress again. After some moments he put it down and turned to Mariposa with a quizzical smile.

"Do you know I'm going to say something very funny, but look at her well. Does she look like anybody you know?"

The girl looked and shook her head:

"Like her father a little," she said, "but no one else I can think of."

"No, not her father. Some one you know intimately and see often—very often, if you're as vain as you ought to be."

"Who?" she demanded, frowning and looking puzzled; "I can't think whom you mean."

"Yourself; she looks like you."

Mariposa gave a quick look at the girl and then at Essex. For the moment she thought he was mocking her, but with her second look at the box, the likeness suddenly struck her.

"She is," she said slowly, reaching for the glass; "yes," putting it down, "I see it—she is. How funny! and fancy your telling me on top of the statement that she was so ugly! I don't see how I can smile again this evening."

She smiled with the words on her lips, the charming smile of a woman who knows her silliest phrases are delightful to one man at least.

"I'm not entirely like her?" she asked, with a somewhat anxious air; "I haven't got those pale-gray, prominent eyes, have I?"

"No, you've got mysterious dark eyes, as deep as wells, and when I look into them, down, down, I sometimes wonder if I can see your heart at the bottom. Can I? Let me see."

He leaned forward as if to look straight into her eyes. Mariposa suddenly flushing and feeling uncomfortable, dropped them. The sensation she so often experienced with Essex, of being awkward and raw, was intensified now by the annoyed embarrassment provoked by the florid gallantry of his words. But she was too inexperienced a little fly to deal with this cunning spider, and tangled herself worse in the web by saying nervously:

"And my nose! I haven't got that kind of nose? Oh, surely not," putting up a gloved hand to feel of its unsatisfactoriness.

"You have the dearest little nose in the world, straight as a Greek statue's. It's a little bit haughty, but I like it that way. And your mouth," he dropped his voice slightly, "your mouth—"

Mariposa made a sudden movement of annoyance. She threw up her head and looked at the curtain with frowning brows.

"Don't," she said sharply, "I don't like you to talk about me like that."

Essex was silent, regarding her profile with a deliberating eye and a slight, amused smile. How crude she was and how handsome! After a moment's silence, he leaned toward her and said in a voice full of good-humored banter:

"Butterfly! Butterfly! Why did they call you Butterfly?"

The change in his tone and manner put her back at once on the old footing of gay bonhomie.

"In English, that way, it sounds dreadful, doesn't it? Fancy me being called Butterfly! I was called after the flower. My whole name is Mariposa Lily."

"Mariposa Lily!" he repeated in amused amazement; "what an absurd name!"

"Absurd!" said Mariposa indignantly. "I don't see

anything absurd about it. I think it very pretty. My mother called me after the flower, the first time she saw it. They couldn't find a suitable name for me for a long time, and then when she saw the flower she decided at once to call me after it. It's the most beautiful wild flower in California."

"It's fortunate you were not called Eschscholtzia," said Essex, who thought the name extremely ridiculous, and who found a somewhat mean amusement in teasing the girl; "you might just as well have been called Eschscholtzia Poppy."

The spirited reply which was on Mariposa's lips was stopped by the rising of the curtain. The crowded, rustling house settled itself into silence, the orchestra's subdued notes rolled out with the voices swelling above them into the listening auditorium.

The rest of the evening was an enchanted dream to her. She had never seen an opera, and for the first time realized what it might mean to possess a voice. She heard the house thunder its applause to Leonora, and thought of herself as singing thus, standing alone on that dim stage, looking out over the sea of faces, all listening, all staring, all spellbound, hanging on the notes that fell, sweet and rich, thrilling and passionate, from her lips. Could there ever be such a life for her? Did they tell the truth when they spoke so admiringly of her voice? Could she ever sing like this? A surge of exultant conviction rose in her, and sent its whisper of hope and ambition to her throbbing brain.

As the opera progressed she grew pale and motionless. The wild thought was gaining possession of her, that she, Mariposa Moreau, with her four pupils and her sixteen dollars a month, could sing as well as this woman of European renown, for whom Essex, the critical, the vastly experienced, had words of praise. Once or twice it seemed to her as if the notes were swelling in her own throat, were pressing to burst out and soar up, higher, fuller, richer than the woman's on the stage. Oh, the rapture of being able to pour out one's voice, to give wild, melodious expression to love or despair, while a thousand people hung this way on one's lips!

As the curtain fell for the third time she turned to Essex, pale and large-eyed, and said breathlessly:

"I could sing as well as that woman if I had more lessons; I know I could! I know it!"

CHAPTER V

TRIAL FLIGHTS

"The music of the moon
Sleeps in the plain eggs of the nightingale."
—TENNYSON.

A week had not passed since the night at the opera when Mariposa received a hasty letter from Mrs. Willers. It was only a few lines scrawled on a piece of the yellow paper affected by the staff of *The Trumpet,* and advising the recipient of the fact that Mr. Shackleton requested her presence at his office at three the following afternoon, yet a suggestion of triumph breathed from its every word. Mrs. Willers was clearly elated at the moment of its production. She hinted, in a closing sentence, that Mariposa's star was rising rapidly. She, herself, would conduct the girl to the presence of the great man, and suggested that Mariposa meet her in her rooms a half-hour before the time set for the interview.

Mariposa was glad to do this, and in the few moments' walk across town toward Third Street, to hear what Mrs. Willers thought was the object of the interview. The girl's cheeks were dyed with excited color as they drew near *The Trumpet* office. Mrs. Willers was certain it was to do with her singing. Shackleton had almost told her as much. He had been immensely impressed by her voice, and now, with the Lepine Opera Company in the city, Mrs. Willers fancied he was going to have Lepine, who was a well-known impresario in a small but respectable way, pass judgment on it. Mariposa's foot lagged when she heard this. It was such a portentous step from the seclusion of a rose-draped cottage in Santa Barbara, even to this talk of singing before a real impresario. She looked down the vista of Third Street where the façade of *The Trumpet* office loomed large from humbler neighbors, and Mrs. Willers saw hesitation and fright in her eyes. Like a sensible guardian she slipped her hand through the young girl's arm and walked her briskly forward, talking of the rare chances life offers to a handicapped humanity.

The Trumpet office, as all old San Franciscans know, stood on Third Street, and was, in its day, considered a fine building. Jake Shackleton had not been its owner six months yet, and all his reforms were not inaugurated. From the yawning arch of its doorway flights of stairs led up and upward, from stories where the presses rattled all night, to the editorial story where the sentiments of *The Trumpet* staff were confided to paper. This latter and most important department was four flights up the dark stairway, which was lit at its turnings with large kerosene lamps, backed by tin reflectors. There was little of the luxury of the modern newspaper office about the barren, business-like building, echoing like an empty shell to the shouts of men and the pounding of machinery.

At the top of the fourth flight the ladies paused. The landing broadened out into a sort of anteroom, bare and windowless, two dejected-looking gas-jets dispensing a tarnished yellow light into the surrounding gloom. A boy, with a sleek, oiled head, sat at a table reading that morning's issue of *The Trumpet.* He put it down as Mrs. Willers rose before his vision and nodded familiarly to her. She gave him a quick word of greeting and swept Mariposa forward through a doorway, down a long passage, from which doors opened into tiny rooms with desks and droplights. The girl now and then had glimpses of men seated at the desks, the radiance of the droplights hard on their faces that had been lifted expectantly as their ears caught the interesting rustle of skirts in the corridor.

Suddenly, at the end of the passage, Mrs. Willers struck with her knuckles on a closed portal. The next moment Mariposa, with the light of a large window shining full on her face, was shaking hands with Shackleton. Then, in response to his motioning hand, she took the chair beside the desk, where she sat, facing the white glare of the window, conscious of his keen eyes critically regarding her. Mrs. Willers took a chair in the background. For a moment she had fears that the nervousness she had noticed in her protégée's countenance on the way down would make her commit some *bêtise* that would antagonize the interest Shackleton so evidently took in her. Mrs. Willers had seen her chief's brusk impatience roused by follies more excusable than those that rise from a young girl's nervous shyness and that would be incomprehensible to his hardy, self-confident nature.

But Mariposa seemed encouragingly composed.

She again felt the curious sense of ease, of being at home with him, that this unknown man had given her before. She had that inspiring sensation that she was approved; that this old-time friend of her father's had a singular unspoken sympathy with her. "As if he might have been an old friend," she told her mother after the first meeting, "or some kind of relation—one of those uncles that come back from India in the English novels."

Now only her fluctuating color told of the inward tumult that possessed her as he told her concisely, but kindly, that he had arranged for her to sing before Lepine, the manager of the opera, at two o'clock on the following day. Several people of experience had told him Lepine was an excellent judge. They would then hear an expert's opinion on her voice.

"I think it's the finest kind of voice," he said, smiling, "but you know my opinion's worth more on ores than on voices. So we won't soar too high till we hear what the fellow whose business it is, has to say. Then, if he's satisfied"—he gave a little shrug—"we'll see."

The interview was brought to an end in a few moments. It seemed to Mariposa that the scenes which Mrs. Willers assured her were so big with promise were incredibly short for moments so fraught with destiny. She seemed hardly to have caught her breath yet from the ascent of the four flights of stairs, when they were once again walking down the corridor, with the writing men looking up with pricked ears at the returning rustle of skirts. It was Mrs. Willers who had wafted her away so quickly.

"Never beat about the bush where you deal with

Jake Shackleton," she said, slipping her hand in Mariposa's arm as they passed down the corridor. "He's got no use for people who gambol round the subject. Say your say and then go. That's the way to get on with him."

In the anteroom the boy was still sitting, his chair tilted back on its hind legs, *The Trumpet* in his hands. Nevertheless, he had made an incursion into the inner regions to find out whom Mrs. Willers was piloting into the sanctum, for he had the curiosity of those who hang on the fringes of the newspaper world.

As the ladies passed him, going toward the stairhead, a young man rose above it, almost colliding with them. Then in the gloom of the dejected gas-jets he stood aside, against the wall, letting them pass out. He wore a long ulster with a turned-up collar. Between the edge of this and the brim of his derby hat, there was the gleam of a pair of eye-glasses and a suggestion of a fair mustache. He raised his hat, holding it above his head during the interval of their transit, disclosing a small pate clothed with smooth blond hair.

"Who was that lady with Mrs. Willers?" he said to the boy, as he walked toward the door into the corridor.

"She's some singing lady," answered that youth drawlingly, tilting his chair still farther back, "what's come to see Mr. Shackleton about singing at the opera-house. Her name's Moreau."

The young man, without further comment, passed into the inner hall, leaving the boy smiling with pride that his carelessly-acquired information should have been so soon of use. For the questioner was Winslow Shackleton, the millionaire's only son.

The next morning was one of feverish excitement in the cottage on Pine Street. Mariposa could not settle herself to anything, at one moment trying her voice at the piano, at the next standing in front of her glass and putting on all her own and her mother's hats in an effort to see in which she presented the most attractive appearance. She thrilled with hope for a space, then sank into a dead apathy of dejection. Lucy was quietly encouraging, but the day was one of hidden anguish to her. The daughter, ignorant of the knowledge and the memories that were wringing the mother's heart, wondered why Lucy was so confident of her winning Shackleton's approval. As the hour came for her to go she wondered, too, at the marble pallor of her mother's face, at the coldness of the hand that clung to hers in a lingering farewell. Lucy was giving back her child to the father who had deserted it and her.

The excitement of the morning reached its climax when a carriage appeared at the curb with Mrs. Willers' face at the window. The hour of fate had struck, and Mariposa, with a last kiss to her mother, ran down the steps feeling like one about to embark on a journey upon perilous seas in which lie enchanted islands.

During the drive Mrs. Willers talked on outside matters. She was business-like and quiet to-day. Even her clothes seemed to partake of her practical mood and were inconspicuous and subdued. As the carriage turned down Mission Street she herself began to experience qualms. What if they had all been mistaken and the girl's voice was nothing out of the ordinary? What a cruel disappointment, and with that sick, helpless mother! What she said was:

"Now, here we are! Remember that you've got the finest voice Lepine's ever likely to hear, and you're going to sing your best."

They alighted, and as they turned into the flagged entrance that led to the foyer, Shackleton came forward to meet them. He looked older in the crude afternoon light, his face showing the lines that his fiercely-lived life had plowed in it. But he smiled reassuringly at Mariposa and pressed her hand.

"Everything's all ready," he said; "Lepine's put back a rehearsal for us, so we mustn't keep him waiting. And are you all ready to surprise us?" he asked, as they walked together toward where the three steps led to the foyer.

"I'm ready to do my best," she answered; "a person can't do more than that."

The answer pleased him, as everything she said did. He saw she was nervous, but that she was going to conquer herself.

"Lots of grit," he said to himself as he gave ear to a remark of Mrs. Willers'. "She won't quit at the first obstacle."

They passed through the opening in the brass rail that led to the foyer. This space, the gathering place of the radiant beings of Mariposa's first night at the opera, was now a dimly-lit and deserted hall, its flagged flooring looking dirty in the raw light. From somewhere, in what seemed a far, dreamy distance, the sound of a piano came, as if muffled by numerous doors. As they crossed the foyer toward the entrance into the auditorium, the door swung open and two men appeared.

One was a short and stout Frenchman, with a turned-over collar, upon which a double chin rested. He had a bald forehead and eyes that gleamed sharply from behind a *pince-nez*. At sight of the trio, he gave an exclamation and came forward.

"Our young lady?" he said to Mariposa, giving her a quick look of scrutiny that seemed to take her in from foot to forehead. Then he greeted Shackleton with slightly exaggerated foreign effusion. He spoke English perfectly, but with the inevitable accent. This was Lepine, the impresario, and the other man, an Italian who spoke little English, was presented as Signor Tojetti, the conductor.

They moved forward talking, and then, pushing the door open, Lepine motioned Mariposa to enter. She did so and for a moment stood amazed, staring into a vast, shadowy space, where, in what seemed a vague, undefined distance, a tiny spot or two of light cut into the darkness. The air was chill and smelt of a stable. From somewhere she heard the sound of voices rising and falling, and then again the notes of a piano, now near and unobscured, carelessly touched and resembling, in the echoing hollow spaciousness of the great building, the thin, tinkling sounds emitted by smitten glass.

Lepine brushed past her and led the way down the aisle. As she followed him her eyes became accustomed to the dimness, and she began to make out the arch of the stage with blackness beyond, into which cut the circles of light of a few gas-jets. The lines of seats stretched before her spectral in linen covers. Now and then a figure crossed the stage, and as they drew nearer, she saw on one side of it a man sitting on a high stool reading a paper book by the light of a shaded lamp. The notes of the piano sounded sharper and closer, and by their proximity more than by her sight, she located it in a dark corner of the orchestra. As they approached, the sound of two voices came from this corner, then suddenly a man's smothered laugh.

"Mr. Martinez," said Lepine, directing his voice toward the darkness whence the laugh had risen, "the lady is here to sing, if you are ready."

Instantly a faintly luminous spark, Mariposa had noticed, bloomed into the full-blown radiance of a gas-jet turned full cock under a sheltering shade. It projected, what seemed in the dimness, a torrent of light on the keyboard of the piano, illuminating a pair of long masculine hands that had been moving over the keys in the darkness. Behind them the girl saw a shadowy shape, and then a spectacled face under a mane of drooping black hair was advanced into the light.

"Has the lady her music?" said the face, in English, but with another variety of accent.

She handed him the two songs she had brought, "Knowest thou the Land," from Mignon, and "Farewell, Lochaber." In the short period of her tuition her teacher had told her that she had sung "Lochaber" admirably. The man opened them, glanced at the names, and placing the "Mignon" aria on the rack, ran his hands lightly and carelessly over the keys in the opening bars of the accompaniment.

"Whenever the lady is ready," he said, with an air of patience, as though he had endured this form of persecution until all spirit of revolt was crushed.

Mariposa drew back from him, wondering if she were to sing there and then. Lepine was behind her, and behind him she saw, with a sense of nostalgic loneliness, that the Italian conductor was shepherding Mrs. Willers and Shackleton into two seats on the aisle. They looked small and far away.

"We will mount to the stage this way, Mademoiselle," said Lepine, and he indicated a small flight of steps that rose from the corner of the orchestra to the lip of the stage above.

He ascended first, she close at his heels, and in a moment found herself on the dark, deserted stage. It seemed enormous to her, stretching back into unseen regions where the half-defined shapes of trees and castles, walls and benches were huddled in dim confusion. Down the aisles between side-scenes she caught glimpses of vistas lit by wavering gleams of light. People moved here and there, across these vistas, their footsteps sounding singularly distinct. As she stood uneasily, looking to the right and left, a sudden sound of hammering arose from somewhere behind, loud and vibrant. Lepine, who was about to descend the stairs, turned and shouted a furious sentence in Italian down the opening. The hammering instantly ceased, and a man in white overalls came and stared at the stage. The impresario, charily—being short and fat—descended the stairs.

"Now, Mademoiselle," he said, speaking from the orchestra, "if you are ready, come forward a little, nearer the footlights there."

Mariposa moved forward. Her heart was beating in her throat, and she felt a sick terror at the thought of what her voice would be like in that huge void space. She was aware that the man who had been reading the paper book had closed it and was leaning his elbow on the lamp-stand, watching her. She was also aware that a woman and a man had suddenly appeared in the lower proscenium box close beside her. She saw the woman dimly, a fat, short figure in a light-colored ulster. Whispering to the man, she drew one of the linen-covered chairs close to the railing and seated herself.

"Is the lady ready?" said the pianist, from his dark corner.

"Quite ready," replied Mariposa, hearing her voice like a tremulous thread of sound in the stillness.

The first bars of the accompaniment sounded thinly. Mariposa stepped forward. She could see in the shadowy emptiness of the auditorium Lepine's bald head where he sat alone, half way up the house, and the two pale faces of Shackleton and Mrs. Willers. The Italian conductor had left them and was sitting by himself at one side of the parquet. In the stillness, the notes of the piano were curiously tinkling and feeble.

Mariposa raised her chest with a deep inspiration.

A sudden excited expectation seized her at the thought of letting her voice swell out into the hushed void before her. The listening people seemed so small and insignificant in it, they suddenly lost their terror. She began to sing.

It seemed to her that her first notes were hardly audible. They seemed as ineffectual as the piano. Then her confidence grew, and delight with it. She never before had felt as if she had enough room. Her voice rolled itself out like a breaking wave, lapping the walls of the building.

The first verse came to an end. The accompaniment ceased. Lepine moved in his distant seat.

"Continue, Mademoiselle," he said sharply; "the second verse, if you please. Again, Mr. Martinez."

Mariposa saw the woman in the box look at the man beside her, raise her eyebrows, and nod.

She began the second verse and sang it through. As its last notes died out there was silence for a moment. In the silence the Italian conductor rose and came forward to where Lepine sat. Mariposa, standing on the stage, saw them conferring for a space. The Italian talked in a low voice, with much gesticulation. Shackleton and Mrs. Willers were motionless and dumb. The woman in the box began to whisper with the man.

"And now the second piece, if Mademoiselle has no objection," came the voice of the impresario across the parquet. "One can not judge well from one song."

The second song, "Lochaber," had been chosen by Mariposa's teacher to show off her lower register—those curious, disturbing notes that were so deep and full of vague melancholy. She had gained such control as she had over her voice and sang with an almost joyous exultation. She had never realized what it was to sing before people who knew and who listened in this way in a place that was large enough.

When the last notes died away, the tinkling of the piano sounding like the frail specters of music after the tones of the rich, vibrant voice, there was a sudden noise of clapping hands. It came from the box on the right, where the woman in the ulster was leaning over the rail, clapping with her bare hands held far out.

"*Brava!*" she cried in a loud, full voice. "*Brava! La belle voix! Et quel volume! Brava!*"

She bounced round on her chair to look at the man beside her, and, leaning forward, clapped again, crying her gay "brava."

Mariposa walked toward the box, feeling suddenly shy. As she drew nearer she saw the woman's face more distinctly. It was a dark French face, with a brunette skin warming to brick-dust red on the cheeks, set in a frame of wiry black hair, and with a big mouth that, laughing, showed strong white teeth, well separated. As Mariposa saw it fairly in the light of an adjacent lamp she recognized it as that of the Leonora of "Il Trovatore." It was the prima donna.

She started forward with flushing cheek and held out a hesitating hand. The fat, ungloved palms of the singer closed on it with Gælic effusion. Mariposa was aware of something delightfully wholesome and kind in the broad, ruddy visage, with its big, smiling mouth and the firm teeth like the halves of cleanly-broken hazelnuts. The singer, leaning over the rail, poured a rumbling volume of French into the girl's blushing, upturned face. Mariposa understood it and was trying to answer in her halting schoolgirl phrases, when the voice of Mrs. Willers, at the bottom of the steps, summoned her.

"Come down, quick! They think it's fine. Oh, dearie," stretching up a helping hand as Mariposa swept her skirts over the line of the footlights, "you did fine. It was great. You've just outdone yourself. And you looked stunning, too. I only wished the place had been full. Heavens! but I thought I'd die at first. While you were standing there waiting to begin I felt seasick. It was an awful moment. And you looked just as cool! Mr. Shackleton don't say much, but I know he's tickled to death."

They walked up the aisle as she talked to where Shackleton and the two men were standing in earnest conversation. As they approached Lepine turned toward her and gave a slight smile.

"We were saying, Mademoiselle," he said, "that you have unquestionably a voice. The lower register is remarkably fine. Of course, it is very untrained; absolutely in the rough. But Signor Tojetti, here, finds that a strong point in your favor."

"Signor Tojetti," said Shackleton, "seems to think that two years of study would be ample to fit you for the operatic stage."

Mariposa looked from one to the other with beaming eyes, hardly able to believe it all.

"You really did like it, then?" she said to Lepine with her most ingenuous air.

He shrugged his shoulders, with a queer French expression of quizzical amusement.

"It was a truly interesting performance, and after a period of study with a good master it should be a truly delightful one."

The Italian, to whom these sentences were only half intelligible, now broke in with a quick series of sonorous phrases, directed to Lepine, but now and then turned upon Shackleton. Mariposa's eyes went from one to the other in an effort to understand. The impresario, listening with frowning intentness, responded with a nod and a word of brusk acquiescence. Turning to Shackleton, he said:

"Tojetti also thinks that the appearance of Mademoiselle is much in her favor. She has an admirable stage presence"—he looked at Mariposa as if she were a piece of furniture he was appraising. "Her height alone is of inestimable value. She would have at least five feet eight or nine inches."

At this moment the lady in the box, who had risen to her feet, and was leaning against the railing, called suddenly:

"*Lepine, vraiment une belle voix, et aussi une belle fille! Vous avez fait une trouvaille.*"

Lepine wheeled round to his star, who in the shadowy light stood, a pale-colored, burly figure, buttoning her ulster over her redundant chest.

"A moment," he said, apologetically to the others, and, running to the box, stood with his head back, talking to her, while the prima donna leaned over and a rapid interchange of French sentences passed between them.

Signor Tojetti turned to Mariposa, and, with solemn effort, produced an English phrase:

"Eet ees time to went." Then he waved his hand toward the stage. The sound of feet echoed therefrom, and as Mariposa looked, an irruption of vague, spectral shapes rose from some unseen cavernous entrance and peopled the orchestra.

"It's the rehearsal," she said. "We must be going."

They moved forward toward the entrance, the auditorium behind them beginning to resound with the noise of the incoming performers. A scraping of strings came from the darkened orchestra, and mingled with the tentative chords struck from the piano. At the door Lepine joined them, falling into step beside Shackleton and conversing with him in low tones. Signor Tojetti escorted them to the brass rail and there withdrew with low bows. The ladies made out that the rehearsal demanded his presence.

Once again in the gray light of the afternoon they stood for a moment at the curb waiting for the carriage.

Lepine offered his farewells to Mariposa and his wishes to see her again.

"In Paris," he said, giving his little quizzical smile—"that is the place in which I should like to see Mademoiselle."

"We'll talk about that again," said Shackleton; "I'm going to see Mr. Lepine before he goes and have another talk about you. You see, you're becoming a very important young lady."

The carriage rolled up and Mariposa was assisted

in, several street boys watching her with wide-eyed interest as evidently a personage of distinction.

Her face at the window smiled a radiant farewell at the group on the sidewalk; then she sank back breathless. What an afternoon! Would the carriage ever get her home, that she might pour it all out to her mother! What a thrilling, wonderful, unheard-of afternoon!

CHAPTER VI

THE VISION AND THE DREAM

"For a dream cometh through the multitude of business."
—ECCLESIASTES.

As the carriage turned the corner into Third Street, Shackleton and Mrs. Willers, bidding their adieux to Lepine, started toward *The Trumpet* office. The building was not ten minutes' walk away, and both the proprietor and the woman reporter had work there that called them.

In their different ways each was exceedingly elated. The man, with his hard, bearded face, the upper half shaded by the brim of his soft felt hat, gave no evidence in appearance or manner of the exultation that possessed him. But the woman, with her more febrile and less self-contained nature, showed her excited gratification in her reddened cheeks and the sparkling animation of her tired eyes. Her state of joyous triumph was witnessed even in her walk, in the way she swished her skirts over the pavements, in the something youthful and buoyant that had crept into the tones of her voice.

"Well," she said, "that *was* an experience worth having! I never heard her sing so before. She just outdid herself."

"She certainly seemed to me to sing well. I was doubtful at the beginning, not knowing any more about singing than I do about Sanskrit, as to whether she really had as fine a voice as we thought. But there don't seem to me to be any doubt about it now."

"Lepine is quite certain, is he?" queried Mrs. Willers, who had tried to listen to the conversation between her chief and the impresario on the way out, but had been foiled by Mariposa's excited chatter.

"He says that she has an unusually fine voice, which, with proper training, would, as far as they can say now, be perfectly suitable for grand opera. It's what they call a dramatic mezzo-soprano, with something particularly good about the lower notes. Lepine is to see me again before he goes."

"Did he suggest what she ought to do?"

"Yes; he spoke of Paris as the best place to send her. He knows some famous teacher there that he says is the proper person for her to study with. He seemed to think that two years of study would be sufficient for her. She'd be ready to make her appearance in grand opera after that time."

"Good heavens!" breathed Mrs. Willers in a transport of pious triumph, "just think of it! And now up in that cottage on Pine Street getting fifty cents a lesson, and with only four pupils."

"In two years," said Shackleton, who was speaking more to himself than to her, "she'll be twenty-seven years old—just in her prime."

"She'll be twenty-six," corrected Mrs. Willers; "she's only twenty-four now."

THE VISION AND THE DREAM 149

He raised his brows with a little air of amused apology.

"Twenty-four, is it?" he said. "Well, that's all the better. Twenty-six is one year better than twenty-seven."

"It'll be like the 'Innocents Abroad' to see her and her mother in Paris," said Mrs. Willers. "They're just two of the most unsophisticated females that ever strayed out of the golden age."

The man vouchsafed no answer to this remark for a moment; then he said:

"The mother's health is very delicate? She's quite an invalid, you say?"

"Quite. But she's one of the sweetest, most uncomplaining women you ever laid eyes on. You'd understand the daughter better if you knew the mother. She's so gentle and girlish. And then they've lived round in such a sort of quiet, secluded way. It's funny to me because they had plenty of money when Mr. Moreau was alive. But they never seemed to go into society, or know many people; they just seemed enough for each other, especially when the father was with them. They simply adored him, and he must have been a fine man. They—"

"Is Mrs. Moreau's state of health too bad to allow her to travel?" said Shackleton, interrupting suddenly and rudely.

Mrs. Willers colored slightly. She knew her chief well enough to realize that his tone indicated annoyance. Why did he so dislike to hear anything about the late Dan Moreau?

"As to that I don't know," she said. "She's so much of an invalid that she rarely goes out. But with good care she might be able to take a journey and benefit by it. A sea trip sometimes cures people."

"Miss Moreau couldn't, and, I have no doubt, wouldn't leave her. It'll therefore be necessary for the mother to go to Paris with the girl, and if she is so complete and helpless an invalid she'll certainly be of no assistance to her daughter—only a care."

"She'd undoubtedly be a care. But a person couldn't separate those two. They're wrapped up in each other. It's a pity you don't know Mrs. Moreau, Mr. Shackleton."

For the second time that afternoon Mrs. Willers was conscious that words she had intended to be gently ingratiating had given mysterious offense to her employer. Now he said, with more than an edge of sharpness to his words:

"I've no doubt it's a pity, Mrs. Willers. But there are so many things and people it's a pity I don't know, that if I came to think it over I'd probably fall into a state of melancholia. Also, let me assure you, that I haven't the least intention of trying to separate Mrs. Moreau and her daughter. What I'm just now bothered about is the fact that this lady is hardly of sufficient worldly experience, and certainly has not sufficient strength to take care of the girl in a strange country."

"Well, no," said Mrs. Willers with slow reluctance, "it would be the other way round, the girl would be taking care of her."

"That's exactly what I thought. The only way out

THE VISION AND THE DREAM 151

of it will be to send some one with them. A woman who could take care of them both, chaperone the daughter and look after the mother."

There was a silence. Mrs. Willers began to understand why Mr. Shackleton had walked down to *The Trumpet* office with her. The walk was over, for they were at the office door, and the conversation had reached the point to which he had evidently intended to bring it before they parted.

As they turned into the arched doorway and began the ascent of the stairs, Mrs. Willers replied:

"I think that would be a very good idea, Mr. Shackleton. That is, if you can find the right woman."

"Oh, I've got her now," he answered, giving her a quick, side-long glance. "I think it would be a good arrangement for all parties. *The Trumpet* wants a Paris correspondent."

The door leading into the press-rooms opened off the landing they had reached, and he turned into this with a word of farewell, and a hand lifted to his hat brim. Mrs. Willers continued the ascent alone. As she mounted upward she said to herself:

"The best thing for me to do is to get a French phrase book on the way home this evening, and begin studying: 'Have you the green pantaloons of the miller's mother?'"

The elation of his mood was still with Shackleton when, two hours later, he alighted from the carriage at the steps of his country house. He went upstairs to his own rooms with a buoyant tread. In his library, with the windows thrown open to the soft, scented air, he sat smoking and thinking. The October dusk was closing in, when he heard the wheels of a carriage on the drive and the sound of voices. His women-folk with the second of the Thurston girls—the one guest the house now contained—were returning from the afternoon round of visits that was the main diversion of their life during the summer months, and swept the country houses from Redwood City to Menlo Park.

It was a small dinner table that evening. Winslow had stayed in town over night, and Shackleton sat at the head of a shrunken board, with Bessie opposite him, his daughter to the left, and Pussy Thurston on his right. Pussy was Maud's best friend and was one of the beauties of San Francisco. To-night she looked especially pretty in a pale green crape dress, with green leaves in her fair hair. Her skin was of a shell-like purity of pink and white, her face was small, with regular features and a sweet, childish smile.

She and her sister were the only children of the famous Judge Beauregard Thurston, in his day one of those brilliant lawyers who brought glory to the California bar. He had made a fortune, lived on it recklessly and magnificently, and died leaving his daughters almost penniless. He had been in the heyday of his splendor when Jake Shackleton, just struggling into the public eye, had come to San Francisco, and the proud Southerner had not scrupled to treat the raw mining man with careless scorn. Shackleton evened the score before Thurston's death, and he still soothed his wounded pride with the thought that the two daughters of the man who had once despised him were largely dependent on his wife's charity. Bessie took them to balls and parties, dressed them, almost fed

THE VISION AND THE DREAM 153

them. The very green crape gown in which Pussy looked so pretty to-night had been included in Maud's bill at a fashionable dressmaker's.

Personally he liked Pussy, whose beauty and winning manners lent a luster to his house. Once or twice to-night she caught him looking at her with a cold, debating glance in which there was little of the admiration she was accustomed to receiving since the days of her first long dress.

He was in truth regarding her critically for the first time, for the Bonanza King was a man on whom the beauty of women cast no spell. He was comparing her with another and a more regally handsome girl. Pussy Thurston would look insipid and insignificant before the stately splendor of his own daughter.

He smiled as he realized Mariposa's superiority. The young girl saw the smile, and said with the privileged coquetry of a maid who all her life has known herself favored above her fellows:

"Why are you smiling all to yourself, Mr. Shackleton? Can't we know if it is something pleasant?"

"I was looking at something pretty," he answered, his eyes full of amusement as they rested on her charming face. "That generally makes people smile."

She was so used to such remarks that her rose-leaf color did not vary the fraction of a shade. Maud, to whom no one ever paid compliments, looked at her with wistful admiration.

"Is that all?" she said with an air of disappointment. "I hoped it was something that would make us all smile."

"Well, I have an idea that may make you all smile"

—he turned to his wife—"how would you like to go to Europe next spring, Bessie?"

Mrs. Shackleton looked surprised and not greatly elated. On their last trip to Europe, two years before, her husband had been so bored by the joys of foreign travel that she had made up her mind she would never ask him to go again. Now she said:

"But you don't want to go to Europe. You said last time you hated it."

"Did I? Yes, I guess I did. Well, I'm prepared to like it this time. We could take a spin over in the spring to London and Paris. We'd make quite a stay in Paris, and you women could buy clothes. You'd come, too, Pussy, wouldn't you?" he said, turning to the girl.

Her color rose now and her eyes sparkled. She had never been even to New York.

"Wouldn't I?" she said. "That *does* make me smile."

"I thought so," he answered good humoredly—"and Maud, you'd like it, of course?"

Maud did not like the thought of going at all. In this little party of four, two were moved in their actions by secret predilections of which the others were ignorant. Maud thought of leaving her love affair at the critical point it had reached, and, with anguish at her heart, looked heavily indifferent.

"I don't know," she said, crumbling her bread, "I don't think it's such fun in Europe. You just travel round in little stuffy trains, and have to live in hotels without baths."

"Well, you and I, Pussy," said Shackleton, "seem to

be the only two who've got any enthusiasm. You'll have to try and put some into Maud, and if the worst comes to the worst we can kidnap the old lady."

He was in an unusually good temper, and the dinner was animated and merry. Only Maud, after the European suggestion, grew more stolidly quiet than ever. But she cheered herself by the thought that the spring was six months off yet, and who could tell what might happen in six months?

After dinner the ladies repaired to the music room, and Shackleton, following a custom of his, passed through one of the long windows into the garden, there to pace up and down while he smoked his cigar.

The night was warm and odorous with the scent of hidden blossoms. Now and then his foot crunched the gravel of a path, as his walk took him back and forth over the long stretch of lawn broken by flower beds and narrow walks. The great bulk of the house, its black mass illumined by congeries of lit windows, showed an inky, irregular outline against the star-strewn sky.

Presently the sound of a piano floated out from the music room. The man stopped his pacing, listened for an instant, and then passed round to the side of the house. The French windows of the music room were opened, throwing elongated squares of light over the balcony and the grass beyond. He paused in the darkness and looked through one of them. There, like a painting framed by the window casing, was Pussy Thurston seated at the piano singing, while Maud sat near by listening. One of Miss Thurston's most admired social graces was the gift of song. She had a small agreeable voice, and had been well taught; but the light, frail tones sounded thin in the wide silence of the night. It was the feebly pretty performance of the "accomplished young lady."

Shackleton listened with a slight smile that increased as the song drew to a close. As it ceased he moved away, the red light of his cigar coming and going in the darkness.

"Singing!" he said to himself, "they call that singing! Wait till they hear my daughter!"

CHAPTER VII

THE REVELATION

"Praised be the fathomless universe
   For life and for joy and for objects and knowledge curious,
   And for love, sweet love—but praise, praise, praise,
For the sure-enwinding arms of cool-enfolding Death,
   The night in silence under many a star,
   The ocean shore and the husky whispering wave whose voice
      I hear,
And the soul turning to thee, O vast and well-veiled Death,
   And the body gratefully nestling close to thee."
                                                    —WHITMAN.

From the day when Mrs. Willers had appeared with the news of Shackleton's interest in her daughter, Lucy's health had steadily waned. The process of decay was so quiet, albeit so sure and swift, that Mariposa, accustomed to the ups and downs of her mother's invalid condition, was unaware that the elder woman's sands were almost run. The pale intensity, the coldness of the hand gripped round hers, that had greeted her account of the recital at the Opera House, seemed to the girl only the reflection of her own eager exultation. She was blind, not only from ignorance, but from the egotistic preoccupations of her youth. It seemed impossible to think of her mother's failing in her loving response, now that the sun was rising on their dark horizon.

But Lucy knew that she was dying. Her feeble body had received its *coup de grâce* on the day that Mrs. Willers brought the news of Shackleton's wish to see his child. Since then she had spent long hours in thought. When her mind was clear enough she had pondered on the situation trying to see what was best to do for Mariposa's welfare. The problem that faced her terrified her. The dying woman was having the last struggle with herself.

One week after the recital at the Opera House she had grown so much worse that Mariposa had called in the doctor they had had in attendance, off and on, since their arrival. He was grave and there was a consultation. When she saw their faces the cold dread that had been slowly growing in the girl's heart seemed suddenly to expand and chill her whole being. Mrs. Moreau was undoubtedly very ill, though there was still hope. Yet their looks were sober and pitying as they listened to the daughter's reiterated asseverations that her mother had often been worse and made a successful rally.

An atmosphere of illness settled down like a fog on the little cottage. A nurse appeared; the doctors seemed to be in the house many times a day. Mrs. Willers, as soon as she heard, came up, no longer overdressed and foolish, but grave and helpful. After a half-hour spent at Lucy's bedside, wherein the sick woman had spoken little, and then only about her daughter, Mrs. Willers had gone to the office of *The*

THE REVELATION

Trumpet, frowning in her sympathetic pain. It was Saturday, and Shackleton had already left for Menlo Park when she reached the office. But she determined to see him early on Monday and tell him of the straits of his old friend's widow and child. Mrs. Willers knew the signs of the scarcity of money, and knew also the overwhelming expenses of sickness. What she did not know was that on Friday morning Mariposa had wept over her check-book, and then gone out and sold the diamond brooch.

The long Sunday—the interminable day of strained anxiety—passed, shrouded in rain. When her mother fell into the light sleep that now marked her condition, Mariposa mechanically went to the window of the bedroom and looked out. It was one of those blinding rains that usher in the San Francisco winter, the water falling in straight lances that show against the light like thin tubes of glass, and strike the pavement with a vicious impact, which splinters them into spray. It drummed on the tin roof above the bedroom with an incessant hollow sound, and ran in a torn ribbon of water from the gutter on the eaves.

The prospect that the window commanded seemed in dreariness to match the girl's thoughts. That part of Pine Street was still in the unfinished condition described by the words "far out." Vacant lots yawned between the houses; the badly paved roadbed was an expanse of deeply rutted mud, with yellow ponds of rain at the sewer mouths. The broken wooden sidewalk gleamed with moisture and was evenly striped with lines of vivid green where the grass sprouted between the boards. Now and then a wayfarer hurried by, crouched under the dome of an umbrella spouting water from every rib.

The gray twilight settled early, and Mariposa, dropping the curtain, turned to the room behind her. The light of a small fire and a shaded lamp sent a softened glow over the apartment, which, despite its poverty, bespoke the taste of gentlewomen in the simple prettiness of its furnishings. The nurse, a middle-aged woman of a kindly and capable aspect, sat by the fire in a wicker rocking-chair, reading a paper. Beside her, on a table, stood the sick-room paraphernalia of glasses and bottles. The regular creak of the rocking-chair, and an occasional snap from the fire, were the only sounds that punctuated the steady drumming of the rain on the tin roof.

A Japanese screen was half-way about the bed, shutting it from the drafts of the door, and in its shelter Lucy lay sleeping her light, breathless sleep. In this shaded light, in the relaxed attitude of unconsciousness, she presented the appearance of a young girl hardly older than her daughter. Yet the hand of death was plainly on her, as even Mariposa could now see.

Without sound the girl passed from the room to her own beyond. Her grief had seized her, and the truth, fought against with the desperate inexperience of youth, forced itself on her. She threw herself on her bed and lay there battling with the sickness of despair that such knowledge brings. Twilight faded and darkness came. In answer to the servant's tap on the door, and announcement of dinner, she called back that she desired none. The room was as dark about her as her own thoughts. From the door that led into the sick chamber, only partly closed, a shaft of light cut the blackness, and on this light she fastened her eyes, swollen with tears, feeling herself stupefied with sorrow.

As she lay thus on the bed, she heard the creaking of the wicker-chair as the nurse arose, then came the clink of the spoon and the glass, and the woman's low voice, and then her mother's, stronger and clearer than it had been for some days. There was an interchange of remarks between nurse and patient, the sound of careful steps, and the crack of light suddenly expanded as the door was opened. Against this background, clear and smoothly yellow as gold leaf, the nurse's figure was revealed in sharp silhouette.

"Are you there, Miss Moreau?" she said in a low voice. Mariposa started with a hurried reply.

"Well, your mother wants to see you and you'd better come. Her mind seems much clearer and it may not be so again."

The girl rose from the bed trying to compose her face. In the light of the open door the woman saw its distress and looked at her pityingly.

"Don't tire her," she said, "but I advise you to say all you have to say. She may not be this way again."

Mariposa crossed the room to the bed. Her mother was lying on her side, pinched, pale and with darkly circled eyes.

"Have you just waked up, darling?" said the girl, tenderly.

"No," she answered, with a curious lack of response in manner and tone; "I have been awake some time. I was thinking."

"Why didn't you send Mrs. Brown for me? I was in my room passing the time till you woke up."

"I was thinking and I wanted to finish. I have been thinking a long time, days and weeks."

Mariposa thought her mind was wandering, and sitting down on a chair by the bedside, took her hand and pressed it gently without speaking. Her mother lay in the same attitude, her profile toward her, her eyes looking vacantly at the screen. Suddenly she said:

"You know my old desk, the little rose-wood one Dan gave me? Take my keys and open it, and in the bottom you'll see two envelopes, with no writing. One looks dirty and old. Bring them to me here."

Mariposa rose wondering, and looking anxiously at her mother. The elder woman saw the look, and said weakly and almost peevishly:

"Go; be quick. I am not strong enough to talk long. The keys are in the work-box."

The girl obeyed as quickly as possible. The desk was a small one resting on the center table. It had been a present of her father's to her mother, and she remembered it from her earliest childhood in a prominent position in her mother's room. She opened it, and in a few moments, under old letters, memoranda and souvenirs, found the two envelopes. Carrying them to the bed she gave them to her mother.

Lucy took them with an unsteady hand, and for a moment lay staring at her daughter and not moving. Then she said:

"Put the pillows under my head. It's easier to breathe when I'm higher," and as Mariposa arranged them, she added, in a lower voice: "And tell Mrs. Brown to go; I want to be alone with you."

Mariposa looked out beyond the screen, and seeing the nurse still reading the paper, told her to go to the kitchen and get her dinner. The woman rose with alacrity, and asking Mariposa to call her if the invalid showed signs of fatigue, or any change, left the room.

The girl turned back to the bedside and took the chair. Lucy had taken from the dirty envelope a worn and faded paper, which she slowly unfolded. As she did so, she looked at her daughter with sunken eyes and said:

"These are my marriage certificates."

Mariposa, again thinking that her mind was wandering, tried to smile, and answered gently:

"Your marriage certificate, dear. You were only married once."

"I was married twice," said Lucy, and handed the girl the two papers.

Still supposing her mother slightly delirious, the daughter took the papers and looked at them. The one her eye first fell on was that of the original marriage. She read the names without at first realizing whose they were. Then the significance of the "Lucy Fraser" came upon her. Her glance leaped to the second paper, and at the first sweep of her eyes over it she saw it was the marriage certificate of her father and mother, Daniel Moreau and Lucy Fraser, dated at Placerville twenty-five years before. She turned back to the other paper, now more than bewildered. She held it near her face, as though it were difficult to read, and in the dead silence of the room it began to rustle with the trembling of her hand. A fear of something hideous and overwhelming seized her. With pale lips she read the names, and the date, antedating by five years the other certificate.

"Mother!" she cried, in a wild voice of inquiry, dropping the paper on the bed.

Lucy, raised on her pillows, was looking at her with a haggard intentness. All the vitality left in her expiring body seemed concentrated in her eyes.

"I was married twice," she said slowly.

"But how? When? What does it mean? Mother, what does it mean?"

"I was married twice," she repeated. "In St. Louis to Jake Shackleton, and in Placerville, five years after, to Dan Moreau. And I was never divorced from Jake. It was not according to the law. I was never Dan's lawful wife."

The girl sat staring, the meaning of the words slowly penetrating her brain. She was too stunned to speak. Her face was as white as her mother's. For a tragic moment these two white faces looked at each other. The mother's, with death waiting to claim her, was void of all stress or emotion. The daughter's, waking to life, was rigid with horrified amaze.

Propped by her pillows, Lucy spoke again; her sentences were short and with pauses between:

"Jake Shackleton married me in St. Louis when I was fifteen. He was soon tired of me. We went to Salt Lake City. He became a Mormon there, and took a second wife. She was a waitress in a hotel. She's his wife now. He brought us both to California twenty-five years ago. On the way across, on the plains of Utah, you were born. He is your father, Mariposa."

She made an effort and sat up. Her breathing was becoming difficult, but her purpose gave her strength. This was the information that for weeks she had been nerving herself to impart.

"He is your father," she repeated. "That's what I wanted to tell you."

Mariposa made no answer, and again she repeated:

"He is your father. Do you understand? Answer me."

"Yes— I don't know. Oh, mother, it's so strange and horrible. And you sitting there and looking at me like that, and telling it to me! Oh,—mother!"

She put her hands over her face for an instant, and then dropping them, leaned over on the bed and grasped her mother's wrists.

"You're wandering in your mind. It's just some hideous dream you've had in your fever. Dearest, tell me it's not true. It can't be true. Why, think of you and me and father always together and with no dreadful secret behind us like that. Oh—it can't be true!"

Lucy looked at the papers lying brown and torn on the white quilt. Mariposa's eyes followed the same direction, and with a groan her head sank on her arms extended along the bed. Her mother's hand, cold and light, was laid on one of hers, but the dying woman's face was held in its quiet, unstirred apathy, as she spoke again:

"Jake was hard to me on the trip. He was a hard man and he never loved me. After Bessie came he got to dislike me. I was always a drag, he said. I couldn't seem to get well after you were born. Coming over the Sierras we stopped at a cabin. Dan was there with another man, a miner, called Fletcher. That was the first time I ever saw Dan."

Mariposa lifted her head and her eyes fastened on her mother's face. The indifference that had held it seemed breaking. A faint smile was on her lips, a light of reminiscence lit its gray pallor.

"He was always good to anything that was sick or weak. He was sorry for me. He tried to make Jake stop longer, so I could get rested. But Jake wouldn't. He said I had to go on. I couldn't, but knew I must, if he said it. We were going to start when Jake said he'd exchange me for the pair of horses the two miners had in the shed. So he left me and took the horses."

"Exchanged you for the horses? Left you there sick and alone?"

"Yes, Jake and Bessie went on with the horses. I stayed. I was too sick to care."

She made a slight pause, either from weakness, or in an effort to arrange the next part of her story.

"I lived there with them for a month. I was sick and they took care of me. Then one day Fletcher stole all the money and the only horse and never came back. We were alone there then, Dan and I. I got better. I came to love him more each day. We were snowed in all winter, and we lived as man and wife. In the spring we rode into Hangtown and were married."

She stopped, a look of ineffable sweetness passed over her face, and she said in a low voice, as if speaking to herself:

THE REVELATION

"Oh, that beautiful winter! There is a God, to be so good to women who have suffered as I had."

Mariposa sat dumbly regarding her. It was like a frightful nightmare. Everything was strange, the sick room, the bed with the screen around it, her mother's face with its hollow eyes and pinched nose. Only the two old dirty papers on the white counterpane seemed to say that this was real.

Lucy's eyes, which had been looking back into that glorified past of love and youth, returned to her daughter's face.

"But Jake is your father," she said. "That's what I had to tell you. He'll be good to you. That was why he wanted to find you and help you."

"Yes," said Mariposa, dully, "I understand that now; that was why he wanted to help me."

"He'll be good to you," went on the low, weak voice, interrupted by quick breaths. "I know Jake. He'll be proud of you. You're handsome and talented, not weak and poor spirited, as I was. You're his only legitimate child; the others are not; they were born in California. They're Bessie's children, and I was his only real wife. You'll let him take care of you? Oh, Mariposa, my darling, I've told you all this that you might understand and let him take care of you."

She made a last call on her strength and leaned forword. Her dying body was re-vivified; all her mother's agony of love appeared on her face. In determining to destroy the illusions of her child to secure her future, she had made the one heroic effort of her life. It was done, and for a last moment of relief and triumph she was thrillingly alive.

Mariposa, in a spasm of despair, threw herself forward on the bed.

"Oh, why did you tell me? Why did you tell me?" she cried. "Why didn't you let me think it was the way it used to be? Why did you tell me?"

Lucy laid her hand on the bowed head.

"Because I wanted you to understand and let him be your father."

"My father! That man! Oh, no, no!"

"You must promise me. Oh, my beloved child, I couldn't leave you alone. It seemed as if God had said to me, 'Die in peace. Her father will care for her.' I couldn't go and leave you this way, without a friend. Now I can rest in peace. Promise to let him take care of you. Promise."

"Oh, mother, don't ask me. What have you just told me? That he sold you to a stranger for a pair of horses, left you to die in a cabin in the mountains! That's not my father. My father was Dan Moreau. I can do nothing but hate that other man now."

"Don't blame him, dear, the past is over. Forgive him. Forgive me. If I sinned there were excuses for me. I had suffered too much. I loved too well."

Her voice suddenly hesitated and broke. A gray pallor ran over her face and a look of terror transfixed her eyes. She straightened her arms out toward her daughter.

"Promise," she gasped, "promise."

With a spring Mariposa snatched the drooping body in her arms and cried into the face, settling into cold rigidity:

THE REVELATION

"Yes—yes—I promise! All—anything. Oh, mother, darling, look at me. I promise."

She gently shook the limp form, but it was nerveless, only the head oscillated slightly from side to side.

"Mother, look at me," she cried frantically. "Look at me, not past me. Come back to me. Speak to me, I promise everything."

But there was no response. Lucy lay, limp and white-lipped, her head lolling back from the support of her daughter's arm. Her strength was exhausted to the last drop. She was unconscious.

The wild figure of Mariposa at the kitchen door summoned Mrs. Brown. Lucy was not dead, but dying. A few moments later Mariposa found herself rushing hatless through the rain for the doctor, and then again, in what seemed a few more minutes, standing, soaked and breathless, by her mother's side. She sat there throughout the night, holding the limp hand and watching for a glimmer of consciousness in the half-shut eyes.

It never came. There was no rally from the collapse which followed the mother's confession. She had lived till this was done. Then, having accomplished the great action of her life, she had loosed her hold and let go. Once, Mrs. Brown being absent, Mariposa had leaned down on the pillow and passionately reiterated the assurance that she would give the promise Lucy had asked. There was a slight quiver of animation in the dying woman's face and she opened her eyes as if startled, but made no other sign of having heard or understood. But Mariposa knew that she had promised.

On the evening of the day after her confession Lucy died, slipping away quietly as if in sleep. The death of the simple and unknown lady made no ripple on the surface of the city's life. Mrs. Willers and a neighbor or two were Mariposa's sole visitors, and the only flowers contributed to Lucy's coffin were those sent by the newspaper woman and Barry Essex. The afternoon of the day on which her mother's death was announced, Mariposa received a package from Jake Shackleton. With it came a short note of condolence, and the offer, kindly and simply worded, of the small sum of money contained in the package, which, it was hoped, Miss Moreau, for the sake of the writer's early acquaintance with her parents and interest in herself, would accept. The packet contained five hundred dollars in coin.

Mariposa's face flamed. The money fell through her fingers and rolled about on the floor. She would have liked to take it, piece by piece, and throw it through the window, into the mud of the street. She felt that her horror of Shackleton augmented with every passing moment, gripped her deeper with every memory of her mother's words, and every moment's perusal of the calm, dead face in its surrounding flowers.

But her promise had been given. She picked up the money and put it away. Her promise had been given. Already she was beginning dimly to realize that it would bind and cramp her for the rest of her life. She was too benumbed now fully to grasp its meaning, but she felt feebly that she would be its slave as long as he or she lived. But she had given it.

The money lay untouched throughout the next few

days, Lucy's simple funeral ceremonies being paid for with the proceeds of the sale of the diamond brooch, which Moreau had given her in the early days of their happiness.

CHAPTER VIII

ITS EFFECT

"Flower o' the peach,
Death for us all, and his own life for each."
—BROWNING.

Jake Shackleton did not come up from San Mateo on Monday, as Mrs. Willers expected, and the first intimation he had of Lucy's death was the short notice in the paper.

He had come down the stairs early on Tuesday morning into the wide hall, with its doors thrown open to the fragrant air. With the paper in his hand, he stood on the balcony looking about and inhaling the freshness of the morning. The rain had washed the country clean of every fleck of dust, burnished every leaf, and had called into being blossoms that had been awaiting its summons.

From beneath the shade made by the long, gnarled limbs of the live oaks, the perfume of the violets rose delicately, their crowding clusters of leaves a clear green against the base of the hoary trunks. The air that drifted in from the idle, yellow fields beyond was impregnated with the breath of the tar-weed—one of the most pungent and impassioned odors Nature has manufactured in her vast laboratory, characteristic scent to rise from the dry, yet fecund grass-lands of California. In the perfect, crystalline stillness these mingled perfumes rose like incense to the new day.

Shackleton looked about him, the paper in his hand. He had little love for Nature, but the tranquil-scented freshness of the hour wrung its tribute of admiration from him. What an irony that the one child he had, worth having gained all this for, should be denied it. Mariposa, thus framed, would have added the last touch to the triumphs of his life.

With an exclamation of impatience he sat down on the top step, and opening the paper, ran his glance down its columns. He had been looking over it for several minutes before the death notice of Lucy struck his eye. It took away his breath. He read it again, at first not crediting it. He was entirely unprepared, having merely thought of Lucy as "delicate." Now she was dead.

He dropped the paper on his knee and sat staring out into the garden. The news was more of a shock than he could have imagined it would be. Was it the lately roused pride in his child that had reawakened some old tenderness for the mother? Or was it that the thought of Lucy, dead, called back memories of that shameful past?

He sat, staring, till a step on the balcony roused him, and turning, he saw his son. Win, though only twenty-three, was of the order of beings who do not look well in the morning. He was slightly built and thin and had a rasped, pink appearance, as though he felt cold. Stories were abroad that Win was dissipated, stories, by the way, that were largely manufactured by himself. He was at that age when a reputation for deviltry has its attractions. In fact, he was amiable, gentle and far too lacking in spirit to be the desperate rake he liked to represent himself. He had a wholesome fear of his father, whose impatience against him was not concealed by surface politeness as in Maud's case.

Standing with his hands in his trousers' pockets, his chest hollowed, his red-rimmed eyes half shut behind the *pince-nez* he always wore, and his slight mustache not sufficient to hide a smile, the foolishness of which rose from embarrassment, he was not a son to fill a father's heart with pride.

"Howdy, Governor," he said, trying to be easy; then, seeing the paper in his father's hand, folded back at the death notices, "anybody new born, dead, or married this morning?"

His voice rasped unbearably on his father's mood. The older man gave him a look over his shoulder, with a face that made the boy quail.

"Get away," he said, savagely; "get in the house and leave me alone."

Win turned and entered the house. The foolish smile was still on his lips. Pride kept it there, but at heart he was bitterly wounded.

At the foot of the stairway he met his mother.

"You'd better not go out there," he said, with a movement of his head in the direction of his father; "it's as much as your life's worth. The old man'll bite your nose off if you do."

"Is your father cross?" asked Bessie.

"Cross? He oughtn't to be let loose when he's like that."

"Something in the paper must have upset him," said Bessie. "He was all right this morning before he came down. Something on the stock market's bothered him."

"Maybe so," said his son, with a certain feeling. "But that's no reason why he should speak to me like a dog. He goes too far when he speaks to me that way. There isn't a servant in the house would stand it."

He balanced back and forth on his toes and heels, looking down, his face flushed. It would have been hard to say—such was the characterless insignificance of his appearance—whether he was really hurt, as a man would be in his heart and his pride, or only momentarily stung by a scornful word.

Bessie passed him and went out on the balcony. Her husband was still sitting on the steps, the paper in his hand.

"What is it, Jake?" she said. "Win says you're cross. Something gone wrong?"

"Lucy's dead," he answered, rising to his feet and handing her the paper.

She paled a little as she read the notice. Then, raising her eyes, they met his. In this look was their knowledge of the secret that both had struggled to keep, and that now, at last, was theirs.

For the second time in a half-year, Death had stepped in and claimed one of the four whose lives had touched so briefly and so momentously twenty-five years before.

"Poor Lucy!" said Bessie, in a low voice. "But they say she was very happy with Moreau. You can do something for your—for the girl now."

"Yes," he said; "I'll think it over. I won't be down to breakfast. Send up some coffee."

He went upstairs and locked himself in his library. He could not understand why the news had affected him so deeply. It seemed to make him feel sick. He did not tell Bessie that he had gone upstairs because he felt too ill and shaken to see any one.

All morning he sat in the library, with frowning brows, thinking. At noon he took the train for the city and, soon after its arrival, despatched to Mariposa the five hundred dollars. He had no doubt of her accepting it, as it never crossed his mind that Lucy, at the last moment, might have told.

The days that followed her mother's funeral passed to Mariposa like a series of gray dreams, dreadful, with an unfamiliar sense of wretchedness. The preoccupation of her mother's illness was gone. There were idle hours, when she sat in her rooms and tried to realize the full meaning of Lucy's last words. She would sit motionless, staring before her, her heart feeling shriveled in her breast. Her life seemed broken to pieces. She shrank from the future, with the impossibilities she had pledged herself to. And the strength and inspiration of the beautiful past were gone. All the memories of that happy childhood and young maidenhood were blasted. It was natural that the shock and the subsequent brooding should make her view of the subject morbid. The father that she had grown up to regard with reverential tenderness, had not been hers. The mother, who had been a cherished idol, had hidden a dark secret. And she, herself, was an outsider from the home she had so deeply loved—child of a brutal and tyrannical father—originally adopted and cared for out of pity.

It was a crucial period in her life. Old ideals were gone, and new ones not yet formed. There seemed only ruins about her, and amid these she sought for something to cling to, and believe in. With secret passion she nursed the thought of Essex—all she had left that had not been swept away in the deluge of this past week.

Fortunately for her, the business calls of the life of a woman left penniless shook her from her state of brooding idleness. The cottage was hers for a month longer, and despite the impoverished condition of the widow, there was a fair amount of furniture still left in it that was sufficiently valuable to be a bait to the larger dealers. Mariposa found her days varied by contentions with men, who came to stare at the great red lacquer cabinet and investigate the interior condition of the marquetry sideboard. When the month was up she was to move to a small boarding-house, kept by Spaniards called Garcia, that Mrs. Willers, in her varying course, included among her habitats. The Garcias would not object to her piano and practising, and it was amazingly cheap. Mrs. Willers herself had lived there in one of her periods of eclipse, and knew them to be respectable denizens of a somewhat battered Bohemia.

"But you're going to be a Bohemian yourself, being

a musical genius," she said cheerfully. "So you won't mind that."

Mariposa did not think she would mind. In the chaotic dimness of the dismantled front parlor she looked like a listless goddess who would not mind anything.

Mrs. Willers thought her state of dreary apathy curious and spoke of it to Shackleton, whom she now recognized as the girl's acknowledged guardian. He had listened to her account of Mariposa's broken condition with expressionless attention.

"Isn't it natural, all things considered, that a girl should be broken-hearted over the death of a devoted mother? And, as I understand it, Miss Moreau is absolutely alone. She has no relatives anywhere. It's a pretty bleak outlook."

"That's true. I never saw a girl left so without connections. But she worries me. She's so silent, and dull, and unlike herself. Of course, it's been a terrible blow. I'd have thought she'd been more prepared."

He shrugged his shoulders, stroking his short beard with his lean, heavily-veined hand. It amused him to see the way Mrs. Willers was quietly pushing him into the position of the girl's sponsor. And at the same time it heightened his opinion of her as a woman of capacity and heart. She would be an ideal chaperone and companion for his unprotected daughter.

"When she feels better," he said, "I wish you'd bring her down here again. Don't bother her until she feels equal to it. But I want to talk to her about Lepine's ideas for her. I saw him again and he gave me a lot of information about Paris and teachers and all the rest of it. Before we make any definite arrangements I'll have to see her and talk it all over."

Mrs. Willers went back triumphant to Mariposa to report this conversation. It really seemed to clinch matters. The Bonanza King had instituted himself her guardian and backer. It meant fortune for Mariposa Moreau, the penniless orphan.

To her intense surprise, Mariposa listened to her with a flushed and frowning face of indignation.

"I won't go," she said, with sudden violence.

"But, my dear!" expostulated Mrs. Willers, "your whole future depends on it. With such an influence to back you as that, your fortune's made. And listen to me, honey, for I know,—it's not an easy job for a woman to get on who's alone and as good-looking as you are."

"I won't go," repeated Mariposa, angry and obstinate.

"But why not, for goodness' sake?"—in blank amaze. "What's come over you? Is it your mourning? You know your mother's the last person who'd want you to sit indoors, moping like a snail in a shell, when your future was waiting for you outside the door."

Her promise rose up before Mariposa's mental vision and checked the angry reiteration that was on her lips. She turned away, suddenly, tremulous and pale.

"Don't talk about it any more," she answered, "but I *can't* go now. Perhaps later on, but not now—I can't go now."

Mrs. Willers shrugged her shoulders, and was wisely silent. Mariposa's grief was making her unreasonable, that was all. To Shackleton she merely said that the girl was too ill and overwrought to see any one just yet. As soon as she was herself again Mrs. Willers would bring her to *The Trumpet* office for the interview that was to be the opening of the new era.

CHAPTER IX

HOW COULD HE

"Man is the hunter; woman is his game,
The sleek and shining creatures of the chase.
We hunt them for the beauty of their skins;
They love us for it, and we ride them down."
—TENNYSON.

The month of Mariposa's tenantry of the cottage was up. It was the last evening there, and she sat crouched over a handful of fire that burned in the front parlor grate. The room was half empty, all the superfluous furniture having been taken that morning by a Jewish second-hand dealer. In one corner stood huddled such relics as she had chosen to keep, and which would be borne away on the morrow to the Garcias' boarding-house. The marquetry sideboard was gone. It had been sold to a Sutter Street dealer for twenty-five dollars. The red lacquer cabinet, though no longer hers, still remained. It, too, would be carried away to-morrow morning by its new owners. She looked at it with melancholy glances as the fire-light found and lost its golden traceries and sent sudden quivering gleams along its scarlet doors. The fire was less a luxury than an economy, to burn the last pieces of coal in the bin.

Bending over the dancing flames, Mariposa held her

hands open to the blaze, absently looking at their backs. They were fine, capable hands, large and white, with strong wrists and a forearm so round that its swell began half-way between elbow and wrist-bone. Pleased by the warmth that soothed the chill always induced by a sojourn in the front parlor, she pulled up her sleeves and watched the gleam of the fire turn the white skin red. She was sitting thus, when a ring at the bell made her start and hurriedly push her sleeves down. Her visitors were so few that she was almost certain of the identity of this one. For all the griefs of the last month she was yet a woman. She sprang to her feet, and as the steps of the servant sounded in the hall, ran to the large mirror in the corner and patted and pulled her hair to the style she thought most becoming.

She had turned from this and was standing by the fire when Essex entered. He had seen her once since her mother's death, but she had then been so preoccupied with grief that, with a selfish man's hatred of all unpleasant things, he had left her as soon as possible. To-night he saw that she was recovering, that, physically at least, she was herself again. But he was struck, almost as soon as his eye fell on her, by a change in her. Some influence had been at work to effect a subtile and curious development in her. The simplicity, the something childish and winning that had always seemed so inconsistent with her stately appearance, was gone. Mariposa was coming to herself. His heart quickened its beats as he realized she was handsomer, richer by some inward growth, more a woman than she had been a month ago.

He took a seat at the other side of the fire, and the tentative conversation of commonplaces occupied them for a few moments. The silence that had held her in a spell of dead dejection on his former visit was broken. She seemed more than usually talkative. In fact, Mariposa was beginning to feel the reaction from the life of grief and seclusion of the last month. She was violently ashamed of the sense of elation that had surged up in her at the sound of Essex's voice. She struggled to hide it, but it lit a light in her eyes, called a color to her cheeks that she could not conceal. The presence of her lover affected her with a sort of embarrassed exultation that she had never experienced before. To hide it she talked rapidly, looking into the fire, to which she still held out her hands.

Essex, from the other side of the hearth, watched her. He saw his arrival had made her nervous, and it only augmented the sentiment that had been growing in him for months.

She began to tell him of her move.

"I'm going to-morrow, in the afternoon. It's a queer place, an old house on Hyde Street, with a big pepper-tree, the biggest in the city, they say, growing in the front garden. It was once quite a fine house, long ago in the early days, and was built by these people, the Garcias, when they still had money. Then they lost it all, and now the old lady and her son's wife take a few people, as the house is too big for them and they are so poor. Young Mrs. Garcia is a widow. Her husband was killed in the mines by a blast."

"It sounds picturesque. Do they speak English?"

"The señora, that's the old lady, doesn't. She has lived here since before the Gringo came, but she can't speak any English at all. The daughter-in-law is an American, a Southerner. She looked very untidy the day I went there. I'm afraid I'll be homesick. You'll come to see me sometimes, won't you?"

There was no coquetry in the remark. Her dread of loneliness was all that spoke.

Essex met her eyes, dark and wistful, and nodded without speaking.

She looked back at the fire and again spread her hands to it, palms out.

"It's—it's—rather a dilapidated sort of place," she continued after a moment's pause, "but perhaps I'll get used to it."

There was distinct pleading for confirmation in this. Her voice was slightly husky. Essex, however, with that perversity which marked all his treatment of her, said:

"Do you think you will? It's difficult for a woman to accommodate herself to such changed conditions— I mean a woman of refinement, like you."

She continued feebly to make her stand.

"But my conditions have changed so much in the last two or three years. I ought to be used to it; it's not as if it was the first time. Before my father got sick we were so comfortable. We were rich and had quantities of beautiful things like that cabinet. And as they have gone, one by one, so we have come down bit by bit, till I am left like this."

She made a gesture to include the empty room and turned back to the fire.

"But you won't stay like this," he said, throwing a glance over the bare walls.

"Don't you think so?" she said, looking into the fire with dejected eyes. "You're kind to try to cheer me up."

"You can be happy, protected and cared for, with your life full of sunshine and joy—"

He stopped. Every step he took was of moment, and he was not the type of man to forgive himself a mistake. Mariposa was looking at him, frowning slightly.

"How do you mean?' she said. "With my voice?"

"No," he answered, in a tone that suddenly thrilled with meaning, "with me."

That quivering pause which falls between a man and woman when the words that will link or sever them for life are to be spoken, held the room. Mariposa felt the terrified desire to arrest the coming words that is the maiden's last instinctive stand for her liberty. But her brain was confused, and her heart beat like a hammer.

"With me," Essex repeated, as the pause grew unbearable. "Is there no happiness for you in that thought?"

She made no answer, and suddenly he moved his chair close to her side. She felt his eyes fastened on her and kept hers on the fire. Her other offers of marriage had not been accomplished with this stifling sense of discomfort.

"I've thought," his deep voice went on, "that you cared for me—a little. I've watched, I've desponded.

But lately—lately—" he leaned toward her and lowered his voice—"I've hoped."

She still made no answer. It seemed to her none was necessary or possible.

"Do you care?" he said softly.

She breathed a "yes" that only the ear of love could have heard.

"Mariposa, dearest, do you mean it?" He leaned over her and laid his hand on hers. His voice was husky and his hand trembling. To the extent that was in him he loved this woman.

"Do you love me?" he whispered.

The "yes" was even fainter this time. He raised the hand he held to his breast and tried to draw her into his arms.

She resisted, and turned on him a pale face, where emotions, never stirred before, were quivering. She was moved to the bottom of her soul. Something in her face made him shrink a little. With her hand against his breast she gave him the beautiful look of a woman's first sense of her surrender. He stifled the sudden twinge of his conscience and again tried to draw her close to him. But she held him off with the hand on his breast and said—as thousands of girls say every year:

"Do you really love me?"

"More than the whole world," he answered glibly, but with the roughened voice of real feeling.

"Why?" she said with a tremulous smile, "why should you?"

"Because you are you."

"But I'm just a small insignificant person here, without any relations, and poor, so poor."

"Those things don't matter when a man loves a woman. It's you I want, not anything you might have or might be."

"But you're so clever and have lived everywhere and seen everything, and I'm so—so countrified and stupid."

"You're Mariposa. That's enough for me."

"All I can bring you for my portion is my heart."

"And that's all I want."

"You love me enough to marry me?"

His eyes that had been looking ardently into her face, shifted.

"I love you enough to be a fool about you. Does that please you?"

Her murmured answer was lost in the first kiss of love that had ever been pressed on her lips. She drew back from it, pale and thrilled, not abashed, but looking at her lover with eyes before which his drooped. It was a sacred moment to her.

"How wonderful," she whispered, "that you should care for me."

"It would have been more wonderful if I hadn't."

"And that you came now, when everything was so dark and lonely. You don't know how horribly lonely I felt this evening, thinking of leaving here to-morrow and going among strangers."

"But that's all over now. You need never be lonely again. I'll always be there to take care of you. We'll always be together."

"Don't you think things often change when they get to their very worst? It seemed to me to-night that I was just about to open a door that led into the world, where nobody cared for me, or knew me, or wanted me."

"One person wanted you, desperately."

"And then, all in a moment, my whole life is changed. It's not an hour ago that I was sitting here looking into the fire thinking how miserable I was, and now—"

"You are in my arms!" he interrupted, and drew her against him for his kiss. She turned her face away and pressed it into his shoulder, as he held her close, and said:

"We'll go to Europe, to Italy—that's the country for you, not this raw Western town where you're like some exotic blossom growing in the sand. You've never seen anything like it, with the gray olive trees like smoke on the hillsides, and the white walls of the villas shining among the cypresses. We'll have a villa, and we can walk on the terrace in the evening and look down on the valley of the Arno. It's the place for lovers, and we're going to be lovers, Mariposa."

Still she did not understand, and said happily:

"Yes, true lovers for always."

"And then we'll go to France, and we'll see Paris— all the great squares with the lights twinkling, and the Rue de Rivoli with gas lamps strung along it like diamonds on a thread. And the river—it's black at night with the bridges arching over it, and the lamps stabbing down into the water with long golden zigzags. We'll go to the theaters and to the opera, and you'll be the handsomest woman there. And we'll drive home in an open carriage under the starlight, not saying much, because we'll be so happy."

"And shall I study singing?"

"Of course, with the best masters. You'll be a great prima donna some day."

"And I sha'n't have to be sent by Mr. Shackleton? Oh, I shall be so glad to tell him I'm going with you."

Essex started—looked at her frowning.

"But you mustn't do that," he said with a sudden, authoritative change of key.

"Why not?" she answered. "You know he was to send me. I promised my mother I would let him take care of me. But now that I'm going to be married, my—my—husband will take care of me."

She looked at him with a girl's charming embarrassment at the first fitting of this word to any breathing man, and blushed deeply and beautifully. Essex felt he must disillusion her. He looked into the fire.

"Married," he said slowly. "Well, of course, if we were married—"

He stopped, gave her a lightning side-glance. She was smiling.

"Well, of course we'll be married," she said. "How could we go to Europe unless we were?"

Still avoiding her eyes, which he knew were fixed on him in smiling inquiry, he said in a lowered voice:

"Oh, yes, we could."

"How—I don't understand?"

For the first time there was a faint note of uneasiness in her voice. Though his glance was still bent on the fire, he knew that she was no longer smiling.

"We could go easily, without making any talk or

fuss. Of course we could not leave here together. I'd meet you in Chicago or New York."

He heard her dress rustle as she instinctively drew away from him.

"Meet me in New York or Chicago?" she repeated. "But why meet me there? I don't understand. Why not be married here?"

He turned toward her and threw up his head as a person does who is going to speak emphatically and at length. Only in raising his head his eyes remained on the ground.

"My dear girl," he said in a suave tone, "you've lived all your life in these small, half-civilized California towns, and there are many things about life in larger and more advanced communities you don't understand. I've just told you I loved you, and you know that your welfare is of more moment to me than anything in the world. I would give my heart's blood to make you happy. But I am just now hardly in a position to marry. You must understand that."

It was said. Mariposa gave a low exclamation and rose to her feet. He rose, too, feeling angry with her that she had forced him to this banal explanation. There were times when her stupidity could be exasperating.

She was very pale, her eyes dark, her nostrils expanded. On her face was an expression of pitiful bewilderment and distress.

"Then—then—you didn't want to *marry* me?" she stammered with trembling lips.

"Oh, I want to," he said with a propitiatory shrug.

"Of course I *want* to. But one can't always do what one wants. Under the circumstances, as I tell you, marriage is impossible."

She could say nothing for a moment, the first stunned moment of comprehension. Then she said in a low voice, still with her senses scattered, "And I thought you meant it all."

"Meant what? that I love you? Don't you trust me? Don't you believe me? You must acknowledge I understand life better than you do."

She looked at him straight in the eyes. The pain and bewilderment had left her face, leaving it white and tense. He realized that she was not going to weep and make moan—the wound had gone deeper. He had stabbed her to the heart.

"You're right," she said. "I don't understand about life as you do. I didn't understand that a man could talk to a woman as you have done to me and then strike her such a blow. It's too new to me to learn quickly. I—I—can't—understand yet. I can't say anything to you, only that I don't ever want to see you, or hear you, or think of you again."

"My dearest girl," he said, going a step toward her, "don't be so severe. You're like a tragedy queen. Now, what have I done?"

"I didn't think that a man could have the heart to wound any woman so—any living creature, and one who cared as I did—" she stopped, unable to continue.

"But I wouldn't wound you for the world. Haven't I just told you I loved you?"

"Oh, go," she said, backing away from him. "Go! go away. Never come near me again. You've debased and humiliated me forever, and I've kissed you and told you I loved you. Why can't I creep into some corner and die?"

"Mariposa, my darling," he said, raising his eyebrows with a theatrical air of incomprehension, "what is it? I'm quite at sea. You speak to me as if I'd done you a wrong, and all I've done is to offer you my deepest devotion. Does that offend you?"

"Yes, horribly—horribly!" she cried furiously. "Go—go out of my sight. If you've got any manliness or decency left, go—I can't bear any more."

She pressed her hands on her face and turned from him.

"Oh, don't do that," he said tenderly, approaching her. "Does my love make you unhappy? A half-hour ago it was not like this."

He suddenly, but gently, attempted to take her in his arms. Though she did not see she felt his touch, and with a cry of horror tore herself away, rushed past him into the adjoining room, and from that into her bedroom beyond. The bang of the closing door fell coldly upon Essex's ear.

He stood for a moment listening and considering. He had a fancy that she might come back. The house was absolutely silent. Then, no sound breaking its stillness, no creak of an opening door echoing through its bare emptiness, he walked out into the hall, put on his hat and overcoat and let himself out. He was angry and disgusted. In his thoughts he inveighed against Mariposa's stupidity. The unfortunately downright explanation had aroused her wrath, and he did not know how deep that might be. Only as he recalled her ordering him from the room he realized that it was not the fictitious rage he had seen before and understood.

Mariposa stood on the inside of her room door, holding the knob and trying to suppress her breathing that she might hear clearly. She heard his steps, echoing on the bare floor with curious distinctness. They were slow at first; then there was decision in them; then the hall door banged. She leaned against the panel, her teeth pressed on her underlip, her head bowed on her breast.

"Oh, how could he? how could he?" she whispered.

A tempest of anguish shook her. She crept to the bed and lay there, her face buried in the pillow, motionless and dry-eyed, till dawn.

CHAPTER X

THE PALE HORSE

"Nicanor lay dead in his harness."
—MACCABEES.

The day broke overcast and damp, one of those depressing days of still, soft grayness that usher in the early rains, when the air has a heavy closeness and the skies seem to sag with the weight of moisture that is slow to fall.

There was much to do yet in the rifled cottage. Mariposa rose to it wan and heavy-eyed. The whirl of her own thoughts during the long, sleepless night had not soothed her shame and distress. She found herself working doggedly, with her heart like lead in her breast, and her mouth feeling dry as the scene of the evening before pressed forward to her attention. She tried to keep it in the background, but it would not down. Words, looks, sentences kept welling up to the surface of her mind, coloring her cheeks with a miserable crimson, filling her being with a sickness of despair. The memory of the kisses followed her from room to room, and task to task. She felt them on her lips as she moved about, the lips that had never known the kiss of a lover, and now seemed soiled and smirched forever.

After luncheon the red lacquer cabinet went away. She watched it off as the last remnant of the old life. She felt strangely indifferent to what yesterday she thought would be so many unbearable wrenches. Finally nothing was left but her own few possessions, gathered together in a corner of the front room—two trunks, a screen, a table, a long, old-fashioned mirror and some pictures. Yesterday morning she had bargained with a cheap carter, picked up on the street corner, to take them for a dollar, and now she sat waiting for him, while the day grew duller outside, and the fog began to sift itself into fine rain.

The servant, who was to close and lock the cottage, begged her to go, promising to see to the shipping of the last load. Mariposa needed no special urging. She felt that an afternoon spent in that dim little parlor, looking out through the bay window at the fine slant of the rain would drive her mad. There was no promise of cheer at the Garcia boarding-house, but it was, at least, not haunted with memories.

A half-hour later, with the precious desk, containing the marriage certificates and Shackleton's gift of money, under her arm, she was climbing the hills from Sutter Street to that part of Hyde Street in which the Garcia house stood. She eyed it with deepening gloom as it revealed itself through the thin rain. It was a house which even then was getting old, standing back from the street on top of a bank, which was held in place by a wooden bulk-head, surmounted by a low balustrade. A gate gave access through this, and a flight of rotting wooden steps led by zigzags to the house. The lower story was skirted in front by a balcony, which, after the fashion of early San Francisco architecture, was encased in glass. Its roof above slanted up to the two long windows of the front bedroom. The pepper-tree, of which Mariposa had spoken to Essex, was sufficient to tell of the age of the property and to give beauty and picturesqueness to the ramshackle old place. It had reached an unusual growth and threw a fountain of drooping foliage over the balustrade and one long limb upon the balcony roof.

To-day it dripped with the rest of the world. As Mariposa let the gate bang the impact shook a shower from the tree, which fell on her as she passed beneath. It seemed to her a bad omen and added to the almost terrifying sensation of gloom that was invading her.

Her ring at the bell brought the whole Garcia family to the door and the hall. A child of ten—the elder of the young Mrs. Garcia's boys—opened it. He was in the condition of moisture and mud consequent on a game of baseball on the way home from school. Behind him crowded a smaller boy—of a cherubic beauty —arrayed in a very dirty sailor blouse, with a still dirtier wide white collar, upon which hung locks of wispy yellow hair. Mrs. Garcia, the younger, came drearily forward. She was a thin, pretty, slatternly, young woman, very baggy about the waist, and with the same wispy yellow hair as her son, which she wore in the popular bang. It had been smartly curled in the morning, but the damp had shown it no respect, and it hung down limply nearly into her eyes. Back of her, in the dim reaches of the hall, Mariposa saw the grandmother, the strange old Spanish woman, who spoke no English. She looked very old, and small, and was wrinkled like a walnut. But as she encountered the girl's miserable gaze she gave her a gentle reassuring smile, full of that curious, patient sweetness which comes in the faces of the old who have lived kindly.

The younger members of the family escorted the new arrival upstairs. She had seen her room before, had already placed therein her piano and many of her smaller ornaments, but its bleakness struck her anew. She stopped on the threshold, looking at its chill, half-furnished extent with a sudden throttling sense of homesickness. It was a large room, evidently once the state bedroom of the house, signs of its past glory lingering in the elaborate gilt chandelier, the white wall-paper, strewed with golden wheat-ears, and the marble mantelpiece, with carvings of fruit at the sides. Now she saw with renewed clearness of vision the threadbare carpet, with a large ink-stain by the table, the rocking-chair with one arm gone, the place on the wall behind the sofa where the heads of previous boarders had left their mark.

"Your clock don't go," said the cherubic boy in a loud voice. "I've tried to make it, but it only ticks a minute and then stops."

"There!" said Mrs. Garcia, with a gesture of collapsed hopelessness, "he's been at your clock! I knew he would. Have you broken her clock?" fiercely to the boy.

"No, I ain't," he returned, not in the least overawed by the maternal onslaught. "It were broke when it came."

"He did break it," said the other boy suddenly. "He opened the back door of it and stuck a hairpin in."

Mrs. Garcia made a rush at her son with the evident intention of administering corporal punishment on the spot. But with a loud, derisive shout, he eluded her and dashed through the doorway. Safe on the stairs, he cried defiantly:

"I ain't done it, and no one can prove it."

"That's the way they always act," said Mrs. Garcia despondently, pushing up her bang so that she could the better see her new guest. "It's no picnic having no husband and having to slave for everybody."

"Grandma slaves, too," said the rebel on the stairway; "she slaves more'n you do, and Uncle Gam slaves the most."

Further revelations were stopped by another ring at the bell. Visitors were evidently rare, for everybody but Mariposa flew to the hall and precipitated themselves down the stairs. In the general interest the recent battle was forgotten, the rebel earning his pardon by getting to the door before any one else. The newcomer was Mariposa's expressman. She had already seen through her window the uncovered cart with her few belongings glistening with rain.

The driver, a grimy youth in a steaming blouse, was standing in the doorway with the wet receipt flapping in his hand.

"It's your things," yelled the boys.

"Tell him to bring them up," said Mariposa, who was now at the stair-head herself.

The man stepped into the hall and looked up at her. He had a singularly red and impudent face.

"Not till I get my two dollars and a half," he said.

"Two dollars and a half!" echoed Mariposa in alarm, for a dollar was beginning to look larger to her than it ever had done before. "It was only a dollar."

"A dollar!" he shouted. "A dollar for that load!"—pointing to the street—"say, you've got a gall!"

Mariposa flushed. She had never been spoken to this way before in her life. She leaned over the balustrade and said haughtily:

"Bring in my things, and when they're up here I will give you the dollar you agreed upon."

The man gave a loud, derisive laugh.

"That beats anything!" he said, and then roared through the door to his pard: "Say, she wants to give us a dollar for that load. Ain't that rich?"

There was a moment's silence in the hall. A vulgar wrangle was almost impossible to the girl at the juncture to which the depressing and hideous events of the last few weeks had brought her. Yet she had still a glimmer of spirit left, and her gorge rose at the impudent swindle.

"I won't pay you two dollars and a half, and I will have my things," she said. "Bring them up at once."

The man laughed again, this time with an uglier note.

"I guess not, young woman," he said, lounging against the balustrade. "I guess you'll have to fork out the two fifty or whistle for your things."

Mariposa made no answer. Her hand shaking with rage, she began to fumble in her pocket for her purse. The whole Garcia family, assembled in the hallway beneath, breathed audibly in the tense excitement of the moment, and kept moving their eyes from her to the expressman and back again. The Chinaman from the kitchen had joined them, listening with the charmed smile which the menials of that race always wear on occasions of domestic strife.

"Say," said the man, coming a step up the stairs and assuming a suddenly threatening air, "I can't stay fooling round here all day. I want my money, and I want it quick. D'ye hear?"

Mariposa's hand closed on the purse. She would have now paid anything to escape from this hateful scene. At the same moment she heard a door open behind her, a quick step in the hall, and a man suddenly stood beside her at the stair-head. He was in his shirt-sleeves and he had a pen in his hand.

The expressman, who had mounted two or three steps, saw him and recoiled, looking startled.

"What's the matter with you?" said the new-comer shortly.

"I want my money," said the man doggedly, but retreating.

"Who owes you money? And what do you mean by making a row like this in this house?"

"I owe him money," said Mariposa. "I agreed to pay him a dollar for carrying my things here, and now he wants two and a half and won't give me my things unless I pay it. But I'll pay what he wants rather than fight this way."

She was conscious of a slight, amused smile in the very keen and clear gray eyes the man beside her fastened for one listening moment on her face.

THE PALE HORSE

"Get your dollar," he said, "and don't bother any more." Then in a loud voice down the stairway: "Here, step out and get the trunks and don't let's have any more talk about it. Ching," to the Chinaman, "go out and help that man with this lady's things."

The Chinaman came forward, still grinning. The expressman for a moment hesitated.

"Look here," said the man in the shirt-sleeves, "I don't want to have to come downstairs, I'm busy."

The expressman, with Ching behind him, hurried out.

Mariposa's deliverer stood at the stair-head watching them and slightly smiling. Then he turned to her. She was again conscious of how gray and clear his eyes looked in his sunburned face.

"I was writing a letter in my room, and I heard the sound of strife long before I realized what was happening. Why didn't you call me?"

"I didn't know there was any one there," she answered.

"Well, the boys ought to have known. Why didn't one of you little beggars come for me?" he said to the two boys, who were clambering slowly up the outside of the balustrade staring from the deliverer to the expressman, now advancing up the steps with Mariposa's belongings.

"I liked to see 'em fight," said the smaller. "I liked it."

"You little scamp," said the man, and, leaning over the stair-rail, caught the ascending cherub by the slack of his knickerbockers and drew him upward, shrieking delightedly. On the landing he gave him a slight shake, and said:

"I don't want to hear any more of that kind of talk. Next time there's a fight, call me."

The expressman and Ching had now entered laden with the luggage. They came staggering up the stairs, scraping the walls with the corners of the trunks and softly swearing. Mariposa started for her room, followed by the strange man and the two boys.

Her deliverer was evidently a person to whom the usages of society were matters of indifference. He entered the room without permission or apology and stood looking inquiringly about him, his glance passing from the bed to the wide, old-fashioned bureau, the rocking-chair with its arm off and the ink-stain on the carpet. As the men entered with their burdens, he said:

"You look as if you'd be short of chairs here. I'll see that you get another rocker to-morrow."

Mariposa wondered if Mrs. Garcia was about to end her widowhood and this was the happy man.

He stood about as the men set down the luggage, and watched the transfer of the dollar from Mariposa's white hand to the dingy one of her late enemy. The boys also eyed this transaction with speechless attention, evidently anticipating a second outbreak of hostilities. But peace had been restored and would evidently rule as long as the sunburned man in the shirt-sleeves remained.

This he appeared to intend doing. He suggested a change in the places of one or two of Mariposa's pieces of furniture, and showed her how she could use her screen to hide the bed. He looked annoyed over a torn strip of loose wall-paper that hung dejected, revealing a long seam of plaster like a seared scar. Then he went to the window and pushed back the curtains of faded rep.

"There's a nice view from here on sunny days down into the garden."

Mariposa felt she must show interest, and went to the window, too. The pane was not clean, and the view commanded nothing but the splendid fountain-like foliage of the pepper-tree and below a sodden strip of garden in which limp chrysanthemums hung their heads, while a ragged nasturtium vine tried to protest its vigor by flaunting a few blossoms from the top of the fence. It seemed to her the acme of forlornness. The crescendo of the afternoon's unutterable despondency had reached its climax. Her sense of desolation welled suddenly up into overwhelming life. It caught her by the throat. She made a supreme effort, and said in a shaken voice:

"It looks rather damp now."

Her companion turned from the window.

"Here, boys, scoot," he said to the two boys who were attempting to open the trunks with the clock key. "You've got no business hanging round here. Go down and study your lessons."

They obediently left the room. Mariposa heard their jubilantly clamorous descent of the stairs. She made no attempt to leave the window, or to speak to the man, who still remained moving about as if looking for something. The light was growing dim in the dark wintry day, but the girl still stood with her face to the pane. She knew that if the tears against which she fought should come there would be a deluge of them. Biting her lips and clenching her hands, she stood peering out, speechless, overwhelmed by her wretchedness.

Presently the man said, as if speaking to himself:

"Where the devil are the matches? Elsie's too careless for anything."

She heard him feeling about on shelves and tables, and after a moment he said:

"Did you see where the matches were? I want to light the gas."

"There aren't any," she answered without turning.

He gave a suppressed exclamation, and, opening the door, left the room.

With the withdrawal of his restraining presence the tension snapped. Mariposa sank down in the chair near the window and the tears poured from her eyes, tears in torrential volume, such as her mother had shed twenty-five years before in front of Dan Moreau's cabin.

Her grief seized her and swept her away. She shook with it. Why could she not die and escape from this hideous world? It bowed her like a reed before a wind, and she bent her face on the chair arm and trembled and throbbed.

She did not hear the door open, nor know that her solitude was again invaded, till she heard the man's step beside her. Then she started up, strangled with sobs and indignation.

"Is it you again?" she cried. "Can't you see how miserable I am?"

"I saw it the moment I came out of my room this afternoon," he answered quietly. "I'm sorry I disturb you. I only wanted to light the gas and get the place a little more cheerful and warm. It's too cold in here. You go on crying. Don't bother about me; I'm going to light the fire."

She obeyed him, too abject in her misery to care. He lit all the gases in the gilt chandelier, and then knelt before the fireplace. Soon the snapping of the wood contested the silence with the small, pathetic noises of the woman's weeping. She felt—at first without consciousness—the grateful warmth of the blaze. Presently she removed the wad of saturated handkerchief from her face. The room was inundated by a flood of light, the leaping gleam of the flames licking the glaze of the few old-fashioned ornaments and evoking uncertain gleams from the long mirror standing on the floor in the corner. The man was sitting before the fire. He had his coat on now, and Mariposa could see that he was tall and powerful, a bronzed and muscular man of about thirty-five years of age, with a face tanned to mahogany color, thick-brown hair and a brown mustache. His hand, as it rested on his knee, caught her eye; it was well formed but worn as a laborer's.

"Don't you want to come and sit near the fire?" he said, without moving his head.

She murmured a negative.

"I see that your clock is all off," he continued. "There's something the matter with it. I'll fix it for you this evening."

He rose and lifted the clock from the mantelpiece.

It was a small timepiece of French gilt, one of the many presents her father had given her mother in their days of affluence.

As he lifted it Mariposa suddenly experienced a return of misery at the thought that he was going. At the idea of being again left to herself her wretchedness rushed back upon her, with redoubled force. She felt that the flood of tears would begin again.

"Oh, don't go," she said, with the imploring urgency of old friendship. "I'm so terribly depressed. Don't go."

Her lips trembled, her swollen eyes were without light or beauty. She was as distinctly unlovely as a handsome woman can be. The man, however, did not look at her. He had opened the door of the clock and was studying its internal machinery. He answered quietly:

"I'll have to go now for a while. I must finish my letter. It's got to go out to-night, but I was going to ask you if you wouldn't like to have your supper up here? It's now a little after five; at six o'clock I'll bring it, and if you don't mind, I'll bring mine up, too. I just take tea and some bread and butter and jam or stuff—whatever Elsie happens to have round. If you'd like it, you fix up the table and get things into some sort of shape."

He walked toward the door. With the handle in his hand he said:

"You don't mind my taking mine up here, too, do you? If you do, just say so."

"No, I don't mind," said Mariposa, in the stifled voice of the weeper.

When he had gone she listlessly tried to create some kind of order in the chaotic room. She felt exhausted and indifferent. Once she found herself looking at her watch with a sort of heavy desire to have the time pass quickly. She dreaded her loneliness. She caught a glimpse of herself in the chimney-piece glass and felt neither shame nor disgust at her unsightly appearance.

At six o'clock she heard the quick, decisive step in the hall that earlier in the afternoon had broken in on her wrangle with the expressman. A knock came on the door that sounded exceedingly like a kick bestowed under difficulties. She opened it, and her new friend entered bearing a large tray set forth with the paraphernalia of a cold supper and with the evening paper laid on top. He put it on the cleared table, and together they lifted off its contents and set them forth. There was cold meat, jam, bread and butter, a brown pottery teapot with the sprout broken and two very beautiful cups, delicate and richly decorated. Then they sat down, one at each side of the table, and the meal began.

Mariposa did not care to eat. Sitting under the blaze of the gilt chandelier, with the firelight gilding one side of her flushed and disfigured face, she poured out the tea, while her companion attacked the cold meat with good appetite. The broken spout leaked, and she found herself guiltily regarding the man opposite, as she surreptitiously tried to sop up with a napkin the streams of tea it sent over the table-cloth.

He appeared to have the capacity for seeing anything that occurred in his vicinity.

"Never mind the teapot," he said, with his mouth full; "it always does that. It's no good getting a new one. I think the boys break them. Elsie says they play boats with them in the bath-tub."

Mariposa made no reply, and the meal progressed in silence. Presently her *vis-à-vis* held out his cup for a second filling.

"What beautiful cups," she said. "It would be a pity to break them."

"They're grandma's. They're the only two left. Grandma had some stunning things, brought round The Horn by her husband in the early days, before the Gringo came. He was a great man in his day, Don Manuel Garcia."

"Is she your grandmother, too?" Mariposa asked. It seemed natural to put pointblank questions to this man, who so completely swept aside the smaller conventions.

"Mine? Oh, Lord, no. My poor old granny died crossing the plains in '49. I was there, but I don't remember it. I call old lady Garcia grandma, because I'm here so much, and because I look upon them as my family."

"Do you live here always?" asked Mariposa, looking with extinguished eyes over the piece of bread she was nibbling.

"No, I live at the mines. I'm a miner. My stamping-ground's the whole Sierra from Siskiyou to Tuolumne."

He looked at her with a queer, whimsical smile. His strong white teeth gleamed for a moment from between his bearded lips.

"I'm up at the Sierra a lot of the time," he continued, "and then I'm down here a lot more of the time. I come here to find my victims. I locate a good prospect in the Sierra, and I come down here to sell it. That's my business."

"What's your name?" asked Mariposa suddenly, hearing herself ask this last and most pertinent question with the dry glibness of an interviewer.

"My name? Great Scott, you don't know it!" he threw back his head and a jolly, sonorous laugh filled the room. "That's great, you and I sitting here together over supper as if we'd grown up together in the same nursery, and you don't know what my name is. It's Gamaliel Barron. Do you like it?"

"Yes," said Mariposa, gravely, "it's a very nice name."

"I'm glad you think so. I can't say I'm much attached to the front end of it. It's a Bible name. I haven't the least idea who the gentleman was, or what he did, but he's in the Bible somewhere."

"Saul sat at his feet," said Mariposa; "he was a great teacher."

"Well, I'm afraid his namesake isn't much like him. I never taught anybody anything, and certainly no one ever sat at my feet, and I'd hate it if they did."

There was another pause, while Barron continued his supper with unabated gusto. He had finished the cold meat and was now spreading jam on bread and butter and eating it, with alternate mouthfuls of tea. Though he ate rapidly, as one accustomed to take his meals alone, he ate like a gentleman. She found herself regarding him with a listless curiosity, faintly wondering what manner of man he was.

Looking up he met her eyes and said:

"You'll be very comfortable here. Don't let the first glimpse discourage you. Elsie's careless, and the boys are pretty wild, but they're all right when you come to know them better, and grandma's fine. There's not many women in San Francisco to match old Señora Garcia. She's the true kind."

"What a pity her son died!" said Mariposa.

He raised his head instantly and an expression of pain passed over his face.

"You're right, there," he said in a low voice. "That was one of the hardest things that ever happened. If there's a God I'd like to know why he let it happen. Juan Garcia was the salt of the earth—a great man. He was the best son, the best husband and the best friend I ever knew. And he was killed offhand, for no reason, by an unnecessary accident, leaving these poor, helpless creatures this way."

He made a gesture with his head toward the door.

"You knew him well?" said Mariposa.

The gray eyes looked into hers very gravely.

"He was my best friend," he answered; "the best friend any man ever had in the world."

The girl saw he was moved.

"The people we love, and depend on, and live for always die," she said gloomily.

"But others come up. They don't quite take their places, but they fill up the holes in the ranks. We're not expected always to love comfortably and be happy. We're expected to work; that's what we're here for,

THE PALE HORSE

and there's plenty of it to do. Haven't I got my work cut out for me," suddenly laughing, "in those two boys?"

Mariposa's pale lips showed the ripple of an assenting smile.

"They're certainly a serious proposition," he continued, "and poor Elsie can't any more manage 'em than she could ride a bucking bronco. But they'll pull out all right. Don't you worry. Those boys are all right."

He was about to return to the remnants of the supper when his eyes fell on the folded paper, which had been pushed to one side of the table.

"Oh, look!" he said; "we forgot the paper. You've finished; wouldn't you like to see it?"

She shook her head. The paper had not much interest for her at the best of times.

"Well, then, if you don't mind, I'll run my eye over it, while you make me another cup of tea. Three cups are my limit—one lump and milk."

He handed her the cup, already shaking the paper out of its folds. She was struggling with the leakage of the broken spout, when he gave a loud ejaculation:

"Great Scott! here's news!"

"What is it?" she queried, the broken teapot suspended over the cup.

"Jake Shackleton's dead!"

The teapot fell with a crash on the table. Her mouth opened, her face turned an amazing pallor, and she sat staring at the astonished man with horror-stricken eyes.

"Dead!" she gasped; "why everybody's dead!"

Barron dropped the paper on the floor.

"I'm so awfully sorry; I didn't know you knew him well. I didn't know he was a friend."

"Friend!" she echoed, almost with a shriek. "Friend! Why, he was my father."

The voice ended in a wild peal of laughter, horrible, almost maniacal.

The man, paying no attention to her words, realized that the strain of the day and her overwhelming depression of spirits had completely unbalanced her. Her wild laughter suddenly gave way to wilder tears. In a moment he ran to the door to summon the señora, but in the next, remembered that Elsie and the boys would undoubtedly accompany her, and that the woman before him was in no state to be exposed to their uncomprehending stares.

Hysterics were new to him, but he had a vague idea that water administered suddenly from a pitcher was the only authorized cure. He seized the pitcher from the wash-stand, began to sprinkle her somewhat timidly with his fingers, and finally ended by pouring a fair amount on her head.

It had the desired effect. Gasping, saturated, but dragged back to some sort of control, by the chill current running from her head in rillets over her body, Mariposa sat up. The man was standing before her, anxiously regarding her, the pitcher held ready for another application. She pushed it away with an icy hand.

"I'm all right now," she gasped. "You'd better go. And—and—if I said anything silly, you understand, I didn't know what I was saying. I meant—that Mr. Shackleton was a *friend* of my father's. He's been very good to me. It gave me an awful shock. Please go."

Barron set down the pitcher and went. He was overcome with pity for the broken creature, and furious with himself for the shock he had given her. The words she had uttered had made little impression on him at first. It was afterward, while he was in the silence of his own room, that they recurred to him with more significance. For a space he thought of the remark and her explanation of it with some wonder. But before he settled to sleep, he had pushed the matter from his mind, setting it down as the meaningless utterance of an hysterical woman.

CHAPTER XI.

BREAKS IN THE RAIN

"I had no time to hate because
The grave would hinder me,
And life was not so simple I
Could finish enmity."
—DICKINSON.

For two days after her hysterical outburst Mariposa kept her room, sick in body and mind. The quick succession of nerve-shattering events, ending with the death of Shackleton, seemed to stun her. She lay on the sofa, white and motionless, irresponsive even to the summons of the boys, who drummed cheerfully on her door as soon as they came home from school.

Fortunately for her, solitude was as difficult to find in that slipshod *ménage* as method or order. When the boys were at school, young Mrs. Garcia, in the disarray that attended the accomplishment of her household tasks, mounted to her first-floor boarder and regaled her with mingled accounts of past splendors and present miseries. Mrs. Garcia spoke freely of her husband and the affluence with which he had surrounded her. The listener, looking at the faded, blond prettiness of her foolish face, wondered how the Juan Garcia that Gamaliel Barron had described could have loved her. Mariposa had yet to learn that

Nature mates the strong men of the world to the feeble women, in an effort to maintain an equilibrium.

Once or twice the old señora came upstairs, carrying some dainty in a covered dish. She had been born at Monterey and had come to San Francisco as a bride in the late fifties, but had never learned English, speaking the sonorous Spanish of her girlhood to every one she met, whether it was understood or not. Even in the complete wreck of fortune and position, in which Mariposa saw her, she was a fine example of the highest class of Spanish Californian, that once brilliant and picturesque race, careless, simple, lazy, happy, lords of a kingdom whose value they never guessed, possessors of limitless acres on which their cattle grazed.

The day after Shackleton's death Mrs. Willers appeared, still aghast at the suddenness of the catastrophe. Mariposa did not know that a few days previously, Shackleton had acquainted the newspaper woman with his intention of sending her to Paris with Miss Moreau, the post of correspondent to *The Trumpet* being assigned to her. It had been the culminating point of Mrs. Willers' life of struggle. Now all that lay shattered. Be it said to her credit her disappointment was more for the girl than for herself. She knew that Shackleton had made no definite arrangements for the starting of Mariposa on her way. All had been *in statu quo*, attending on the daughter's recovery from her mother's loss. Now death had stepped in and forever closed the door upon these hopes.

Mrs. Willers found Mariposa strangely apathetic. She had tried to cheer her and then had seen, to her amazement, that the girl showed little disappointment.

That the sudden blow had upset her was obvious. She undoubtedly looked ill. But the wrenching from her hand of liberty, independence, possibilities of fame, seemed to affect her little. She listened in silence to Mrs. Willers' account of the Bonanza King's death. As an "inside writer" on *The Trumpet* the newspaper woman had heard every detail of the tragic event discussed threadbare in the perturbed office. Shackleton had been found, as the paper stated, sitting at his desk in the library at Menlo Park. He had been writing letters when death called him. His wife had come in late at night and found him thus, leaning on the desk as if tired. It was an aneurism, the doctors said. The heart had been diseased for years. No one, however, had had any idea of it. Poor Mrs. Shackleton was completely prostrated. It was not newspaper talk that she was in a state of collapse.

"And it was enough to collapse any woman," said Mrs. Willers, with a sympathetic wag of the head, "to come in and find your husband sitting up at his desk stone dead. And a good husband, too. It would have given me a shock to have found Willers that way, and even an obituary notice in the paper of which he was proprietor could hardly have called Willers a good husband."

Two days' rest restored Mariposa to some sort of balance. She still felt weak and stunned in heart and brain. The lack of interest she had shown to Mrs. Willers had been the outward sign of this internal benumbed condition. But as she slowly dressed on the morning of the third day, she felt a slight ripple of returning life, a thawing of these congealed faculties.

She heard the quick, decisive step of Barron in the hallway outside, and then its stoppage at her door, and his call through the crack, "How are you this morning? Better?"

"Much," she answered; "I'm getting up."

"First-rate. Couldn't do better. Get a move on and go out. It's a day that would put life into a mummy. I'd take you out myself, but I've got to go down town and lasso one of my victims."

Then he clattered down the stairs. Mariposa had not seen him since their supper together. Every morning he had stopped and called a greeting of some sort through the door. She shrank from meeting him again. The extraordinary remark she had made to him haunted her. The only thing that appeased her was the memory of his face, in which there was no consciousness of the meaning of her words, only consternation and amaze at the effect his news had produced.

It was, indeed, a wonderful day. Through her parted curtains she saw details of the splendor in the bits of turquoise sky between the houses, and the vivid greens of the rain-washed gardens. When the sun was well up, and the opened window let in delicious earth scents, she put on her hat and jacket and went out, turning her steps to that high spine of the city along the crest of which California Street runs.

Has any place been found where there are finer days than those San Francisco can show in winter? "The breaks in the rain," old Californians call them. It is the rain that gives them their glory, for the whole world has been washed clean and gleams like an agate beneath a wave. The skies reflect this clearness of tint. There are no clouds. The whole arch is a rich blue, fading at the horizon to a thin, pale transparency. The landscape is painted with a few washes of fresh primary colors, each one deep, but limpid, like the tints in the heart of a gem. And in this crystalline purity of atmosphere every line is cut with unfaltering distinctness. There is no faintness, no breath of haze, or forgotten film of fog. Nature seems even jealous of the smoke-wreaths that rise from the city to blur the beauty of the mighty picture, and the gray spirals are hurriedly dispersed.

Mariposa walked slowly, ascending by a zigzag course from street to street, idly looking at the houses and gardens as she passed. People of consideration had for some time been on the move from South Park to this side of town. The streets through which the young girl's course led her were now the gathering place of the city's successful citizens. On the heights above them, the new millionaires were raising palaces, which they were emulating on the ascending slopes. Great houses reared themselves on every sunny corner. The architecture of the bay-windowed mansion with the two lions sleeping on the front steps had supplanted that of the dignified, plastered-brick fronts, with the long lines of windows opening on wrought-iron balconies.

These huge wooden edifices housed the wealth and fashion of the city. Mariposa paused and stood with knit brows, looking down from a vantage-point on the glittering curve of greenhouse and the velvet lawns of Jake Shackleton's town house; there was no sign of life or occupation about it. Curtains of lace veiled its innumerable windows. Only in the angle of lawn and garden that abutted on the intersection of two streets, a man, in his shirt-sleeves, was cutting calla lilies from the hedge that topped the high stone wall which rose from the sidewalk.

Finally, on the crest of the hill, where California Street runs between its palaces, the girl paused and looked about her. The great buildings were new, and stood, vast, awe-compelling monuments to California's material glory. Their owners were still trying to make themselves comfortable in them. There were sons and daughters to be married from them. Perched high above the city, in these many-windowed aeries, they could look down on the town they had seen grow from a village in the days when they, too, had been young, poor and struggling. What memories must have crowded their minds as they thought of the San Francisco they had first seen, and the San Francisco they saw now; of themselves as they had been then, and as they were now!

Mariposa leaned against a convenient wall top and looked down. The city lay clear-edged and gray in the cup made by its encircling hills. It had not yet thrown out feelers toward the Mission hills, and they rose above the varied sweep of roof and chimney, in undulating greenness, flecked here and there by the white dot of a cottage. The girdle of the bay shone sapphire-blue on this day of still sunshine. From its farther side other hills were revealed, each peak and shoulder clear cut against its neighbor and defining themselves in a crumpled, cobalt line against the faint sky. Over all Mount Diavolo rose, a purple point, pricking up above the green of newly grassed hills, about whose feet hung a white fringe of little towns.

Turning her eyes again on the descending walls and roofs, the watcher saw a long cortège passing soberly between the gray house-fronts on a street a few blocks below her. As she looked the boom of solemn music rose to her. It was a funeral, and one of unusual length, she thought, as her eyes caught the slow line of carriages far back through breaks in the houses. Presently, in the opening where two streets crossed, the hearse came into view, black and gloomy, with its nodding tufts of feathers and somberly caparisoned horses. Men walked behind it, and the measured music swelled louder, melancholy and yet inspiring.

Suddenly she realized whose it was. The rich man was going splendidly to his rest.

"My father!" she whispered to herself. "My father! How strange! how strange!"

The cortège passed on, the music swelling grandiosely and then dying down into fitful snatches of sweetness. The long line of carriages moved slowly forward, at a crawling foot-pace.

The daughter leaned on the coping of the wall, watching this last passage through the city of the father she had known so slightly and toward whom she felt a bitter and silent resentment.

She watched the nodding plumes till they were out of sight. How strangely death had drawn together the three that life had separated! In six months the woman and two men, tied together by a twist of the hand of Fate, had been summoned, one after the other, into the darkness beyond. Would they meet there? Mariposa shuddered and turned away. The black plumes had disappeared, but the music still boomed fitfully in measured majesty.

The whistles were blowing for midday when she retraced her steps to the Garcia house. As she mounted the stairs to the front door she became aware that there were several people grouped on the balcony, their forms dimly visible through the grimy glass and behind the rampart of long-stemmed geraniums that grew there in straggling neglect. The opening of the outer door let her in on them. She started and slightly changed color when she saw that one of the figures was that of Gamaliel Barron. He was sitting on the arm of a dilapidated rocker, frowningly staring at Benito, the younger Garcia boy, against whom, it appeared, a charge of some moment had just been brought. The case was being placed before Barron, who evidently acted as judge, by a person Mariposa had not seen before—a tall, thin young man of some thirty years, with a stoop in the shoulders, a shock of fine black hair, and a pair of very soft and beautiful blue eyes.

They were so preoccupied in the matter before them that no effort was made to introduce the stranger to Mariposa, though Barron offered her his armchair, retiring to a seat on the balcony railing, whence he loomed darkly severe, from among the straggling geraniums. Benito, in his sailor collar and wispy curls, maintained an air of smiling innocence, but

Miguel, the elder boy, who was an interested witness, bore evidence of uneasiness of mind in the strained attention of the face turned toward Barron.

Mariposa paused, her hand on the back of the rocking-chair. Benito had already inserted himself into her affections. She looked from one to the other to ascertain his offense. Both men were regarding the culprit, Barron with frowning disapproval, the other with eyes full of amusement. It was he who proceeded to state the case against the accused:

"She leaned over the railing and said to me, 'Them little boys will be sick if they eat that crab.' 'What crab and what little boys?' I asked, quite innocently, and she answered, 'Them little boys in the vacant lot!' Then I turned and saw Benito and Miguel squatting in the grass among the tomato cans and fragments of the daily press, with a crab that they were breaking up between them, a crab about as big as a cart-wheel."

"We found it there," said Benito. "It were just lying there."

"'If they eat that crab,' the lady continued, 'they'll be sick. It ain't no good. I threw it out myself. And I've been hollerin' to them to stop, and that little one with the curls, just turned round on me and says, "Oh, you go to the devil!"'"

The complainant paused, looked at Mariposa with an eye in which she saw laughter dancing, and said:

"That's rather a startling way for a gentleman to speak to a lady, isn't it?"

Though the language used by the accused was hard to associate with his cherubic appearance, and had somewhat shocked Mariposa's affection, she could hardly repress a smile. Benito grinning, as if with pride at the prowess he had shown in the encounter with the strange female, looked at his brother and emitted an explosive laugh. Miguel, however, had more clearly guessed the seriousness of the offense, and looked uneasy. Barron was regarding the younger boy with unmoved and angry gravity. Mariposa saw that the man was not in the least inclined to treat the matter humorously.

"Did you really say that, Benito?" he said.

"Well," said Benito, swaying his body from side to side, and fastening his eyes on a knife he had carelessly extracted from his pocket, "I didn't see what she had to do with that crab. It was all alone in the vacant lot. How was we to know it was her crab?"

"But," to Miguel, "she told you before not to touch it, that it was bad, didn't she?"

"Yes," returned the elder boy, exceedingly uncomfortable. "She come and leaned over the railing and hollered at us not to touch it, that it was bad and it 'ud make us sick. Then I stopped 'cause I didn't want to get sick. But Ben wouldn't, and she hollered again, and then he told her to go to the devil, and Mr. Pierpont came along just then, and she told him, and Ben got skairt and stopped."

There was a moment's silence. The younger boy continued to smile and finger his knife, but it was evident he was not so easy in his mind. The stranger, now with difficulty restraining his laughter, turned again to Mariposa and said:

"If the lady had been in any way aggressing on the

young gentleman's comfort or convenience, it would not have been exactly justifiable, but comprehensible. But when you consider that her sole desire was to save him from eating something that would make him sick, then you begin to realize the seriousness of the offense. Oh, Benito, you're in a bad way, I'm afraid!"

"I ain't nothing of the kind," said Benito, smiling and showing his dimples. "I ain't done nothing more than Miguel."

"I didn't tell her to go to the devil," exclaimed Miguel, in a loud, combative voice.

"'Cause I said it first," replied his brother, calmly. "You didn't have time."

"Well, Benito," said Barron, "I've got no use for you when you behave that way. There's no excuse for it. You've used the worst kind of language to a lady who was trying to do a decent thing. I won't take you this afternoon."

The change on Benito's face was sudden and piteous. The smile was frozen on his lips, he turned crimson, and said stammeringly, evidently hardly believing his ears:

"To see the balloon? Oh, Uncle Gam, you promised it for a week. Oh, I'd rather see the balloon than anything. Oh, Uncle Gam!"

"There's no use talking; I won't take a boy who behaves that way. I'm angry with you."

The man was absolutely grave and, Mariposa saw, spoke the truth when he said he was angry. The boy was about to plead, when probably a knowledge of the hopelessness of such a course silenced him. With a flushed face, he stood before the tribunal fighting with his tears, proud and silent. When he could no longer control them he turned and rushed into the house, his bursting sobs issuing from the hallway. Miguel charged after him.

"Oh, poor little fellow!" cried Mariposa; "how could you? Take him to see the balloon; do, please."

Barron made no reply, sitting on the railing, frowning and abstracted. She turned her eyes on the other man. He was still smiling.

"Barron's bringing up the boys," he said, "and he takes it hard."

"If I didn't," said the man from the railing, "who would? Heaven knows I don't want to disappoint the poor little cuss, but somebody's got to try and keep him in order."

"Can't you punish him some other way? He's been talking about seeing the balloon for days."

"I wish to goodness I'd somebody to help me," said the judge moodily; "I'm not up to this sort of work. It makes me feel the meanest thing that walks to get up and punish a boy for things that are just what I did when I was the same age. But what's a man to do? I can't see those children go to the devil."

The howls of Benito had been rising loudly from the house for some minutes. They now suffered a sudden check; there was a quick step in the hall and Mrs. Garcia appeared in the doorway, red and angry. Benito was at her side, eating a large slice of cake.

"What d'ye mean, Gam Barron," she said in a high key, "by making my son cry that way? Ain't you got no better use for your time than to tease and torment a poor, little, helpless boy, who's got no father to protect him?"

"I wasn't teasing him, Elsie," he answered quietly; "I only said I wouldn't take him out this afternoon because he behaved badly."

"Well, ain't that teasing, when you promised it for a week and more? That's what I call a snide trick. It's just because you want to go somewhere else, I know. And so you put it off on that woman and the crab. Much good she is, anyway; I know her, too. Never mind, my baby," fondly to Benito, stroking his hair with her hand, "mother'll take you to see the balloon herself."

Benito jerked himself away from the maternal hand and said, with his mouth full of cake:

"I don't want to go with you; I want to go with Uncle Gam. He lets me ride in the goat-cart and buy peanuts."

"You'll go with me," said Mrs. Garcia with asperity, "or you'll not go at all."

"I don't want to go with you," said Benito, beginning to grow clamorous; "I don't have fun when I go with you."

"You'll go with me, or stay home shut up in the cupboard all afternoon."

"I won't; no, I won't."

Benito was both tearful and enraged. His mother caught his hand and, holding it in a tense grip, bent her face down to his and said with set emphasis:

"Do you want to stay all afternoon in the kitchen cupboard?"

He struggled to be free, reiterating:

"No, I don't, and I ain't goin' to. I think you're real mean to me; I ain't goin' to go nowhere with you."

"You mean, ungrateful little boy," said his parent, furiously, shaking the hand she held. "Don't talk back to me. You'll go with me this afternoon and see that balloon if I have to drag you all the way. Yes, you will."

"I won't," roared Benito, now enraged past all control; and in his frenzy to escape he kicked at his mother's ankles through her intervening skirts.

This was too much for Mrs. Garcia's feelings as a mother. She took her free hand and boxed Benito smartly on the ear. Then for a moment there was war. Benito kicked, roaring lustily, while his mother cuffed. The din of combat was loud on the balcony, and several of the geranium pots were knocked over.

It remained for Barron to descend from the railing and drag the boy away from his wrathful parent.

"Here, stop kicking your mother," he said peremptorily; "that won't do at all."

"Then make her stop slapping me," howled Benito. "Ain't I got a right to kick back? I guess you'd kick all right if you was slapped that way."

"All right," said his mother from the doorway, "next time you come to me, Benito Garcia, to be taken to the circus or the fair, you'll find out that you've barked up the wrong tree."

"I don't care," responded Benito defiantly; "grandma or Uncle Gam will."

Five minutes after her irate withdrawal she reappeared, calm and smiling, the memory of her recent combat showing only in her heightened color, and announced that lunch was ready.

At lunch the stranger was introduced to Mariposa, and she learned that he was Isaac Pierpont, a singing teacher living in the house.

CHAPTER XII

DRIFT AND CROSSCUT

"A living dog is better than a dead lion."
—ECCLESIASTES.

On the evening of the day when Jake Shackleton went to his account Essex had walked slowly to Bertrand's *rôtisserie,* his head drooped, the evening paper in his hand.

Two hours before the cries of the newsboys announcing the sudden demise of his chief had struck on his ear, for the first moment freezing him into motionless amazement. Standing under a lamp, he had read the short report, then hurried down to the office of *The Trumpet.* There in the turmoil and hubbub which marks the first portentous movement of the great daily making ready to go to press, he had heard fuller details. The office was in an uproar, shaken to its foundation by the startling news, every man and woman ready with a speculation or a rumor as to the ultimate fate of *The Trumpet,* on which their own little fates hung.

At his table in the far corner of Bertrand's he mused over the various reports he had heard. The death of Shackleton would undoubtedly throw the present make-up of *The Trumpet* out of gear. Its sale would be inevitable. From what he had heard of him, Win Shackleton would be quite incapable of taking his father's place as proprietor and manager of the paper that Jake Shackleton, the man of brain and initiative, was transforming into a powerful organ of public opinion. And in the general weeding out of men which would unquestionably occur, why should not Barry Essex mount to a top place?

The Trumpet had always paid its capable men large salaries. It was worth while considering. Essex had now decided to remain in San Francisco, at least throughout the winter. The climate pleased him; the cosmopolitan atmosphere of the remote, picturesque city continued to exert its charm. The very duck he was now eating, far beyond his purse in any other American city, was an inducement to remain. But the real one was the woman, all the more desperately desired because denied him. Her indignation had not repelled him, but he saw it would mean a long wooing.

Once in his own room, he kindled the fire and drew toward him a pile of reference books he had to consult for an article on the great actresses of the French stage from Clairon to Rachel. These light and brilliant essays had been an experiment of Shackleton's, who maintained that the Sunday edition should furnish food for all types of minds. Essex had produced exactly the class of matter wanted, and received for it the generous pay that the proprietor of *The Trumpet* was always ready to give for good work.

The reader was fluttering the leaves of the first book of the pile when a knock at the door stopped him. He knew it was his neighbor across the hall, who had been in bed for over a week, sick with bronchitis. Essex had seen the man several times during his seclusion and had conceived a carelessly cynical interest in him.

When sober, he had developed remarkable anecdotal capacity, which had immensely amused his new acquaintance. Tales of '49 and the early Comstock days, scandals of those now in high places, discreditable accounts of the making of fortunes, flowed from his lips in a high-colored and diverting stream. If they were lies they were exceedingly ingenious ones. Essex saw material for a dozen novels in the man's revealing and lurid recitals. Of his own personal history he was reticent, merely saying that his name was George Harney, and his trade that of job-printer. Drink had almost destroyed him. Physically he was a mere bunch of nerves covered by flabby, sallow flesh.

In answer to Essex's "come in," the door opened and Harney shambled into the room. He was fully dressed, but showed the evidences of illness in his hollowed cheeks and eyes, and the yellow skin hanging flaccid round jaw and throat. His hand shook and his gait was uncertain, but he was perfectly sober.

"I came to have a squint at the paper, Doc," he said in a hoarse voice. "I can't go out with this blasted wheezing on me. Don't want to die in my prime."

Essex threw the paper across the table at him.

"There's news to-night," he said, taking up his book; "Shackleton's dead."

The man stopped as if electrified.

"Shackleton? Jake Shackleton?" he said in a loud voice.

"Jake Shackleton," answered Essex, surprised at

the startled astonishment of his face. "Did you know him?"

Harney snatched the paper and opened it with an unsteady hand. He ran his eyes over the lines under the black-lettered heading of the first page.

"By gosh!" he said to himself, "so he is; so he is!"

He sat down in the chair at the opposite side of the table, smoothed out the sheet and read the account slowly and carefully.

"By gosh!" he said again when he had finished, "who'd a thought Jake'd go off like that!"

"Did you know him?" repeated Essex.

"Once up in the Sierra, when we was all mining up there."

He spoke absently and sat looking into the fire for a moment, then said:

"It's pretty tough luck to be whisked off that way when you just got everything in the palm of your hand."

Essex made no reply, and after a pause he added:

"Between fifteen and twenty millions it says there," indicating the paper, "and when I saw Jake Shackleton first you wouldn't er hired him to sweep down the steps of *The Trumpet* office. But that was twenty-five years ago at least."

"Oh, Shackleton was an able man. There's no question about that. They were saying in the office to-night that twenty million is a conservative figure to put his money at."

"Who does it go to? Do you know that?" queried the man by the fire.

"Widow and children, I suppose. There are two children. Don't amount to anything, I believe."

"No; there are three."

Harney turned from the fire and looked over his shoulder. He was sitting in a hunched position, his back rounded, his chin depressed. His black eyes, that drew close to the nose, were instinct with eager cunning. The skin across the bridge of the nose was drawn in wrinkles. As he looked the wheezing of his disturbed breathing was distinctly audible. Essex was struck by the sly and malevolent intelligence of his face.

"Three children!" he said. "Well, I've always heard the death of a bonanza king was the signal for a large crop of widows and orphans to take the field."

"There won't be any widow this time. She's dead. But the girl's alive, and I've seen her."

He accompanied this remark with a second look, significant with the same malicious intensity of meaning. Then he rose to his feet and walked toward the door.

"Good night, Doc," he said as he reached it; "ain't well enough to talk to-night."

Essex gave him a return good night and the door closed on him. The younger man cogitated over his books for a space. It did not strike him as interesting or remarkable that Shackleton should have had an unacknowledged child, of whose existence George Harney, the drunken job-printer, knew. He was becoming accustomed to the extraordinary intermingling of classes and conditions that marked the pioneer period of California life. But should the unacknowledged child attempt to establish its claim to part of the great estate left by the bonanza king, what a complication that might lead to! These Californians were certainly a picturesque people, with their dramatic ups and downs of fortune, their disdain of accepted standards, their indifference to tradition, and their magnificently disreputable pasts.

As one of the special writers of *The Trumpet,* Essex attended the funeral of his chief. He and Mrs. Willers and Edna, in company with the young woman who did the "Fashions and Foibles" column, were in one of the carriages that Mariposa had seen from the hilltop. Mrs. Willers was silent on the long, slow drive. She had honored her chief, who had been just to her. Miss Peebles, the "Fashions and Foibles" young woman, was so engrossed by her fears that a change of ownership in *The Trumpet* would rob her of her employment that she could talk of nothing else. To Edna, the sensation of being in a carriage was so novel it occupied her to the exclusion of all other matters, and she looked out of the window with a face of sparkling interest.

That evening, after the funeral, Essex was preparing to work late. He had "gutted" the pile of books, and with their contents well assimilated was ready to write his three columns. There was no car line on the street, and traffic at that hour on that quiet thoroughfare was over for the day. For an hour he wrote easily and fluently. The sheets, glistening with damp ink, were pushed in front of him in a careless pile. Now and then he paused to consult his books, which were arranged round him on the table, open at the places he needed for reference. The smoke wreaths were thick round his head and the room was hot. It was nearly ten o'clock when he heard the noisy entrance of his fellow lodger. Harney was evidently sufficiently well to go to work again and to come home drunk. Essex listened with suspended pen and a half-smile on his dark face, which turned to a frown as he realized that the stumbling feet had turned his way. The knock on the door came next, and simultaneously it opened and Harney's head was thrust in.

"What the devil do you want?" said the scribe, sitting erect, his pipe in his hand, the other waving the smoke strata that hung before his face.

"Let me come and get warm a minute. I'm wheezing again, and my room's cold as a tomb. Don't mind me—all I want is to set before the fire for a spell."

He sidled in before the permission was granted and sank down in the armchair, hitching it nearer to the grate. He was a man to whom intoxication lent a curiously amiable and humorous quality. The ugliness and evil that were so evidently part of his nature were not so apparent, and he became cheerful, almost genial.

Sitting close to the fire, he held out his hands to the blaze, then, stealing a look at Essex over his shoulder, saw that he was refilling his pipe.

"Be'n to the funeral?" he said.

Essex grunted an assent.

"The family there?"

"None of the ladies; only Win Shackleton."

Harney was silent; then, with the greatest care, he

took up a piece of coal and set it on the fire. The action required all the ingenuity of which he was master. His body responded to his intoxication, while, save for an unusual fluency of speech, his mind appeared to remain unaffected. After he had set the coal in place he looked again at Essex, who was staring vacantly at him, thinking of the second part of his article.

"Did you notice a tall, fine-looking young lady there with dark red hair?" said Harney, without removing his glassy gaze from the man at the table.

Essex did not move his eyes, but their absent fixity suddenly seemed to snap into a change of focus betokening attention. Gazing at Harney, he answered coldly:

"No; I saw no one like that. To whom are you referring?"

"Oh, I dunno, I dunno," responded the other with a clumsy shrug of his shoulders, and turning back to the fire over which he cowered.

"But you know her anyhow," he added, half to himself.

"Whom do I know? Turn around."

The man turned, looking a little defiant.

"Now, what are you trying to say?"

"I ain't tryin' to say nuthin'. All I done is to ask yer if yer saw a lady—tall, with red hair—at the funeral. You know her, 'cause I've seen you with her."

"Who is she?"

"Well," slowly and uneasily, "she's called Moreau."

"You mean Miss Mariposa Moreau, the daughter of a mining man, who died last spring in Santa Barbara?"

"Yes; that's her all right. She's called Moreau, but it ain't her name."

"Moreau isn't her name? What is her name, then?"

"I dunno," he spoke stubbornly and turned back to the fire.

"Turn back here," said Essex in a suddenly authoritative tone; "explain to me what you mean by that."

"I don't mean nuthin'," said the other, looking sullenly defiant, "and I don't know nuthin' only that that ain't her true name."

"What is her name? Answer me at once, and no fooling."

"I dunno."

Essex rose. Harney, looking frightened, staggered to his feet, clutching the mantelpiece. He half-raised his arm as if expecting to be struck and said loudly:

"If you want to know ask Shackleton's widow. *She* knows."

Essex stood a few paces from him, suddenly stilled by the phrase. The drunkard, alarmed and yet defiant, could only dimly understand what the expression on the face of the man before him meant.

"Sit down," said Essex quietly; "I'm not going to touch you. I'm going to get some whisky. That'll tone you up a bit. The bronchitis has taken it out of you more than you think."

He went to a cupboard and brought out a bottle and glasses. Pouring some whisky into one, he pushed it toward Harney.

"There, that'll brace you up. You'll feel more yourself in a minute."

He diluted his own with water and only touched the

glass's rim to his lips. His eyes, glistening and intent, were on the drunkard's now darkly flushing face. The glass rattled against the table as Harney set it down.

"That puts mettle into me again. Makes me feel like the old times before the malaria got into my bones. Malaria was my ruin. Got it in the Sierra mining. People think it's drink that done it, but it's malaria."

"That was when you knew Moreau? What sort of man was he?"

"Poor sort; not any grit. Had a good claim up there beyond Placerville, he and I. Took out 's much as eight thousand in that first summer. Moreau stayed by it, but I quit. Both had our reasons."

"And Miss Moreau, you say, is not Dan Moreau's daughter. Is she a step-daughter?"

"Well—in a sort of a way you might say so. Anyway, she ain't got no legal right to that name."

"I didn't know the mother was a widow when she married Moreau?"

"She weren't. She married twict, and she weren't divorced. There ain't but two people in the world that knows it. One's Jake Shackleton's widow,"— he rose, and, putting an unsteady hand on the table, leaned forward and almost whispered into his interlocutor's face,—"and the other's me."

"Are you trying to tell me," said Essex quietly, "that Miss Moreau is Jake Shackleton's daughter?"

"That's what she is." The man turned round like a character on the stage and swept the room with an investigating look—"And she's more'n that. She's his lawful daughter, born in wedlock."

The two faces stared at each other. The drunken

man was not too far beyond himself to realize the importance of what he was saying. In a second's retrospect Essex's mind flew back over the hitherto puzzling interest Shackleton had taken in Mariposa Moreau. Could it be possible the man before him was telling the truth?

"How does she come to be known as Moreau's daughter? Why didn't Shackleton acknowledge her if she was his legitimate child? That's a fairy tale."

"There was complications. Have you ever heard that Shackleton was once a Mormon?"

Essex had heard the gossip which had persistently followed Shackleton's ascending course. He nodded his head, gazing at Harney, a presentiment of coming revelations holding him silent.

"Well, that's true. He was. I seen him when he was. Jake Shackleton crossed the Sierra with two wives. One—the first one—was the lady who died here a month ago, and passed as Mrs. Moreau. The other's the widow. But she was the second wife. She didn't have no children then. But the first wife had one, a girl baby, born on the plains in Utah. It weren't three weeks old when I seen it."

"Where did you see it?"

"In the Sierra back of Hangtown. Me and Dan Moreau was workin' a stream bed there. And one day two emigrants, a man and a woman, with a sick woman inside the wagon, came down from the summit. They was Jake Shackleton and his two wives, and they was the worst looking outfit you've ever clapped your eyes on. They was pretty near dead. One er their horses did die, in front of our cabin, and the sick woman—

she that afterwards was called Mrs. Moreau—was too beat out to move on. Shackleton, who didn't care who died, so long's they got into the settlements, calkalated to make her ride a spell, and when the other horse dropped make her walk. She was the orneriest lookin' scarecrow you ever seen, and she hadn't no more life'n a mummy. But she was ready to do just what they said. She was just so beat out. And then Moreau—he was just that kind of a fool—"

He paused and looked at Essex, with his beady, dark eyes glistening with a sense of the importance of his communication. His hand sought the glass and he drained it. Then he leaned forward to deliver the climax of his story:—

"Bought her from Shackleton for a pair of horses."

"Bought her for a pair of horses! How could he?"

"I'm not sayin' how he could; I'm sayin' what he did."

"What did he do it for?"

"The Lord knows. He was that kind of a fool. We had her in the cabin sick for days, with me and him waitin' on her hand and foot, and the cussed baby yellin' like a coyote. She wasn't good for anything. Just ust ter lie round sick and peaked and sorter pine. But Moreau got a crazy liking for her, and he was sot on the baby same's if it was his own. I caught on pretty soon to the way the cat was goin' to jump. I lit out and left 'em."

"Why did you leave if the claim was good?"

"It weren't no good when no one worked it, and there weren't more'n enough in it for Moreau alone, with a woman and a baby on his hands. He said first off he was only goin' to get her cured up and send her to the Eldorado Hotel to be a waitress, but I seen fast enough what was goin' to happen. And it did happen. They was snowed in up there all winter. In the spring he took her into Hangtown and married her—said he was marryin' a widow woman whose husband died on the plains. I heard that afterwards from some er the boys, but it weren't my business to give 'em away. So I shut my mouth and ain't opened it till now. But Moreau's dead, and the woman's dead, and now Shackleton's dead. There ain't no one what knows but me and Shackleton's widow."

"And what makes you think this is the same child? The baby you saw may have died and this may be a child born a year or two later."

"It ain't. It's the same. There weren't never any other children. I kep' my eye on 'em. Moreau was mining round among the camps and afterward was in Sacramento for a spell, and I was round in them places off and on myself. I saw him, but I dodged him 'cause I knew he didn't want to run up against me, knowin' as how I was onter what he'd done. He was safe for me. But I seen the girl often; seen her grow up. And I knew her in a minute the day I saw you walkin' with her on Sutter Street, and I thinks to myself, 'You're with the biggest heiress in San Francisco if you and she only knew it.' And that's what she is, if there was somethin' else but my word to prove it."

Essex sat pushed back from the table, his hands in his pockets, his pipe nipped between his teeth, his face partly obscured by the floating clouds of smoke that hung about his head.

A first-rate story," he said slowly; "have some more whisky."

And he pushed the bottle toward Harney, who seized it and fumblingly poured the fiery liquor into the glass.

"And it's true," he said hoarsely—"every blamed word."

He drank what he had poured out, set down the glass and stared at Essex with his face puckered into its expression of evil cunning.

"And *she* don't know anything about it, does she?" he asked.

"If you mean Miss Moreau, she certainly appears to think she is the child of the man who brought her up."

"That's what I heard. But Shackleton, when Moreau died, was goin' to do the square thing by her. At least, I heard talk of his sendin' her to Europe to be a singer. Ain't it so?"

"I heard something about it myself. But I'm no authority."

There was a pause. Harney settled back in his chair. The room was exceedingly hot, and impregnated with the odor of whisky and the smoke from Essex's pipe.

"He couldn't acknowledge her. It would er given the other children too big a black eye. But it seemed like he wanted to square things up when he was taken off suddent like that."

He paused. The other, smoking, with frowning brows and wide eyes, made no response, his own thoughts holding him in tense immobility.

"And the other wife wouldn't er stood it, anyway. She's a pretty competent woman, I guess. Oh, he couldn't have acknowledged her, nohow. But she's his legitimate daughter, all right. She's the lawful heir to—most er them—millions. She's—"

His voice broke and trailed off into silence, which was suddenly interrupted by a guttural snort and then heavy, regular breathing. Essex rose, and, going to the window, opened it. A keen-edged breeze of air entered, seeming all the fresher from the dense atmosphere of the room. Its hurried entrance sent the smoke wreaths skurrying about in fantastic whorls and curls. The dying fire threw out a frightened flame.

Essex moved toward it, saying as he approached:

"Yes; it's a good story. You ought to be a novelist, Harney."

There was no answer, and, looking into the chair, he saw that Harney had fallen into a sodden sleep, curled against the chair-back, his chin sunk on his breast, the hollows in his face looking black in the hard light of the gas. The younger man gazed at him for a moment with an expression of slight, cold disgust, then turned back to the table and sat down.

He wrote no more, but sat motionless, his eyes fixed on vacancy, the thick, curling smoke oozing from the bowl of his pipe and issuing from between his lips. His thoughts reviewed every part of the story he had heard. He felt certain of its truth. The drunken job-printer had never imagined it.

It explained many things that before had puzzled him. Why the Moreaus, even in the days of their affluence, had lived in such uneventful quietude, bringing up their beautiful and talented daughter in a jealous and unusual seclusion. It explained Shackleton's interest in the girl. He even saw now, recalling the two faces, the likeness that the father himself had seen in Mariposa's firmly modeled jaw and chin, which did not belong to the soft, feminine prettiness of Lucy.

It must be true.

And, being true, what possibilities might it not develop? Mrs. Shackleton knew it, too—that this penniless girl was the bonanza king's eldest and only legitimate child, with power, if not entirely to dispossess her own children, at least to claim the lion's share of the vast fortune. If Mariposa had proof of her mother's marriage to Shackleton and of her own identity as the child of that marriage, she could rise and claim her heritage—her part of the twenty millions!

The thought, and what it opened before him, dizzied him. He drank some of the diluted whisky in the glass beside him and sat on motionless. It was evident Mariposa did not know. She had been brought up in ignorance of the whole extraordinary story. The man and woman she had been taught to regard as her parents had committed an offense against the law, which they had hidden from her, secure in the thought that the other participants in the strange proceeding would never dare to confess.

The minutes and hours ticked by and Essex still sat thinking, while the drunkard breathed stertorously in his heavy sleep, and the coals dropped softly in the grate as the fire sank into clinkers and ashes.

CHAPTER XIII

THE SEED OF BANQUO

"What says the married woman?"
—SHAKESPEARE.

As soon as Mrs. Shackleton was sufficiently recovered, the family had moved from Menlo Park to their town house.

The long work of settling up the great estate which had been left to the widow and her children, required their presence in the city, and the shock which Bessie had suffered in finding her husband dead, had rendered the country place unbearable to her.

The day after the funeral the women had moved to town. Win, however, remained at Menlo Park, to go over such documents of his father's as had been left there. Shackleton had lived so much at his country place for the last two or three years that many of his papers and letters were kept in the library, which had been his especial sanctum.

Among these, the son had come upon a small package of letters, which, fastened together with an elastic, and bearing a note of their contents on one end, had roused his interest. They were the letters exchanged between his father and the chief of the detective bureau when the latter had been commissioned to locate the widow and daughter of Daniel Moreau.

Shackleton, a man of exceedingly methodical habits, had kept copies of his letters. There were only seven of them altogether—three from him; four in reply. The first ones were short, only a few lines, containing the request to find the ladies who, the writer understood, were in San Francisco, and ascertain their circumstances and position. Then came the acknowledgment of that, and then in a few days, the answer stating the whereabouts of Mrs. Moreau and her daughter, their means, and such small facts about them as that the mother was in delicate health and the daughter "a handsome, accomplished, and estimable young lady."

Win looked over this correspondence, puzzled and wondering. He remembered the girl he had seen in *The Trumpet* office that dark afternoon, and how the office boy had told him it was a Miss Moreau, a friend of Mrs. Willers, and a singer. What motive could his father have had in seeking out this girl and her mother in this secret and effectual way? He read over the letters again. Moreau had died in Santa Barbara in the spring, the widow and her daughter had then come to San Francisco, and by the wording of the second letter he inferred that his father had been ignorant of their means, and of the girl's appearance, style and character. It was evidently not the result of an interest in people he had once known and then lost sight of. It seemed to be an interest, for some outside reason, in two women of whom he knew absolutely nothing.

Win had heard that his father contemplated offering a musical education to some singing girl, of whom the young man knew nothing, and had seen only for a moment that day in *The Trumpet* office. This was undoubtedly the girl. But Shackleton evidently had not heard of her through Mrs. Willers, who was known to be an energetic boomer of obscure genius. He had hunted her out himself; had undoubtedly had some ulterior interest in, or knowledge of her some time before the day Win had seen her. It was odd, the boy thought, meditating over the correspondence. What could have led his father to search for, and then attempt to assist, a woman who seemed to be a complete stranger to him? It looked like the secret paying of an old debt.

Win put the letters in his pocket and went up to town. There was more work for him to do now than there had ever been before, and he rose to it with a spirit and energy that surprised himself. Neither he nor any one else had ever realized how paralyzing to him had been his father's cold scorn. From boyhood, Win had felt himself to be an aggravating failure. The elder man had not scrupled to make him understand his inferiority. The mere presence of his father seemed to numb his brain and make his tongue stammer over the simplest phrases. Now, he felt himself free and full of energy, as though bands that had cramped his mind and confined his body were broken. His old attitude of posing as a fast young man of fashion lost its charm. Life grew suddenly to mean something, to be full of use and purpose.

He was left very much to himself, his mother being still too much broken to attend to business, and Maud being absorbed in her affair with Latimer, which had recently culminated in a secret engagement. This she had been afraid to tell to her domineering father and ambitious mother, and her opportunities of seeing her fiancé had been of the briefest until now. Latimer haunted the house of evenings, when Bessie was lying on the sofa in an upstairs boudoir and Win was locked in his father's study going over the interminable documents.

The first darkness of her grief and horror past, Bessie, in her seclusion, thought of many things. One of these was the fate of Mariposa Moreau. The bonanza king's widow, with all her faults, had that lavish and reckless generosity, where money was concerned, that marked the early Californians. This forceful woman, who had made the blighting journey across the plains without complaint, faced the fierce hardships of her early married life with a smile, borne her children amid the rude discomforts of remote mining camps, was an adept in the art of luxurious living. She knew by instinct how to be magnificent, and one of her magnificences was the careless munificence of her generosity.

Now, she felt for Mariposa. She knew Shackleton's plans for her, and realized the girl's disappointment. In her heart she had been bitterly jealous of the other wife's child, who had the beauty and gifts her own lacked. It would be to everybody's advantage to remove the girl to another country and sphere. And because her husband had died there was was no reason why his plans should remain unfulfilled. Though Shackleton had assured her that the girl knew nothing, though every one connected with the shameful bargain but herself was dead, it was best to be prudent, especially when prudence was the course most agreeable to all concerned. She would rest easier; her children would seem more secure in their positions and possessions, if Mariposa Moreau, well provided for, were safe in Paris studying singing.

When she was fully decided as to the wisdom of her course, she wrote Mariposa a short but friendly letter, speaking of her knowledge of Mr. Shackleton's plans for her advancement, of her desire to carry out her late husband's wishes, and naming a day and hour at which she begged the young girl to call on her. It was a simple matter to ascertain Miss Moreau's address from Mrs. Willers, and the letter was duly sent.

It roused wrath in its recipient. Mariposa was learning worldly wisdom at a rate of which her tardy development had not given promise. Great changes were taking place in her simple nature. She had been wakened to life with savage abruptness. Dormant characteristics, passions unsuspected, had risen to the surface. The powerful feelings of a rich, but undeveloped womanhood had suddenly been shaken from their sleep by a grip of the hand of destiny. The unfamiliarity of a bitter anger against the Shackletons struggled with the creeping disgust of Essex, that grew daily.

Morning after morning she woke when the first gray light was faintly defining the squares of the windows. The leaden sense of wretchedness that seemed to draw her out of sleep, gave place to the living hatred and shame that the upheaval of her life had left behind. She watched the golden wheat-ears dimly glimmering on the pale walls, while she lay and thought of all she had learned of life, her faith and happy ignorance destroyed forever.

Six weeks ago Mrs. Shackleton's letter would have represented no more to her than what its words expressed. Now, she saw Bessie's anxiety to be rid of her, to push her out of sight as a menace. How much more readily would the widow have gone to work, with what zest of alarm and energy, would she have contrived for her expulsion, had she guessed what Mariposa knew. The girl vacillated for a day, hating the thought of an interview with any member of the family whose wrongs to her beloved mother were seared scars in her brain; but finally concluding that it would be better to end her connection with them by an interview with Mrs. Shackleton, she answered the letter, stating that she would come at the appointed hour.

Two days later, at the time set in the afternoon, she stood in the small reception-room, to the left of the wide marble hall, waiting. The hushed splendor of the house would have impressed and awed her at any other time. But to-day her heart beat loud and her brain was preoccupied with its effort to keep her purpose clear, and yet not to be angered into revealing too much. The vast lower floor was loftier and more spacious than anything she had ever seen before. There were glimpses through many doors, and artificial elongations of perspective by means of mirrors. The long receding vista was touched with gleams of light on parquet flooring, reflections on the gray surfaces of mirrors, the curves of porcelain vases, the bosses of gilded frames. Over all hung the scent of flowers, that were massed here and there in Chinese bowls.

Bessie's step, and the accompanying rustle of brushing silks, brought the girl to her feet, rigid and cold. The widow swept into the room with extended hand. She was richly and correctly garbed in lusterless black, that sent out the nervous whisperings of crushed silks and exhaled a faint perfume. It was impossible to ignore the hand, and Mariposa touched it with her own for a minute. She had seen Bessie only once before, on the evening of the opera. The change wrought in her by grief and illness was noticeable. Her fine, healthy color had faded; her eyes were darkened, and there were many deep lines on her forehead and about her mouth. Nevertheless, a casual eye would have still noticed her as a woman of vigor, mental and physical. It was easy to understand how she had stood shoulder to shoulder with her husband in his fight for fortune.

She motioned Mariposa to a chair facing the window, and studied her as she glibly accomplished the commonplaces of greeting. Her heart drew together with a renewed spasm of jealousy as she noted the girl's superiority to her own daughter. What subtly finer qualities had Lucy had, that her child should be thus distinguished from the other children of Jake Shackleton? The indignation working against this woman gave a last touch of stateliness to poor Mariposa's natural dignity of demeanor. She seemed to belong, by nature and birth, to these princely surroundings, which completely dwarfed Maud, and even made the adaptive Bessie look common.

"My husband," said the elder woman, when the beginnings of the conversation were disposed of, "was very much interested in you. He knew your father, Dan Moreau, very well."

Mariposa was becoming used to this phrase and could listen to it without the stare of surprise, or the blush of consciousness.

"So Mr. Shackleton told me," she answered.

"Your father"—Bessie looked down at the deeply-bordered handkerchief in her hand—"was a man of great kindliness and generosity. Mr. Shackleton knew him in the Sierras, mining, a long time ago, when he" —she paused, not from embarrassment, but in order to choose her words carefully—"was very kind to my husband and others of our party. It was an obligation Mr. Shackleton never forgot."

Mariposa could make no answer. Shackleton had never spoken to her with this daring. Bessie looked at her for a response, and saw her with her eyes on the ground, pale and slightly frowning. She wanted to sweep away any possible suspicion from the girl's mind by making her understand that the attitude of the family toward her rose from gratitude for a past benefit.

"Mr. Shackleton," she went on, "often talked to me about his plans for you. He wanted to have you study in Paris, under some teacher Lepine spoke to him about. I understand you've got a remarkable voice. I wanted, several times, to hear you, but it couldn't seem to be managed, living in the country, and always so busy. In his sudden—passing away, all these plans came to an end. He hadn't regularly arranged anything. There were such a lot of delays."

Mariposa nodded, then feeling that she must say something, she murmured:

"My mother died. I was not well, and I couldn't see him."

"Exactly, I understand just how it was. And it wasn't a bit fair, that simply because you didn't happen to be able to go to the office at that time, you should lose your chance of a musical education and all that might have come out of it. Now, Miss Moreau, it's my intention to carry out my husband's wishes."

She looked at Mariposa, not smiling, nor condescending, but with a hard earnestness. The girl raised her eyes and the two glances met.

"His wishes with regard to me?" said Mariposa, with a questioning inflection.

"That's it. I want you to go to Paris, as he wanted you to go. I want you to study to be a singer. I'll pay it all—education, masters, and a monthly sum for living besides. I don't think, from what I hear, that it would be necessary for you to study more than two or three years. Then you would make your appearance as a grand opera prima donna, or concert singer, as your teachers thought fit. I don't know much about it, but I believe they can't always tell about a voice right off at the start. Anyway, I'd see to it that yours got every chance for the best development."

She paused.

"I—I'm—afraid it will be impossible," said Mariposa, in a low voice.

"Impossible!" exclaimed the elder woman, sitting upright in her surprise. "Why?"

Mariposa had come to the house of Mrs. Shackleton burning with a sense of the wrongs her mother had suffered at the hands of this woman and her dead husband. She had thought little of what the interview would be like, and now, with the keen, hard, and astonished eyes of Bessie upon her, she felt that something more than pride and indignation must help her through. The world's diplomacy of tongue and brain was an unsuspected art to her.

"I—I—"she stammered irresolutely, "have changed my mind since I talked with Mr. Shackleton."

"Changed your mind! But why? What's made you change your mind in so short a time?"

"Many things," said the girl, with her face flushing deeply under Bessie's unflinching stare. "There have been changes—in—in—circumstances—and in me. My mother was anxious for my advancement. Now she is dead and—it doesn't matter."

It was certainly not a brilliant way out of the difficulty. A faint smile wrinkled the loose skin round Mrs. Shackleton's eyes.

"Oh, my dear," she said, with a slight touch of impatience in her voice. "If that's all, I guess we needn't worry about it. People die, and we lose our energies and ambition, so we just want to lie round and mourn. But at your age that don't last long. You've got to make your future yourself, and now's your chance. It just comes once or twice in a lifetime, and the people who get there are the people who know enough to snatch it as it comes by."

THE SEED OF BANQUO   255

Mariposa's irresolution had passed. She realized that she had not merely to state her intentions, but to fight a will unused to defeat.

"I can't go," she said quietly; "I understand that all you say is perfectly true. You probably think I am silly and ungrateful. I don't think I am either, but that's because I know what I feel. I thank you very much, but I can't accept it."

She rose to her feet. Bessie saw that she was pale —evidently agitated.

"Sit down," she said, indicating the chair again. "Now let me hear your reasons, my dear girl. People don't throw up the chance of a lifetime for nothing. What's behind all this?"

There was a pause. Mariposa said slowly:

"I don't want to accept it. I don't want to take the money or be under any obligation."

"You were willing to be under the obligation, as you call it, a few weeks ago?"

Bessie's voice was as cold as steel. From the moment she had entered the room she had felt an instinctive antagonism between herself and her husband's eldest child. It would become a hatred in time. The girl's slow and reluctant way of speaking seemed to indicate that she expressed herself with difficulty, like one who, under pressure, tells the truth.

"My mother wanted me to accept anything that was for my own benefit. Now she is dead. I am my own mistress. I grieve or hurt no one but myself if I refuse your offer. And, as things are now, it is better for me to refuse it."

"What do you mean by 'as things are now'? Has

anything happened to change your ideas since my husband first made the suggestion to you?"

Mariposa told her lie as a woman does, with reservations. It was creditably done, for it was the first lie she had ever told in her life.

"Nothing has actually happened, but—I—I—have changed."

"And are you going to let a girl's whims stand in the way of your future success in life? I can't believe that. My dear, you're handsome and you've a fine voice, but do you think those two things, without a cent behind them, are going to put you on top of the heap? You're not the woman to get there without a lot of boosting."

"Why should I want to get on top of the heap?"

"Oh, if you *want* to stay at the bottom—"

Mrs. Shackleton gave a shrug and rose to her feet. The girl was incomprehensible. She was either very subtle and deep, or she was extraordinarily dull and shallow. Shackleton had said to her once that she seemed to him childish and undeveloped, for her age. The woman's keen eye saw deeper. If Mariposa was not disingenuous, she would always, on the side of shrewdness and worldly wisdom, be undeveloped.

"Well, my dear," she said coldly, "it all rests with yourself. But I can't, conscientiously, let you throw your best chances away. We won't speak of this any more to-day. But go home and think about it, and in a week or two let me know what conclusion you've come to. Don't ever throw a chance away, even if you don't happen to like the person who offers it."

She gave Mariposa a shrewd and good-natured smile.

THE SEED OF BANQUO

The girl, her face crimsoning, was about to answer, when the hall door opened, and, with a sound of laughter and a whiff of violets, Maud and the Count de Lamolle entered the room.

In her heavy mourning, Maud looked more nearly pretty than she had ever done before. It was not the dress that beautified her, but the happiness of her engagement to Latimer, with whom she was deeply in love, which had lent her the fleeting grace and charm that only love, well bestowed, can give. She carried a large bunch of violets in her hand, and her face was slightly flushed.

The count, who had attentively read the will of Jake Shackleton in the papers, was staying on in San Francisco. His attentions to Maud were not more assiduous, but they were more "serious," to use the technical phrase, than heretofore. She would make him an ideal wife, he thought. Even her lack of beauty was an advantage. When an American girl was both rich and pretty, she was more than even the most tactful and sophisticated Frenchman could manage. Maud, ugly, gentle, and not clever, would be a delightful wife, ready to love humbly, unexacting, easy to make happy.

The count, a handsome, polished Parisian, speaking excellent English, bowed over Mrs. Shackleton's hand, and then, in answer to her words of introduction, shot an exploring look, warmed by a glimmer of discreet admiration, at Mariposa. He wondered who she was, for his practised eye took in at a glance that she was shabbily dressed and evidently not of the world of bonanza millions. He wished that he knew her, now that he had made up his mind to spend some months in San Francisco, paying court to the heiress who would make him such an admirable wife, and in whose society time hung so heavily on his hands.

Mariposa excused herself and hurried away. She was angry and confused. It seemed to her she had done nothing but be rude and obstinately stupid, while the cold and composed older woman had eyed her with wary attentiveness. What did Mrs. Shackleton think she had meant? She felt that the widow had not, for a moment, abandoned the scheme of sending her away. Descending the wide steps in the early dark, the girl realized that the woman she had just left was not going to be beaten from her purpose by what appeared a girl's unreasonable caprice.

A man coming up the steps brushed by her, paused for a moment, and then mechanically raised his hat. In the gleam of the lamps, held aloft at the top of the flight, she recognized the thin face and eye-glasses of Win Shackleton. She did not return the salute, as it was completely unexpected, and from the foot of the stairs she heard the hall door bang behind him.

"Who was that girl I met on the steps just now, going out?" Win asked his mother, as they went upstairs together.

"That Miss Moreau your father was interested in. He was going to send her to Paris to learn singing."

"What was she doing here?"

"I sent for her. I wanted to talk over things with her. I intended sending her."

"And did you fix it?"

"No," with a little laugh, "she's a very changeable

young woman. She says she doesn't want to go now; that she's come to the conclusion she doesn't want to be under the obligation."

"That's funny," said Win. "She must be sort of original. Mommer, why did the governor want to send her to Paris? What was it made him so interested in her?"

"He knew her father long ago, mining, in the Sierra, and Moreau did him a good turn up there. Your father had never forgotten it and was anxious to repay it by helping the daughter. She don't seem to be easy to help."

Win, as he dressed for dinner, meditated on his mother's explanation. It sounded reasonable enough, only a thirst to repay past obligations was not—according to his experience and memories—a peculiarity that had troubled his father. Both he and Maud knew that all the generosities and charities of the household had been inspired by their mother. His childish memory was stocked by recollections of her urging the advantage of the bestowal of pecuniary aid to this and that person, association and charity. It was she who had saved Jake Shackleton from the accusation of meanness, which California society invariably makes against its rich men.

CHAPTER XIV

VAIN PLEADINGS

> "Are there not, * * *
> Two points in the adventure of the diver:
> One—when a beggar he prepares to plunge;
> One—when a prince he rises with his pearl?"
> —BROWNING.

To the astonishment of his world, Win Shackleton announced his intention of retaining *The Trumpet*, and conducting it, himself, on the lines laid down by his father. There was a slight shifting of positions, in which some were advanced and one or two heads were unexpectedly lopped off and thrown in the basket. The new ruler took control with a decision that startled those who had regarded him as a typical millionaire's son. The men on the paper, who had seen the time of their lives coming in the managership of a feeble and inexperienced boy, were awakened from their dreams by feeling a hand on the reins, as tight as that of Jake Shackleton himself. Win had ideas. Mrs. Willers was advanced to the managership of the Woman's Page, into which she swept triumphant, with Miss Peebles, the young woman of the "Foibles and Fancies" column, in her wake. Barry Essex was lifted to a staff position, at a high salary, and had to himself one of the little cells that branch off the main passage.

Here he worked hard, for Win permitted no drones in his hive. The luck was with Essex, as it had been often before in his varied career. Things had fallen together exactly as they should for the furthering of his designs. It would take a long wooing to win over Mariposa. Now, he could save money against the day when he and she would leave together for the Europe where they were to conquer fame and fortune.

He had had other talks with Harney since the evening of his revelation. He was convinced that the man was telling the truth. He had known men before of Harney's type and wondered why the drunkard had not made use of his knowledge for his own advancement. He had evidently kept his eye on both Shackleton and Moreau, and it was strange, that, as the two men rose to affluence, he had not used the ugly secret he held. The only explanation of it was that they held an even greater power over him. He had undoubtedly had reason to fear both men. Shackleton, once arrived at the pinnacle of his success, would have crushed like a beetle in his path this drunken threatener of his peace. Moreau, whose every movement he seemed to have followed, had evidently had a hold over him. Hold or no hold, Shackleton would have swept him aside by the power of his money and his position, into the oblivion that awaits the enemies of rich and unscrupulous men.

Now both were dead. But the day of Harney's power was over. Enfeebled in mind and body by drink and disease, he had neither the force nor the brain to be dangerous. His uses were merely those of an instrument in daring hands. And those hands had found him. There were long talks in Essex's room in the evenings, during which the story was threshed out. George Harney, drunk or sober, neither contradicted himself nor varied in his details. His mind, confused and addled on other matters, retained this memory with unblurred clearness.

So Essex deliberated, carefully and without haste, for there was plenty of time.

The bright days continued. On a radiant Saturday afternoon, Mariposa, tired with a morning's teaching, started forth to spend an hour or two in the park. She had done this several times before, finding the green peace and solitude of that beautiful spot soothing to her harassed spirit. It was a long ride in those days, and this had its charm, the little steam dummy cresting the tops of sandy hills, clothed with lupins and tiny frightened oaks, crouching before the sea winds. On this occasion she had invited the escort of Benito, who had been hanging drearily about the house, thinking with mingled triumph and envy of Miguel, who had gone with his mother to have a tooth pulled out.

"Pulling the tooth's bad, of course," Benito had said to Mariposa, as he trotted by her side to the car, "but then afterward there's candy. I dunno but what it's worth while. And then you have the tooth."

"Have the tooth!" said Mariposa. "What do you want the tooth for?"

"You can show it to the boys in school, and you can generally trade it. I traded mine for a knife with two blades, but both of 'em was broke."

VAIN PLEADINGS 263

Benito was becoming very friendly with Mariposa. He was a cheerful and expansive soul. Could they have heard him, Uncle Gam and his mother might have suffered some embarrassment on the score of his revelations as to their quarrels concerning his upbringing. Benito had thoroughly gaged the capacity of each of them in resisting his charms and urging him to higher and better things. He was already at the stage when his mother appealed slightly to his commiseration and largely to his sense of humor. Mariposa saw that while he had grasped the great fact that his Uncle Gam had an unfortunately soft heart, he also knew there was a stage when it was resolutely hardened and his most practised wiles fell baffled from its surface.

They alighted from the car at what was then the main entrance, and, side by side, Benito fluently talking, made toward the gate. Here a peanut vender had artfully placed his stall, and the fumes from the roasted nuts rose gratefully to the nostrils of the small boy. He said nothing, but sniffed with an ostentatious noise, and then looked sidewise at Mariposa. One of the sources of his respect for her was that she was so quick in reading the language of the eye. One did not vulgarly have to demand things of her. He felt the nickel in his hand and galloped off to the stand, to return slowly, his head on one side, an eye investigating the contents of the opened paper bag he carried.

Being a gentleman of gallant forbears, he offered this to Mariposa, listening with some uneasiness to the scraping of her fingers among its contents. He had an awful thought that she might be like Miguel, who could never be trusted to withdraw his hand until it was full to bursting. But Mariposa's eventually emerged with one small nut between thumb and finger. This she nibbled gingerly as they passed under the odorous, dark shade of the cypresses. Benito spread a trail of shells behind him, dragging his feet in silent happiness, his eyes fixed on the brilliant prospect of sunlit green that filled in the end of the vista like a drop-curtain.

As they emerged from the cypress shadows the lawns and shrubberies of the park lay before them radiantly vivid in their variegated greens. The scene suggested a picture in its motionless beauty, the sunlight sleeping on stretches of shaven turf where the peacocks strutted, the red dust of the drive unstirred by wind or wheel. Rich earth scents mingled with the perfume of the winter blossoms, delicate breaths of violets from beneath the trees, spices exhaled by belated roses still bravely blossoming in November, and now and then a whiff of the acrid, animal odor of the eucalyptus.

Following pathways, now damp beneath the shade of melancholy spruce and pine, now hard and dry between velvety lawns, they came out on a large circular opening. Here Mariposa sat down on a bench, with her back to a sheltering mass of fir and hemlock, the splendid sunshine pouring on her. Benito, with his bag in his hand, trotted off to the grassy slope opposite where custom has ordained that little boys may roll about and play. He had hardly settled himself there to the further enjoyment of his nuts when another little boy appeared and made friendly overtures,

VAIN PLEADINGS   265

with his eyes on the bag. Mariposa could not hear them, but she could see the first advance and Benito's somewhat wary eyings of the stranger. In a few moments the formalities of introduction were over, and they were both lying on their stomachs on the grass, kicking gently with their toes, while the bag stood between them.

Mariposa had intended to read, but her book lay unopened in her lap. The sun in California is something more than warming and cheerful. It is medicinal. There is some unnamed balm in its light that soothes the tormented spirit and rests and revivifies the wearied body. It is at once a stimulant and a sedative. It seems to have sucked up healing breaths from the resinous forests inland and to be exhaling them again upon those who can not seek their aid.

As the soothing rays enveloped her, Mariposa felt the strain of mind and body relax and a sense of rest suffuse her. She stretched herself into a more reposeful attitude, one arm thrown along the back of the bench. Her book lay beside her on the seat. To keep the blinding light from her eyes she tilted her hat forward till the shade of its brim cut cleanly across the middle of her face.

Her mouth, which was plainly in view, had the expression of suffering that is acquired by the mouths of those who have been forced to endure suddenly and silently. Her thoughts reverted to Essex and the scene in the cottage. She wondered if the smart and shame of it would ever lessen—if she would ever see him again, and what he would say. She could not imagine him as anything but master of himself. But he was no longer master of her. The subtile spell he had once exercised was forever broken.

She heard a foot on the gravel, but did not look up; several people had passed close to her crossing to the main drive. The new-comer advanced toward her idly, noting the grace of her attitude, the rich and yet elegant proportions of her figure. Her face was turned from him, but he saw the roll of rust-colored hair beneath her hat, started, and quickened his pace. He had come to a halt beside her before she looked up startled. A quick red rushed into her face. He, for his part, stood suave and smiling, holding his hat in one hand, no expression on his face but one of frank pleasure. Even in his eyes there was not a shade of consciousness.

"What a piece of luck!" he said. "Who'd have thought of meeting you here?"

Mariposa had nothing to respond. In a desperate desire for flight and protection she looked for Benito, but he was at the top of the slope, well out of earshot of anything but a scream.

Essex surveyed her face with fond attention.

"You're looking better than you did before you moved," he said; "you were just a little too pale then. You know, I didn't know it was you at all. I was looking at you as I came across the drive, and I hadn't the least idea it was you till I saw your hair"—his eye lighted on it caressingly—"I knew there was only one woman in San Francisco with hair like that."

His voice seemed to mesmerize her at first. Now her volition came back and she rose.

"Benito!" she cried; "come at once."

VAIN PLEADINGS 267

The two little boys had their heads close together and neither turned.

"What are you going to go for?" said Essex in surprise.

"What a question!" she said, picking up her book with a trembling hand, and thinking in her ignorance that he spoke honestly; "what an insulting question!"

"Insulting! What on earth do you mean by that?" coaxingly. "Please tell me why you are going?"

"Because I don't want ever to see you or speak to you again," she said in a voice shaken with anger. "I couldn't have believed any man could be so lacking in decency as—as—to do this."

"Do what?" he asked with an air of blank surprise. "What am I doing?"

"Thrusting yourself on me this way when—when—you know that the sight of you is humiliating and hateful to me."

"Oh, Mariposa!" he said softly. He looked into her face with eyes brimming with teasing tenderness. "How can you say that to me when my greatest fault has been to love you?"

"Love me!" she ejaculated with breathless scorn; "love me! Oh, Benito,"—calling with all her force—"come; do come. I want you!"

Benito, who undoubtedly must have heard, was too pleasantly engaged with the companionship of his new friend to make any response. Early in life he had learned the value of an occasional attack of deafness.

Mariposa made a motion to go to him, but Essex gently moved in front of her. She drew away from him, knitting her brows in helpless, heated rage.

"You know you're treating me very badly," he said.

"Treating you very badly," she now fairly gasped, once more a bewildered fly in the net of this subtle spider, "how else should I treat you?"

"Kindly," he said, softly bending his compelling glance on her, "as a woman treats a man who loves her."

"Mr. Essex," she said, turning on him with all the dignity she had at her command, "we don't seem to understand each other. The last time I saw you, you insulted and humiliated me. I don't know how it can be, but you seem to have forgotten all about it. I haven't. I never can, and I don't want to see you or speak to you or think of you ever again in this world."

"What makes you think I've forgotten?" he said, suddenly dropping his voice to a key that thrilled with meaning.

He saw the remark shake her into startled half-comprehension. That she still took his words at their face value proved to him again how strangely simple she was.

"What makes you think I've forgotten?" he repeated.

She raised her eyes in arrested astonishment and met his, now seeming suddenly to have become charged with memories of the scene in the cottage.

"How could I forget?" he murmured. "Do you really think I could ever forget that evening?"

She turned away speechless with embarrassment and anger, recollections of the kisses of that ill-omened interview burning in her face.

"When a man wounds the one woman in the world he cares for, can he ever forget, do you think?"

He again had the gratification of seeing her flash a look of artless surprise at him.

"Then—then—" she stammered, completely bewildered, "if you know that you wounded me so, why do you come back? Why do you speak to me now? There is nothing more to be said between us."

"Yes, there is; much more."

She drew back, frowning, on the alert to go. For a second he thought he was to lose this precious and unlooked-for chance of righting himself with her.

"Sit down," he said entreatingly; "sit down; I must speak to you."

She turned from him and sent a quick glance toward Benito. She was going.

"Mariposa," he said, desperately catching at her arm, "please—a moment. Give me one moment. You *must* listen to me."

She tried to draw her arm away, but he held it, and pleaded, genuine feeling flushing his face and roughening his voice.

"I beg—I implore—of you to listen to me. I only ask a moment. Don't condemn me without hearing what I have to say. I behaved like a blackguard. I know it. It's haunted me ever since. Sit down and listen to me while I try to explain and make you forgive me."

He was really stirred; the sincerity of his appeal touched the heart, once so warm, now grown so cold toward him. She sat down on the bench, at the end farthest from him, her whole bearing suggesting self-contained aloofness.

"I know I shocked and hurt you. I know it's just and natural for you to treat me this way. I was mad. I didn't know what I was saying. If you knew how I have suffered since you would at least have some pity for me. Can you guess what it means to give a blow to the being who is more to you than all the rest of the world? I was mad for that one evening."

He paused, looking at her. Her profile was toward him, pale and immovable. She neither turned nor spoke. He continued with a slight diminution of confidence:

"I've been a wild sort of fellow, consorting with all sorts of riffraff and thinking lightly of women. I've met lots of all kinds. It was all right to talk to them that way. You were different. I knew it from the first. But that night in the cottage I lost my head. You looked so pale and sad; my love broke the bonds I had put upon it. Can't you understand and forgive me?"

He leaned toward her, his face tense and pale. As he became agitated and fell into the position of pleader, she grew calm and regained her hold on herself. There was a chill poise about her that frightened him. He felt that if he attempted to touch her she would draw away with quick, instinctive repugnance.

She turned and looked into his face with cold eyes.

"No, I don't think I understand. I should think those very things you mention would appeal to the chivalry of a man even if he didn't care for a woman."

"Do you doubt that I love you?"

"Yes," she said, turning away; "I don't think that you ever could love me or any other woman."

"Why do you say that?"

She looked out over the grassy slope in front of them.

"Because you don't understand the first principles of it. When you're fond of people you don't want to hurt and humiliate them. You don't want to drag them down to shame and misery. You'd die to save them from those things. You want to protect them, help them, take care of them, be proud of them and say to all the world: 'Here, look; this is the person I love!'"

Her simplicity, that once would have amused him, now had something in it that at once touched and alarmed him. There was a downright conviction in it, that argument, eloquence, passion even, would not be able to shake.

"And that, Mariposa," he said, ardently, "is the way I love you."

"That the way!" she echoed scornfully. "No—your way is to ask me to destroy myself, body and soul. You ask me to give you everything, while you give nothing. You say you love me, and yet you're so ashamed of me and your love, that it would have to be a hateful secret thing, that you told lies about, and would expect me to tell lies about, too. I can't understand how you can dare to call it love. I can't understand. Oh, don't talk about it any more. It's all too horrible and cruel and false!"

Her words still further alarmed the man. He knew

they were not those of a woman swayed by sentiment, far less by passion.

"That's all true," he said hastily, "that's all true of what I said to you that night in the cottage. Now it's different. Aren't you large-hearted enough to forgive a man whose greatest weakness has been his infatuation for you? I was a ruffian and you an unsuspecting angel. Now I want to offer you the only kind of love that ever should be offered you. Will you be my wife?"

Mariposa started perceptibly. She turned and looked with amazed eyes into his face. He seemed another man from the one who had so bitterly humiliated her at their last interview. He was pale and in earnest.

"Will you?" he repeated.

"No," she said with slow decisiveness, "I will not."

"No?" he exclaimed, in loud-voiced incredulity and bending his head to look into her face. "No?"

"No," she reiterated; "I said no."

She felt with every moment that their positions were changing more and more. She was gradually ascending to the command, while he was slowly coming under her will.

"Why do you say no?" he demanded.

"Because I want to say no."

"But—but—why? Are you still angry?"

"I want to say no," she repeated. "I couldn't say anything else."

"But you love me?" with angry persistence.

"No, I don't love you."

"You do," he said in a low voice. "You're not telling the truth. You do love me. You know you do."

She looked at him with cold defiance, and said steadily:

"I do not."

He drew nearer her along the bench and said with his eyes hard upon her:

"I didn't think you were the kind of woman to kiss a man you didn't care for."

He knew when he spoke the words they were foolish and jeopardized his cause, but his fury at her disdainful attitude forced them from him.

She turned pale and her nostrils quivered. He had given her a body blow. For a moment they sat side by side looking at each other like two enraged animals animated by equally violent if different passions.

"Thank you for saying that," she said, when she could command her voice; "now I understand what your love for me means."

She rose from the bench. He seized her hand and attempted to draw her back, saying:

"Mariposa, listen to me. You drive me distracted. You force me to say things like that to you, when you know that I'm mad with love for you. Listen—"

She tore her hand out of his grasp and ran across the space to the slope, calling wildly to Benito. The boy at last could feign deafness no longer and sat up on his heels in well-simulated surprise.

"Come, come," she cried angrily. "Come at once. I want you."

He rose, dusting his nether parts and shouting:

"Why? why? we're havin' an awful nice time up here."

"Come," she reiterated; "it's late and we must go."

He trotted down the slope, extremely reluctant, and inclined to be rebellious.

Mariposa caught him by the hand and swept him back toward the path between the spruces. Essex was still standing near the bench, an elegant figure with a darkly sinister face. As they passed him he raised his hat. Mariposa, whose face was bent down, did not return the salute; so Benito did, as he was hauled by. She continued to drag the unwilling little boy along, while he hung loosely from her hand, staring backward for a last look at his playmate.

"What's your name?" he roared as he was dragged toward the shadowy path that plunged into the trees. "I forget what your name is."

The answer was lost in the intervening space, and the next moment he and Mariposa disappeared behind the screen of thick-growing evergreens.

"Say," said Benito, "leggo my hand. What's the sense 'er hauling me this way?"

Mariposa did not heed, and they went on at a feverish pace.

"What makes your hand shake that way?" was his next observation. "It's like grandma's when she came home from Los Angeles with the chills."

There was something in this harmless comment that caused Mariposa suddenly to loosen her hold.

"My hand often does that way," she said with an air of embarrassment.

"What makes it?" asked Benito, suddenly interested.

"I don't know; perhaps playing the piano," she said, feeling the necessity of having to dissemble.

"I'd like to be able to make my hand shake that

way," Benito observed enviously. "When grandma had the chills I used to watch her. But she shook all over. Sometimes her teeth used to click. Do your teeth ever click?"

The subject interested him and furnished food for conversation till they reached their car and were swept homeward over the low hills, breaking here and there into sand, and with the little oaks crouching in grotesque fear before the winds.

CHAPTER XV

THROUGH A GLASS DARKLY

"Thou hast made us to drink the wine of astonishment. Thou hast showed thy people hard things."—PSALMS.

The third boarder at the Garcias' was Isaac Pierpont, the teacher of singing. The Garcia house offered, at least, the one recommendation of being a place wherein musically inclined lodgers might make the welkin ring with the sounds of their industry and no voice be raised in protest. Between the pounding of her own pupils Mariposa could hear the voices of Pierpont's as they performed vocal prodigies under their teacher's goadings.

The young man was unusual and interesting. He had a "method" which he expounded to Mariposa during the process of meals. It was founded on a large experience of voices in general and a close anatomical study of the vocal chords. All he wanted, he said, to demonstrate its excellence to the world was a voice. Mrs. Garcia, who used to drop in on Mariposa with her head tied up in white swathings and a broom in her hand, had early in their acquaintance given her a life history of the two other boarders, with a running accompaniment of her own comments. Pierpont had not her highest approval, as he was exasperatingly indifferent to money, being bound, to the exclusion of all lesser interests, on the search for his voice. Half his pupils were taught for nothing and the other half forgot to pay, or Pierpont forgot to send in his bills, which was the same thing in the end, Mrs. Garcia thought.

"I can't see what's the good of working," she said, daintily brushing the surface of the carpet with her broom, "if you don't make anything by your work. What's the sense of it, I'd like to know?"

As soon as the singing teacher heard that Mariposa had a voice he had espied in her the object of his search and begged her to sing for him. But she had refused. She had not sung a note since her mother's death. The series of unforeseen and disastrous developments that had followed the opening scene of the drama in which she found herself the central figure had robbed her of all desire to use the gift which was her one source of fortune. Sometimes, alone in her room, her fingers running over the keys of the piano, she wondered dreamily what it would be like once again to hear the full, vibrating sounds booming out from her chest. Now and then she had tried a note or two or an old familiar strain, then had stopped, repelled and disenchanted. Her voice sounded coarse and strange. And while it quivered on the air there came a rush of exquisitely painful memories.

But one afternoon, a few days after her encounter with Essex, she had come in early to find the lower hall full of the sound of a high, crystal clear soprano, which was pouring from the teacher's room. She listened interested, held in a spell of envious attention. It was evidently a girl of whom Pierpont had spoken to her, who possessed the one voice of promise he had yet found, and who was studying for the stage. Leaning over the stair-rail, Mariposa felt, with a tingling at her heart, that this singing had a finish and poise hers entirely lacked, and yet the voice was thin, colorless and fragile compared with her own. With all its flawless ease and fluency it had not the same splendor of tone, the same passionate thrill.

She went slowly upstairs, pursued by the beautiful sounds, bending over the railing to catch them more fully, with, for the first time since her mother's death, the desire to emulate, to be up and doing, to hear once more the rich notes swelling from her throat.

"Some day *I'll* sing for him," she said to herself, with her head up and her eyes bright, "and he'll see that none of them has a voice like mine."

The stir of enthusiasm was still on her when she shut the door of her own room. It was hard to settle to anything with this sudden welling up of old ambitions disturbing the apathy following on grief. She was standing, looking down on the garden—a prospect which had long lost its forlornness to her accustomed eyes—when a knock at the door fell gratefully on her ears. Even the society of Mrs. Garcia, with her head tied up in the white duster, had its advantages now and then.

But it was not Mrs. Garcia, but Mrs. Willers whom the opening door revealed. Mariposa's welcome was warmed not only by the desire for companionship but by genuine affection. She had come to regard Mrs. Willers as her best friend.

They did not see each other as often as formerly, for the newspaper woman found all her time occupied by her new work. To-day being Monday, she had managed to get off for the afternoon, as it was in the Sunday edition that the Woman's Page attained its most imposing proportions. Monday was a day off. But Mrs. Willers did not always avail herself of it. She was having the first real chance of her life and was working harder than she had ever done before. Her bank account was mounting weekly. On the occasions when she had time to consult the little book she saw through the line of figures Edna going to a fine school in New York, and then, perhaps, a still finer one abroad, and back of that again—dimly, as became a blissful vision—Edna grown a woman, accomplished, graceful, beautiful, a glorified figure in a haze of wealth and success.

She had no war-paint on to-day, but was in her working clothes, dark and serviceable, showing lapses between skirt and waist-band, and tag ends of tape appearing in unexpected places. She had dressed in such a hurry that morning that only three buttons of each boot were fastened, though the evening before Edna had seen to it that they were all on. She had come up the hill on what she would have called "a dead run," and was still fetching her breath with gasps.

Sitting opposite Mariposa, in the bright light of the window, she let her eyes dwell fondly on the girl's face.

"Well, young woman, do you know I've come up here on the full jump to lecture you?"

"Lecture me?" said Mariposa, laughing and bending

forward to give Mrs. Willers' hand a friendly squeeze. "What have I been doing now?"

"That's just what I've come to find out. Left a desk full of work, and Miss Peebles hopping round like a chicken with its head off, to find out what you've been doing. I'd have come up before only I couldn't get away. Mariposa, my dear, I've had a letter from Mrs. Shackleton."

Mariposa's color deepened. A line appeared between her eyebrows, and she looked out of the window.

"Well," she said; "and did she say anything about me?"

"That's what she did—a lot. A lot that sorter stumped me. And I've come up here to-day to find out what's the matter with you. What is it that's making you act like several different kinds of fool all at once?"

"What do you mean?" said Mariposa weakly, trying to gain time. "What did she tell you?"

"My dear, you know as well as I do what she told me. And I can't make head or tail of it. What's come over you?"

"I don't know," said the girl in a low voice. "I suppose I've changed."

"Stuff!" observed Mrs. Willers briskly. "Don't try to tell lies; you don't know how. One's got to have some natural capacity for it. You've had an offer that makes it possible for you to go to Europe, educate your voice, study French and German, and become a prima donna. Everything's to be paid—no limit set on time or money. Now, what in heaven's name made you refuse that?"

Facing her in the bright light, the questioner's eyes were like gimlets on her face. Mrs. Willers saw its distressed uneasiness, but could read no further. Three days before she had received Mrs. Shackleton's letter, and had been amazed by its contents. She could neither assign to herself nor to Mrs. Shackleton a reason for the girl's unexplainable conduct.

"I can't explain it to you," said Mariposa. "I—I—didn't want to go. That was all."

"But you wanted to go only a month or two before, when Shackleton himself made you the offer?"

Mariposa nodded without answering.

"But why? That's the part that's so extraordinary. You'd take it from him, but not from his wife."

"A person might change her mind, mightn't she?"

"A fool might, but a reasonable woman, without a cent, with hardly a friend, how could she?"

"Well, she has."

"Mariposa, look me in the eye."

Mrs. Willers met the amber-clear eyes and saw, with an uneasy thrill, that there was knowledge in them there had not been before. It was not the limpid glance of the candid, unspoiled youth it had once been. She felt a contraction of pain at her heart, as though she had read the same change in Edna's eyes.

"What made you change your mind?—that's what I want to know."

Mariposa lowered her lids.

"I can't tell. What makes anybody change his mind?

You think differently. Things happen that make you think differently."

"Well, what's happened to make *you* think differently?"

The lines appeared again on the smooth forehead. She shifted her glance to the window and then back to the hands on her lap.

"Suppose I don't want to tell? I'm not a little girl like Edna, to have to tell every thought I have. Mayn't I have a secret, Mrs. Willers?"

She looked at her interlocutor with an attempt at a coaxing smile. Mrs. Willers saw that it was an effort, and remained grave.

"I don't want you to have secrets from me, dear, no more than I would Edna. Mariposa," she said in a lowered voice, leaning forward and putting her hand on the girl's knee, "is it because of some man?"

Mariposa looked up quickly. The elder woman saw that, for a moment, she was startled.

"Some man!" she exclaimed. "What man?"

"You haven't changed your mind because of Essex?"

"Essex!" She slowly crimsoned, and Mrs. Willers kept her pitiless eyes on the rising flood of color.

"Oh, my dear girl," she said almost in an agony, "don't say you've got fond of him."

"I don't like Mr. Essex. I—I—can't bear him."

Mrs. Willers knew enough of human nature not to be at all convinced by this remark.

"He's not the man for any woman to give her heart to. He's not the man to take seriously. He's never loved anything in his life but himself. Don't let yourself be fooled by him. He's handsome, and he's about the smoothest talker I ever ran up against. But don't you be crazy enough to fall in love with him."

"I tell you, I don't like him."

"My goodness, I wish there was somebody in this world to take care of you. You've got no sense, and you're so unfortunately good-looking. Some day you'll be fooled just as I was with Willers. Are you telling the truth? It isn't Essex that's made you change your mind?"

These repeated accusations exasperated Mariposa.

"No, it is not," she said angrily; and then, in the heat of her annoyance, "if anything would make me accept Mrs. Shackleton's offer it would be the hope of getting away from that man."

There was no doubt she was speaking the truth now. Mrs. Willers' point of view of the situation underwent a kaleidoscopic upsetting.

"Oh," she said, in a subdued voice, "then it's *he* that's in love?"

The girl made no answer. She felt hot and sore, pricked by this insistent probing of spots that were still raw.

"Does he—does he—bother you?" the elder woman said in an incredulous voice. Somehow she could not reconcile the picture of Essex as a repulsed and suppliant wooer with her knowledge of him as such a very self-assured and debonair person.

"I don't know what you mean by 'bother me,'" said Mariposa, still heated. "He makes love to me, and I don't like it. I don't like him."

"Makes love to you? What do you mean by 'makes love to you?'"

"He has asked me to be his wife," said the victim, goaded to desperation by this tormenting catechism.

She could not have confessed that Essex had entertained other designs with regard to her, any more than she could have told her real reason for refusing Mrs. Shackleton's offer. But she felt ashamed and miserable at these half-truths, which her friend was giving ear to with the wide eyes of wonder.

"Humph!" said Mrs. Willers, "I never thought that man would want to marry a poor girl. But that's not as surprising as that you had sense enough to refuse him."

"I don't like him. I know I'm stupid, but I know when I like a person and when I don't. And I'd rather stand on the corner of Kearney and Sutter Streets with a tin cup begging for nickels than marry Mr. Essex, or be sent to Europe by Mrs. Shackleton."

"Well, you're a combination of smartness and folly I never expect to see beaten. You've got sense enough to refuse to marry a man who's bound to make you miserable. That's astonishing in any girl. And then, on the other hand, you throw up the chance of a lifetime for nothing. That would be astonishing in a candidate for entrance into an asylum for the feeble-minded."

"Perhaps I am feeble-minded," said Mariposa humbly. "I certainly don't think I'm very clever, especially now with everybody telling me what a fool I am."

"You're only a fool on that one point, honey. And

that's what makes it so aggravating. It's just a kink in your brain, for you've got no reason to act the way you do."

She spoke positively, but her pleading look at Mariposa showed that she was not yet willing to give up the search for a reason. Mariposa leaned forward and took her hand.

"Oh, dear Mrs. Willers," she said, "don't ask me any more. Don't tease me. I do love you, and you've been so kind to me I can never stop loving you, no matter what you did. But let me be. Perhaps I have a reason, and perhaps I am only a fool, but whichever way it is, be sure I haven't acted hastily; and I've suffered, too, trying to do what seemed to me right."

Her eyes suddenly filled with tears, and she got up quickly to hide them, and stood looking out of the window. Mrs. Willers rose, too, and, putting an arm around her, kissed her cheek.

"All right," she said, "I'll try not to bother. But you want to tell me whatever you think you can. You're too good-looking, Mariposa, and you're such —a—"

She stopped.

"A fool," came from Mariposa, in the stifled tones of imminent tears. There was a moment's pause, and then their simultaneous laughter filled the room.

"You see you can't help saying it," said Mariposa, laughing foolishly, with the tears hanging on her lashes. "It's like any other bad habit—its getting entire control of you."

A few moments later Mrs. Willers was walking quickly down the hill toward Sutter Street, her brows knit in thought. She had certainly discovered nothing. In her pocket was Mrs. Shackleton's letter telling of Miss Moreau's refusal of her offer and asking if Mrs. Willers knew the reason of it. Mrs. Shackleton had wondered if Miss Moreau's affections had been engaged, which could perhaps account for her otherwise unaccountable rejection of an opportunity upon which her whole future might depend.

Mrs. Willers had been relieved to find there was certainly no man influencing Miss Moreau's decision. For unless it was Essex, it could be no one. Mrs. Willers knew the paucity of Mariposa's social circle. That Essex had asked the girl to marry him and been refused was astonishing. The rejection was only a little more surprising than the offer. For a man like Essex to want to marry a penniless orphan was only exceeded in singularity by a girl like Mariposa refusing a man of Essex's indisputable attractions. But there was always something to be thankful for in the darkest situation, and Mariposa undoubtedly had no intention of marrying him. Providence was guiding her, at least, in that respect.

It was still early when Mrs. Willers approached *The Trumpet* office. The sky was leaden and hung with low clouds. As she drew near the door the first few drops of rain fell, spotting the sidewalk here and there as though they were slowly and reluctantly wrung from the swollen heavens. It would be a storm, she thought, as she turned into the doorway and began the ascent of the dark stairs with the lanterns on the landings. In her own cubby-hole she answered Mrs. Shackleton's letter, and then passed along the passageway to the sanctum of the proprietor, who was still in his office.

Win, in his father's swivel chair, looked very small and insignificant. The wide window behind him let a flood of pale light over his bullet-shaped head with its thatch of limp, blond hair, and his thin shoulders bowed over the desk. His eyes narrowed behind his glasses as he looked up in answer to Mrs. Willers' knock, and then, when he saw who it was, he smiled, for Win liked Mrs. Willers.

She handed him the letter with the request that he give it to his mother that evening, and sat down in the chair beside him, facing the long white panes of the window, which the rain was beginning to lash.

"My mother and you seem to be having a lively correspondence," said Win, who had brought down Mrs. Shackleton's letter some days before.

"Yes, we've got an untractable young lady on our hands, and it's a large order."

"Miss Moreau?" said the proprietor of *The Trumpet*. "My mother told me. She's very independent, isn't she?"

"She's a strange girl. You can tell your mother, as I've told her in this letter, that I don't understand her at all. She's got some idea in her head, but I can't make it out."

"Mightn't a girl just be independent?" said the young man, putting up a long, thin hand to press his glasses against his nose with a first and second finger. "Just independent, and nothing else?"

"There's no knowing what a girl mightn't be, Mr.

Shackleton," Mrs. Willers responded gloomily. "I was one myself once, but it's so long ago I've forgotten what it's like; and, thank heaven, it's a stage that's soon passed."

It so happened that this little conversation set Win's mind once more to thinking of the girl his father had been so determined to find and benefit. As he left *The Trumpet* office, shortly after the withdrawal of Mrs. Willers, his mind was full of the queries the finding of the letters had aroused in it. The handsome girl he had seen that afternoon, three months ago, appeared before his mental vision, and this time as her face flashed out on him from the dark places of memory it had a sudden tantalizing suggestion of familiarity. The question came that so often teases us with the sudden glimpse of a vaguely recognized face: "Where have I seen it before?"

Win walked slowly up Third Street meditating under a spread umbrella. It was raining hard now, a level downpour that beat pugnaciously on the city, which gleamed and ran rillets of water under the onslaught. People were scurrying away in every direction, women with umbrellas low against their heads, one hand gripping up their skirts, from beneath which came and went glimpses of muddy boots and wet petticoats. Loafers were standing under eaves, looking out with yellow, apathetic faces. The merchants of the quarter came to the doorways of the smaller shops that Win passed, and stood looking out and then up into the sky with musing smiles. It was a heavy rain, and no mistake.

Win had a commission to execute before he went

home, and so passed up Kearney Street to Post, where, a few doors from the corner, he entered a photographer's. He was having a copy made on ivory of an old daguerreotype of his father, to be given as a present to his mother, and to-day it was to be finished.

The photographer, a clever and capable man, had started the innovation of having his studio roughly lined with burlaps, upon which photographs of local belles and celebrities were fastened with brass-headed nails. Win, waiting for his appearance, loitered round the room looking at these, recognizing a friend here, and there a proud beauty who had endured him as a partner at the cotillion because he was the only son of Jake Shackleton. Farther on was one of Edna Willers, looking very lovely and seraphic in her large-eyed innocence.

On a small slip of wall between two windows there was only one picture fastened, and as his eye fell on this he started. It was Mariposa Moreau, in the lace dress she had worn at the opera, the face looking directly and gravely into his. At the moment that his glance, fresh from other faces, fell on it, the haunting suggestion of familiarity, of having some intimate connection with or memory of it, possessed him with sudden, startling force. Of whom did she remind him?

He backed away from it, and, as he did so, was conscious that he knew exactly the way her lips would open if she had been going to speak, of the precise manner she had of lifting her chin. Yet he had seen her only twice in his life that he knew of, and then in the half-dark. It was not she that was known to him, but some one that she looked like—some one he knew well, that had some vague, yet close connection with his life. He felt in an eery way that his mind was gropingly approaching the solution, had almost seized it, when the photographer's voice behind him broke the thread.

"It will be ready in a moment, Mr. Shackleton," he said. "You're looking at that picture. It's a Miss Moreau, a young lady who, I believe, is a singer. I put it there by itself, as I was just a little proud of it."

"It's a stunning picture and no mistake," said Win, arranging his glasses, "but it must be easy to make a picture of a girl like that."

"On the contrary, I think it's hard. Miss Moreau's handsome, but it's a beauty that's more suitable to a painter than a photographer. It's the coloring that's so remarkable, so rich and yet so refined—that white skin and dark red hair. That's why I am proud of the picture. It suggests the coloring, I think. It seems to me there's something warm about that hair."

Win said vaguely, yes, he guessed there must be, wondering what the fellow meant about there being something warm about the hair. Further comment was ended by an attendant coming forward with the picture and handing it to the photographer.

The man held it out to Win with a proud smile. It was an enlargement of a small daguerreotype, taken some twenty years previously, and representing Shackleton in full face and without his beard. The work had been excellently done. It was a faithful and spirited likeness.

As his eye fell on it Win suffered a sudden and amazing revelation. It was like a dazzling flash of light tearing away the shadows of a dark place. Through the obscurity of his mind enlightenment rent like a current of electricity. That was what the memory was, that dim sense of previous knowledge, that groping after something well known and yet elusive.

He stared at the picture, and then turned and looked at Mariposa's hanging on the wall. The photographer, looking commiseratingly at him, evidently mistaking his obvious perturbation of mind for a rush of filial affection, recalled him to himself. He did not know that he was pale, but he saw that the plate of ivory in his hand trembled.

"It's—it's—first-rate," he said in a low voice. "I'm tremendously pleased. Send it to *The Trumpet* office to-morrow, and the bill with it, please. You've done an A number one job."

He turned away and went slowly out, the photographer and his assistant looking curiously after him. There were steps to go down before he regained the street, and he descended them in a maze, the rain pouring on his head, his closed umbrella in his hand. It was all as clear as daylight now—the secret searching out of the mother and daughter, the interest taken by his father in the beautiful and talented girl, his desire to educate and provide for her. It was all as plain as A, B, C.

"She was so different from Maud and me," Win thought humbly, as he moved forward in the blinding rain. "No wonder he was fond of her."

It was so astonishing, so simple, and yet so hard to realize in the first moment of discovery this way, that he stopped and stood staring at the pavement.

Two of his friends, umbrellaed and mackintoshed, bore down on him, not recognizing the motionless figure with the water running off its hat brim till they were close on him.

"Win, gone crazy!" cried one gaily. "When did it come on, Winnie boy?"

He looked up startled, and had presence of mind enough not to open his umbrella.

"Win's trying to grow," said the other, knowing that his insignificant size was a mortification to the young man. "So he's standing out in the rain like a plant."

"Rain's all right," said Win. "I like it."

"No doubt about that, sonny. Only thing to doubt's your sanity."

"Cute little day, ain't it?" said his companion.

"Win likes it," said the first. "Keep it up, old chap, and you'll be six feet high before the winter's over."

And they went off cackling to the club to tell the story of Win, with the water pouring off his hat and his glasses damp, standing staring at the pavement on Post Street.

Win opened his umbrella and went on. He walked home slowly and by a circuitous route. His mind traversed the subject back and forth, and at each moment he became more convinced, as all the muddle of puzzling circumstances fell into place in logical sequence.

She was his half-sister, older than he was—his father's first-born. By this accident of birth she was an outcast, penniless and unacknowledged, from the home and fortune he and Maud had inherited. At the very moment when the father had found her free to accept his bounty he had been snatched away. And she knew it. That was the explanation of her changeable conduct. She had found it out in some way between the deaths of her mother and Shackleton. Some one had told her or she had discovered it herself.

In the dripping dark Win pondered it all, going up and down the ascending streets in a tortuous route homeward, wondering at fate, communing with himself.

CHAPTER XVI

REBELLIOUS HEARTS

"Constant you are,
But yet a woman; and for secrecy,
No lady closer, for I will believe
Thou wilt not utter what thou dost not know."
—SHAKESPEARE.

Win found his mother in her boudoir and delivered Mrs. Willers' letter to her without comment. He saw her read it and then sit silent, her brows drawn, looking into the fire beside which she sat. It was impossible just then for him to allude to the subject of the letter, and, after standing by the mantelpiece awkwardly warming his wet feet, he went upstairs to his own rooms.

At dinner the family trio was unusually quiet. Under the blaze of light that fell from the great crystal chandelier over the table with its weight of glass and silver, the three participants looked preoccupied and stupid. The two Chinese servants, soft-footed as cats, and spotless in their crisp white, moved about the table noiselessly, offering dish after dish to their impassive employers.

It was one of those irritating occasions when everything seems to combine for the purpose of exasperating. Bessie, annoyed by the contents of Mrs. Willers' letter, found her annoyance augmented by the fact that Maud looked particularly plain that evening, and the Count de Lamolle was expected after dinner. Worry had robbed her face of such sparkle as it possessed and had accentuated its ungirlish heaviness. She felt that her engagement to Latimer must be announced, for the Count de Lamolle was exhibiting those signs of a coming proposal that she knew well, and what excuse could she give her mother for rejecting him? She must tell the truth, and the thought alarmed her shrinking and peaceable soul. She sat silent, crumbling her bread with a nervous hand and wondering how she could possibly avert the offer if the count showed symptoms of making it that evening.

After dinner her mother left her in the small reception-room, a rich and ornate apartment, furnished in an oriental manner with divans, cushions, and Moorish hangings. The zeal for chaperonage had not yet penetrated to the West, and Bessie considered that to leave her daughter thus alone was to discharge her duties as a parent with delicate correctness. She retired to the adjoining library, where the count, on entering, had a glimpse of her sitting in a low chair, languidly turning the pages of a magazine. He, on his part, had lived in the West long enough to know that the disposal of the family in these segregated units was what custom and conventionality dictated.

The count was a clever man and had studied the United States from other points of vantage than the window of a Pullman car.

With the murmur of his greetings to Maud in her

ears, Bessie rose from her chair. She found the library chill and cheerless after her cozy boudoir on the floor above, and decided to go there. Glancing over her shoulder, as she mounted the stairs, she could see the count standing with his back to the fire, discoursing with a smile—a handsome, personable man, with his dark face and pointed beard looking darker than ever over his gleaming expanse of shirt bosom. It would be an entirely desirable marriage for Maud. Bessie had found out all about the count's position and title in his native land, and both were all that he said they were, which had satisfied and surprised her.

In her own room she sat down before the fire to think. Maud's future was in her own hands now, molding itself into shape downstairs in the reception-room. Bessie could do no more toward directing it than she had already done, and her active mind immediately seized on the other subject that had been engrossing it. She drew out Mrs. Willers' letter and read it again. Then crumpling it in her hand, she looked into the fire with eyes of somber perplexity.

What was the matter with the girl? Mrs. Willers stated positively that, as far as she could ascertain, there was no man that had the slightest influence over Mariposa Moreau's affections. She was acting entirely on her own volition. But what had made her change her mind, Mrs. Willers did not know. Something had undoubtedly occurred, she thought, that had influenced Mariposa to a total reversal of opinion. Mrs. Willers said she could not imagine what this was, but it had changed the girl, not only in ambition and point of view, but in character.

The letter frightened Bessie. It had made her silent all through dinner, and now brooding over the fire, she thought of what it might mean and felt a cold apprehension seize her. Could Mariposa know? Her behavior and conduct since Shackleton's death suggested such a possibility. It was incredible to think of, but Lucy might have told. And also, might not the girl, in arranging her mother's effects after her death, have come on something, letters or papers, which had revealed the past?

A memory rose up in Bessie's mind of the girl wife she had supplanted, clinging to the marriage certificate, which was all that remained to remind her of the days when she had been the one lawful wife. Bessie knew that this paper had been carefully tied in the bundle which held Lucy's few possessions when they left Salt Lake. She knew it was still in the bundle when she, herself, had handed it to the deserted girl in front of Moreau's cabin. Might not Mariposa have found it?

She rose and walked about the room, feeling sick at the thought. She was no longer young, and her iron nerve had been permanently shaken by the suddenness of her husband's death. Mariposa, with her mother's marriage certificate, might be plotting some desperate *coup*. No wonder she refused to go to Paris! If she could establish her claim as Shackleton's eldest and only legitimate child, she would not only sweep from Win and Maud the lion's share of their inheritance, but, equally unbearable, she would drag to the light the ugly story—the terrible story that Jake Shackleton and his second wife had so successfully hidden.

Her thoughts were suddenly broken in on by the

bang of the front door. She looked at the clock and saw it was only nine. If it was the count who was going he had stayed less than an hour. What had happened? She moved to the door and listened.

She heard a light step, slowly and furtively mounting the stairs. It was Maud, for, though she could attempt to deaden her footfall, she could not hush the rustling of her silken skirts. As the sweeping sound reached the stair-head, Bessie opened her door. Maud stopped short, her black dress fading into the darkness about her, so that her white face seemed to be floating unattached through the air like an optical delusion.

"Why, mommer," she said, falteringly, "I thought you were in bed."

"Has the count gone?" queried her mother, with an unusual sternness of tone.

"Yes," said the girl, "he's gone. He—he—went early to-night."

"Why did he go so early?"

"He didn't want to stay any longer."

Maud was terrified. Her hand clutching the balustrade was trembling and icy. In her father's lifetime she had known that she would never dare to tell of her engagement to Latimer. She would have ended by eloping. Now, the fear of her mother, who had always been the gentler parent, froze her timid soul, and even the joy of her love seemed swamped in this dreadful moment of confession.

"Did the count ask you to marry him?" said Bessie.

"Yes! and—" with tremulous desperation, "I said no, I couldn't."

"You said no! that's not possible. You couldn't be such a fool."

"Well, I was, and I said it."

"Come in here, Maud," said her mother, standing back from the doorway; "we can't talk sensibly this way."

But Maud did not move.

"No, I don't want to go in there," she said, like a naughty child; "there's nothing to talk about. I don't want to marry him and I told him so and he's gone, and that's the end of it."

"The end of it! That's nonsense. I want you to marry Count de Lamolle. I don't want to hear silly talk like this. I'll write to him to-morrow."

"Well, it won't do you or him any good," said Maud, to whom fear was giving courage, "for I won't marry him, and neither you nor he can drag me to the altar if I won't go. It's not the time of the Crusades."

If Maud's allusion was not precisely illuminating, her mother understood it.

"It may not be the time of the Crusades," she said, grimly, "but neither is it a time when girls can be fools and no one hold out a hand to check them. Do you realize what this marriage means for you? Position, title, an entrance into society that you never in any other way could put as much as the end of your nose into."

"If I don't want to put even the end of my nose into it, what good does it do me? You know I hate society. I hate going to dinners and sitting beside people who talk to me about things I don't understand or care for.

I hate going to balls and dancing round and round like a teetotum with men I don't like. And if it's bad here, what would it be over there where I don't speak their language or know their ways, and they'd think I was just something queer and savage the count had caught over here with a lasso."

Fears and doubts she had never spoken of to any one but Latimer came glibly to her lips in this moment of misery. Her mother was surprised at her fluency.

"You're piling up objections out of nothing," she said. "When those people over in France know what your fortune is, make no mistake, they'll be only too glad to know you and be your friend. They'll not think you queer and savage. You'll be on the top of everything over there, not just one of a bunch of bonanza heiresses, as you are here. And the count? Do you know any one so handsome, so gentlemanly, so elegant and polite in San Francisco?"

"I know a man I like better," said Maud, in a muffled voice.

The white face, with its dimly suggested figure, looked whiter than ever.

"What do you mean by that?" said her mother, stiffening.

"I mean Jack Latimer."

"Jack Latimer? One of your father's clerks! Maud, come in here at once. I can't stand talking in the hall of things like this."

"No, I won't come in," cried Maud, backing away against the baluster, and feeling as she used to do in her juvenile days, when she was hauled by the hand to the scene of punishment. "There's nothing more to talk about. I'm engaged to Jack Latimer, and I'm going to marry him, and that's the beginning and the end of it all."

She felt desperately defiant, standing there in the darkness looking at her mother's massive shape against the glow of the lit doorway.

"Jack Latimer!" reiterated Mrs. Shackleton, "who only gets a hundred and fifty dollars a month and has to give some of it to his people."

"Well, haven't I got enough for two?"

"Maud, you've gone crazy. All I know is that I'll not let you spoil your future. I'll write to Count de Lamolle to-morrow, and I'll write to Jack Latimer, too."

"What good will that do anybody? Count de Lamolle can't marry me if I don't want to. And why should Jack Latimer throw me over because you ask him to? He," she made a tremulous hesitation that would have touched a softer heart, and then added, "he likes me."

"Likes you!" repeated her mother, with furious scorn, "he likes the five million dollars."

"It's me," said Maud, passionately; "it isn't the money. And he's the only person in the world except Win who has ever really liked me. I don't feel when I'm with him that I'm so ugly and stupid, the way I feel with everybody else. He likes to hear me talk, and when he looks at me I don't feel as if he was saying to himself, 'What an ugly girl she is, anyway.' But I feel that he doesn't know whether I'm pretty or ugly. He only knows he loves me the way I am."

She burst into wild tears, and before her mother could answer or arrest her, had brushed past her and fled up the next flight of stairs, the sound of her sobs floating down from the upper darkness to the listener's ears. Bessie retreated into the boudoir and shut the door.

Maud ran on and burst into her own room, there to throw herself on the bed and weep despairingly for hours. She thought of her lover, the one human being besides her brother who had never made her feel her inferiority, and lying limp and shaken among the pillows, thought, with a wild thrill of longing of the time when she would be free to creep into his arms and hide the ugly face he found so satisfactory upon his heart.

In the morning, before she was up, Bessie visited her and renewed the conversation of the night before. Poor Maud, with a throbbing head and heavy eyes, lay helpless, answering questions that probed the tender secrets of the clandestine courtship, which had been to her an oasis of almost terrifying happiness in the lonely repression of her life. Finally, unable longer to endure her mother's sarcastic allusions to Latimer's disingenuousness, she sprang out of bed and ran into the bath-room, which was part of the suite she occupied. Here she turned on both taps, the sound of the rushing water completely drowning her mother's voice, and sitting on the side of the tub, looked drearily down into the bath, while Bessie's concluding and indignant sentences rose from the outer side of the door.

Mrs. Shackleton lunched alone that day. Win generally went to his club for his midday meal, and Maud had gone out early and found hospitality at the house of Pussy Thurston. Bessie had done more thinking that morning in the intervals of her domestic duties— she was a notable housekeeper and personally superintended every department of her establishment— and had decided to dedicate part of the afternoon to the society of Mrs. Willers. One of the secrets of Mrs. Shackleton's success in life had been her power to control and retain interests in divers matters at the same time. Maud's unpleasant news had not pushed the even more weighty subject of Mariposa into abeyance. It was as prominent as ever in the widow's mind.

She drove down to *The Trumpet* office soon after lunch and slowly mounted the long stairs. It would have been a hardship for any other woman of her years and weight, but Bessie's bodily energy was still remarkable, and she had never indulged herself in the luxury of laziness. At the top of the fourth flight she paused, panting, while the astonished office-boy stared at her, recognizing her as the chief's mother.

Mrs. Willers was in her cubby-hole, with a droplight sending a little circle of yellow radiance over the middle of the desk. A litter of newspaper cuttings surrounded her, and Miss Peebles, at the moment of Mrs. Shackleton's entrance, was in the cane-bottomed chair, in which aspirants for journalistic honors usually sat. The rustle of Mrs. Shackleton's silks and the faint advancing perfume that preceded her, announced an arrival of unusual distinction, and Miss Peebles had turned uneasily in the chair and Mrs. Willers was peering out from the circle of the drop-light, when the lady entered the room.

Miss Peebles rose with a flurried haste and thrust forward the chair, and Mrs. Willers extricated herself from the heaped up newspapers and extended a welcoming hand. The greetings ended, the younger woman bowed herself out, her opinion of Mrs. Willers, if possible, higher even than it had been before.

Mrs. Willers was surprised, but discreetly refrained from showing it. She had known Mrs. Shackleton for several years, and had once heard, from her late chief, that his wife approved her matter and counseled her advancement.

But to have her appear thus unannounced in the intimate heat and burden of office hours was decidedly unexpected. Mrs. Shackleton knew this and proceeded to explain.

"You must think it queer, my coming down on you this way, when you're up to your neck in work, but I won't keep you ten minutes." She looked at the small nickel clock that ticked aggressively in the middle of the desk. "And I know you are too busy a woman to ask you to come all the way up to my house. So I've come down to you."

"Pleased and flattered," murmured Mrs Willers, pushing back her chair, and kicking a space in the newspapers, so that she could cross her knees at ease. "But, don't hurry, Mrs. Shackleton. Work's well on and I'm at your disposal for a good many ten minutes."

"It's just to talk over that letter you sent me by Win.

What do you understand by Miss Moreau's behavior, Mrs. Willers?"

"I don't understand anything by it. I don't understand it at all."

"That's the way it seems to me. There's only one explanation of it that I can see, and you say that isn't the right one."

"What was that?"

"That there's some man here she's interested in. When a girl of that age, without a cent, or a friend or a prospect, refuses an offer that means a successful and maybe a famous future, what's a person to think? Something's stopping her. And the only thing I know of that would stop her is that she's fallen in love. But you say she hasn't."

"She don't strike me as being so. She don't talk like a girl in love."

"Is there any man who is interested in her and sees her continually?"

Mrs. Willers was naturally a truthful woman, but a hard experience of life had taught her to prevaricate with skill and coolness when she thought the occasion demanded it. She saw no menace now, however, and was entirely in sympathy with Mrs. Shackleton in her annoyance at Mariposa's irritating behavior.

"Yes," she said, nodding with grave eyes, "there *is* a man."

"Oh, there *is*," said the other, bending forward with a sudden eager interest that was not lost upon Mrs. Willers. "Who?"

"One of our men here, Barry Essex."

"Essex!" exclaimed the widow, with a sudden light of relieved comprehension suffusing her glance. "Of course. I know him. That dark, foreign-looking man that nobody knows anything about. Mr. Shackleton thought a great deal of him; said he was thrown away on *The Trumpet*. He's not a bit an ordinary sort of person."

"That's the one," said Mrs. Willers, nodding her head in somber acquiescence. "And you're right about nobody knowing anything about him. He's a dark mystery, I think."

"And you say he's in love with her?"

"That's what I'd infer from what she tells me."

"What *does* she tell you?"

"He's asked her to marry him."

"Then they're engaged. That accounts for the whole thing."

"No, they're not engaged. She's refused him."

"Refused him? That girl who's been living in an adobe at Santa Barbara, refuse that fine-looking fellow? Why, she'll never see a man like that again in her life. *She's* not refused him? Of course, she's engaged to him."

"No, you're mistaken. She's not. She doesn't like him."

"That's what she tells you. Girls always say that sort of thing. That explains the way she's acted from the start. He hadn't asked her when Mr. Shackleton was alive. She's engaged to him now and doesn't want to leave him. She struck me as just that soft, sentimental sort."

"You're wrong, Mrs. Shackleton; I know Mariposa

Moreau. She tells the truth; all of it. That's why it's so hard sometimes to understand what she means. We're not used to it. She doesn't like that man, and she wouldn't marry him if he was hung all over with diamonds and was going to give her the Con Virginia for a wedding present."

"Bosh!" ejaculated her companion, with sudden, sharp irritation. "That's what she says. They have no money to marry on, I suppose, and she's trying to keep her engagement secret. It explains everything. I must say I'm relieved. I had the girl on my mind, and it seemed to me she was so senseless and fly-away that you didn't know where she'd fetch up."

Mrs. Willers was annoyed. It was not pleasant to her to hear Mariposa spoken of this way. But a long life of struggle and misfortune had taught her, among other valuable things, the art of hiding unprofitable anger under a bland smile.

"Well, all I can say," she said, laughing quite naturally, "is that I hope you're wrong. I'm sure I don't want to see her married to that man."

"Why not?" queried Mrs. Shackleton, with the sudden arrested glance of surprised curiosity. "What is there to object to in such a marriage?"

"Hundreds of things," answered Mrs. Willers, feeling that there are many disadvantages in having to converse with your employer's mother on the subject of one of your best friends. "Who knows anything about Barry Essex? No one knows where he comes from, or who he is, or even if Essex is his name. I don't believe it is, at all. I think he just took it because it sounds like the aristocracy. And what's his record?

I'll lay ten to one there are things behind him he wouldn't like to see published on the front page of *The Trumpet*. He's no man to make a girl happy."

"You seem to be taking a good deal for granted. Because you don't know anything about him, it's no reason to suppose the worst. He certainly looks and acts like a gentleman, and he's finely educated. And isn't it better for a girl like Miss Moreau to have a husband to take care of her than to go roaming around by herself, throwing away every chance she gets, for some crazy notion? That young woman's not able to take care of herself. The best thing for her is to get Barry Essex to do it for her."

"I've known women," said Mrs. Willers, judicially, "who thought that a bad husband was better than no husband at all. But I'm not of that opinion myself, having had one of the bad ones. Solomon said a corner of a housetop and a dinner of herbs was better than a wide house with a brawling woman. And I tell you that one room in Tar Flat and beef's liver for every meal is better than a palace on Nob Hill with a husband that's no account."

"I'm afraid you're inclined to look on the dark side of matrimony," said Mrs. Shackleton, laughing, as she rose from her chair.

"May be so," said the other; "but after my experience I don't think it such a blissful state that I want to round up all my friends and drive them into the corral, whether they want to go or not."

Mrs. Shackleton looked down for a pondering moment. She was evidently not listening. Raising her head she met Mrs. Willers' half-sad, half-twinkling eyes with a gaze of keen scrutiny, and said:

"Then if it isn't a love affair, what is it that's made Miss Moreau change her mind?"

"Ah!" Mrs. Willers shrugged her shoulders. "That's what I'd like to know as well as you. I can only say what it's not."

"And that's Barry Essex. Well, Mrs. Willers, you're a smart woman, but you know your business better than you do the vagaries of young girls. I don't know Miss Moreau well, but I'd like to bet that I understand her this time better than you do."

She smiled genially and held out her hand.

"My ten minutes are up," nodding at the clock. "And I'm too much of a business woman to outstay my time limit. No"—in answer to Mrs. Willers' polite demur—"I must go."

She moved toward the door, then paused and said:

"Isn't Essex a sort of Frenchman? Or wasn't he, anyway, brought up in Paris, or had a French mother, or something?"

"As to his mother," said Mrs. Willers, sourly, "the Lord alone knows who she was. I've heard she was everything from the daughter of a duke to a snake-charmer in a dime museum. But he told me he was born and partly educated in Paris, and Madame Bertrand, at the Rôtisserie, tells me he must have been, as he talks real French French, not the kind you learn out of a book."

"He certainly looks like a Frenchman," said the departing guest. "Well, good by. It's a sort of bond between us to try to settle to her advantage this silly girl who doesn't want to be settled. If you hear any more of her affair with Essex, you might let me know. In spite of my criticisms, I take the greatest interest in her. I wouldn't criticize if I didn't."

As Mrs. Shackleton was slowly descending the long stairs, Mrs. Willers still stood beside her desk, thinking. The visit had surprised her in the beginning. Now it left her feeling puzzled and vaguely disturbed. Why did Mrs. Shackleton seem to be so desirous of thinking that Mariposa was betrothed to Essex? The bonanza king's widow was a woman of large charities and carelessly magnificent generosities, but she was also a woman of keen insight and unwavering common sense. Her interest in Mariposa was as strong as her husband's, and was entirely explainable as his had been, in the light of their old acquaintance with the girl's father. What Mrs. Willers could not understand was how any person, who had Mariposa Moreau's welfare at heart, could derive satisfaction from the thought of her marrying Barry Essex.

CHAPTER XVII

FRIEND AND BROTHER

"Wisdom is good with an inheritance, and by it there is profit to them that see the sun."—ECCLESIASTES.

Mariposa's sixteen dollars a month had been augmented to twenty-eight by the accession of three new pupils. These had been acquired through Isaac Pierpont, who was glad to find a cheap teacher for his potential prima donnas, who were frequently lacking in the simplest knowledge of instrumental music.

Mariposa was impressed and flattered by her extended clientele, and at first felt some embarrassment in finding that one of the pupils was a woman ten years older than herself. The worry she had felt on the score of her living was now at rest, for Pierpont had promised her his continued aid, and her new scholars professed themselves much pleased with her efforts.

Her monthly earnings were sufficient to cover her exceedingly modest living expenses. The remnants of her fortune—the few dollars left after her mother's funeral and the money realized by the sale of the jewelry and furniture that were the last relics of their *beaux jours*—made up the amount of three hundred and twenty dollars. This was in the bank. In the little desk that stood on a table in her room was the five hundred dollars in gold Shackleton had sent her. She had not touched it and never intended to, seeming to repudiate its possession by keeping it thus secret and apart from her other store.

The time was wearing on toward mid-December. Christmas was beginning to figure in the conversation of Miguel and Benito, and with an eye to its approach they had both joined a Sunday-school, to which they piously repaired every Sabbath morn. They had introduced the question of presents in their conversations with Mariposa with such smiling persistence that she had finally promised them that, on her first free afternoon, she would go down town and price certain articles they coveted. The afternoon came within a few days after her promise, one of her pupils sending her word that she was invited out of town for the holidays, and her lessons would cease till after New Year's.

The pricing had evidently been satisfactory, for, late in the afternoon, Mariposa turned her face homeward, her hands full of small packages. It was one of the clear, hazeless days of thin atmosphere, with an edge of cold, that are scattered through the San Francisco winter. There is no frost in the air, but the chill has a searching quality which suggests winter, as does the wild radiance of the sunset spread over the west in a transparent wash of red. The invigorating breath of cold made the young girl's blood glow, and she walked rapidly along Kearney Street, the exercise in the sharp air causing a faint, unusual pink to tint her cheeks. Her intention was to walk to Clay Street and then take the cable-car, which in those days slid slowly up the long hills, past the Plaza and through Chinatown.

She was near the Plaza, when a hail behind her fell on her ear, and turning, she saw Barron close on her heels, his hands also full of small packages. He had been at the mines for two weeks, and she could but notice the unaffected gladness of his greeting. She felt glad, too, a circumstance of which, for some occult reason, she was ashamed, and the shame and the gladness combined lent a reserved and yet conscious quality to her smile and kindled a charming embarrassment in her eye. They stood by the curb, he looking at her with glances of naïve admiration, while she looked down at her parcels. Passers-by noticed them, setting them down, she in her humble dress, he in his unmetropolitan roughness of aspect, as a couple from the country, a rancher or miner and his handsome sweetheart.

He took her parcels away from her, and they started forward toward the Plaza.

"Do you hear me panting?" he said, laying his free hand on his chest.

"No, why should you pant?"

"Because I've been running all down Kearney Street for blocks after you. I never knew any one to walk as fast in my life. I thought even if I didn't catch you you'd hear me panting behind you and think it was some new kind of fire-engine and turn round and look. But you never wavered—simply went on like a racer headed for the goal. Did you walk so fast because you knew I was behind you?"

She looked at him quickly with a side glance of

protest and met his eyes full of quizzical humor and yet with a gleam of something eager and earnest in them.

"I like to walk fast in this cold air. It makes me feel so alive. For a long time I've felt as though I were half dead, and you don't know how exhilarating it is to feel life come creeping back. It's like being able to breathe freely after you've been almost suffocated. But where did you see me on Kearney Street?"

"I was in a place buying things for the boys. I was looking at a drum for Benito, and I just happened to glance up, and there you were passing. I dropped the drum and ran."

"A *drum* for Benito! Oh, Mr. Barron, don't get Benito a drum!"

He could not control his laughter at the sight of her expression of horrified protest. He laughed so loudly that people looked at him. She smiled herself, not quite knowing why, and insensibly, both feeling curiously light-hearted, they drew closer together.

"What can I get?" he said. "I looked at knives and guns, and I knew that they wouldn't do. Benito would certainly kill Miguel and probably grandma. I thought of a bat and ball, and then I knew he'd break all the windows. The man in the store wanted me to buy a bow and arrow, but I saw him taking his revenge on the crab lady. Benito's a serious problem any way you take him."

They had come to the Plaza, once an open space of sand, round which the wild, pioneer city swept in whirlpool currents, now already showing the lichened brick and dropping plaster, the sober line of house fronts, of an aging locality. Where Chinatown backed on the square the houses had grown oriental, their western ugliness, disguised by the touch of gilding that, here and there, incrusted their fronts, the swaying of crimson lanterns, the green zigzags of dwarf trees. Over the top of the Clay Street hill the west shone red through smoke which filled the air with a keen, acrid smell. It told of hearth-fires. And oozing out of a thousand chimneys and streaming across the twilight city it told of homes where the good wife made ready for her man.

"Let's not take the cars," said Barron. "Let's walk home. Can you manage those hills?"

She gave a laughing assent, and they turned upward, walking slowly as befitted the climb. Chinatown opened before them like the mysterious, medieval haunt of robbers in an old drawing. The murky night was settling on it, shot through with red gleams at the end of streets, where the sunset pried into its peopled darkness. The blackness of yawning doorway and stealthy alley succeeded the brilliancy of a gilded interior, or a lantern-lit balcony. Strange smells were in the air, aromatic and noisome, as though the dwellers in this domain were concocting their wizard brews. There was a sound of shifting feet, a chatter of guttural voices, and a vision of faces passing from light to shadow, marked by a weird similarity, and with eyes like bits of onyx let into the tight-drawn skin.

It was an alien city, a bit of the oldest civilization in the world, imbedded in the heart of the newest. Touches of bizarre, of sinister picturesqueness filled it with arresting interest. On the window-sills lilies, their stalks bound with strips of crimson paper, grew in blue and white china bowls filled with pebbles round which their white roots clung. Miniature pine-trees, in pots of brass, thrust their boughs between the rusty ironwork of old balconies. Through an open doorway a glimpse was given down a dark hallway, narrow, black, a gas-jet, like a tiny golden tear, diffusing a frightened gleam of light. From some dim angle the glow of a blood-red lantern mottled a space of leprous wall. On a tottering balcony a woman's face, rounded like a child's, crimson lipped, crowned with peach blossoms, looked down from shadows, the light of a lantern catching and loosening the golden traceries of her rich robe, the trail of peach blossoms against her cheek.

The ascent was long and steep, and they walked slowly, talking in a desultory fashion. Mariposa recounted the trivial incidents that had taken place in the Garcia house during her companion's absence. As they breasted the last hill the light grew brighter, for the sunset still lingered in a reluctant glow.

"Take my arm," said Barron. "You're out of breath."

She took it, and they began slowly to mount the last steep blocks. She glanced up at him to smile her thanks for his support, and met his eyes, looking intently at her. The red light strengthened on her face as they ascended.

"You've the strangest eyes," he said suddenly. "Do you know what they're the color of?"

"My father used to say they were like a dog's," she

answered, feeling unable to drop them and yet uneasy under his unflinching gaze.

"They're the color of sherry—exactly the same."

"I won't let you see them any more if that's the best you can say of them," she said, dropping them.

"I could say they were the color of beer," he answered, "but I thought sherry sounded better."

"Beer!" she exclaimed, averting not only her eyes, but her face. "That's an insult."

"Well, then, I'll only say in the simplest way what I think. I'm not the kind of man who makes fine speeches—they're the most beautiful eyes in the world."

"That's the worst of all," she answered, extremely confused and not made more comfortable by the thought that she had brought it on herself. "Let's leave my eyes out of the question."

"All right, I'll not speak of them again. But I'll want to see them now and then."

He saw her color mounting, and in the joy of her close proximity, loitering arm in arm up the sordid street, he laughed again in his happiness and said:

"When a person owns something that's rare and beautiful he oughtn't to be mean about it."

"I suppose not," said the owner of the rare and beautiful possessions, keeping them sternly out of sight.

He continued to look ardently at her, not conscious of what he was doing, his step growing slower and slower.

"It's a long climb," he said at length.

"Yes," she assented. "Is that why you're going so slowly?"

"Are we going so slowly?" he asked, and as if to demonstrate how slow had been their progress, they both came to a stop like a piece of run-down machinery.

They looked at each other for a questioning moment, then burst into simultaneous peals of laughter.

One of the last and daintiest charms that nature can give a woman is a lovely laugh. It suggests unexplored riches of tenderness and sweetness, unrevealed capacity for joy and pain, as a harsh and unmusical laugh tells of an arid nature, hard, without juice, devoid of imagination, mystery and passion. Like her mother before her, Mariposa possessed this charm in its highest form. The ripple of sound that flowed from her lips was music, and it cast a spell over the man at whose side she stood, as Lucy's laugh, twenty-five years before, had cast one over Dan Moreau.

"I never heard you laugh before," he said in delight. "What can I say to make you do it again?"

"You didn't say anything that time," said Mariposa. "So I suppose the best way is for you to be silent."

Barron took her advice and surveyed her mutely with dancing eyes. For a moment her lips, puckered into a tremulous pout, twitched with the premonitory symptoms of a second outburst. But she controlled them, moved by some perverse instinct of coquetry, while the laughter welled up in the eyes that were fixed on him.

"I see I'll have to make a joke," he said, "and I can't think of any."

"Mrs. Garcia's got a book full. You might borrow it."

"Couldn't you tell me one that's made you laugh before and loan it to me?"

"But it mightn't work a second time. I might take it quite solemnly. A sense of humor's a very capricious thing."

"I think the lady who's got it is even more so," he said.

And then once again they laughed in concert, foolishly and gaily and without knowing why.

They had gained the top of the hill, and the blaze of red that swept across the west shone on their faces. They were within a few minutes' walk of the house now and they continued, arm in arm, as was the custom of the day, and at the same loitering gait.

"Didn't you tell me your people came originally from Eldorado County, somewhere up near Hangtown?" he asked. "I've just been up that way, and if I'd known the place I might have stopped there."

"Oh, you never could have found it," said Mariposa hastily. "It was only a cabin miles back in the foothills. My mother often told me of it—just a cabin by a stream. It has probably disappeared now. My father and mother met and were married there among the mines, and—and—I was born there," she ended, stammeringly, hating the lies upon which her youthful traditions had been built.

"If I'd known you had been born there I'd have gone on a pilgrimage to find that cabin if it had taken a month."

"But I tell you it can't be standing yet. I'm twenty-four years old—" she suddenly realized that this, too, was part of the necessary web of misstatement in which she was caught. The color deepened on her face into a conscious blush. She dropped her eyes, then raising them to his with a curious defiance, said:

"No—that's a mistake. I'm—I'm—more than that, I'm twenty-five, nearly twenty-six."

Barron, who saw nothing in the equivocation but a girl's foolish desire to understate her age, burst into delighted laughter, and pressing the hand on his arm against his side, said:

"Why, I always thought you were *years* older than that—thirty to thirty-five at least."

And he looked with teasing eyes into her face. But this time Mariposa did not laugh, nor even smile. The joy had suddenly gone out of her, and she walked on in silence, her head drooped, seeming in some mysterious way to have grown suddenly anxious and preoccupied.

"There's the house," she said at length. "I was getting tired."

"There's a light in the parlor," said Barron, as he opened the gate. "What can be the matter? Has Benito killed grandma, or is there a party?"

Their doubts on this point were soon set at rest. Their approaching footsteps evidently were heard by a listening ear within, for the hall door opened and Benito appeared in the aperture.

"There's a man to see you in the parlor," he announced to Mariposa.

Inside the hallway the door on the left that led to Mrs. Garcia's apartments opened and the young woman thrust out her head, and said in a hissing whisper:

"There's a gentleman waiting for you in the parlor, Miss Moreau."

At the same time Miguel imparted similar information from the top of the stairs, and the Chinaman appeared at the kitchen door and cried from thence, with the laconic dryness peculiar to his race:

"One man see you, parlor."

Mariposa stood looking from one to the other with the raised eyebrows of inquiring astonishment. The only person who had visitors in the Garcia house was Pierpont, and they did not come at such a fashionably late hour.

"He's a thin, consumpted-looking young man with eye-glasses," said Mrs. Garcia, curling round the door the better to project the hissing whisper she employed, "and he said he'd wait till you came in."

Mariposa turned toward the parlor door, leaving the family, with Barron, on the stairs, and the Chinaman, peering from the kitchen regions, watching her with tense interest, as if they half expected they would never see her again.

Two of the gases in the old chandelier were lit and cast a sickly light over the large room, which had the close, musty smell of an unaired apartment. The last relics of Señora Garcia's grandeur were congregated here—bronzes that once had cost large sums of money, a gilt console that had been brought from a rifled French château round the Horn in a sailing ship, a buhl cabinet with its delicate silvery inlaying gleaming in the half-light, and two huge Japanese vases, with blue and white dragons crawling round their necks, flanking the fireplace.

On the edge of a chair, just under the chandelier, sat a young man. He had his hat in his hand, and his head drooped so that the light fell smoothly on the crown of blond hair. He looked small and meager in the surrounding folds of a very large and loose ulster. As the sound of the approaching step caught his ear he started and looked up, with the narrowed eyes of the near-sighted, and then jumped to his feet.

"Miss Moreau?" he said inquiringly, and extended a long, thin hand which, closing on hers, felt to her warm, soft grasp like a bunch of chilled sticks. She had not the slightest idea who he was, and looking at him under the wan light, saw he was some one from that world of wealth with which she had so few affiliations. Something about him—the coldness of his hand, an indescribable trepidation of manner—suggested to her that he was exceedingly ill at ease. She looked at him wonderingly, and said:

"Won't you sit down?"

He sat at her bidding on the chair he had risen from, subsiding into the small, shrunken figure in the middle of enveloping folds of overcoat. One hand hung down between his knees holding his hat. He looked at Mariposa and then looked down at the hat.

"Cold afternoon, isn't it?" he said.

"Very cold," she responded, "but I like it. I hope you haven't been waiting long."

"Not very," he looked up at her, blinking near-sightedly through the glasses; "I don't know whether you know what my name is, Miss Moreau? It's Shackleton—Winslow Shackleton. I forgot my card."

Mariposa felt a lightning-like change come over

her face, in which there was a sudden stiffening of her features into something hard and repellent. To Win, at that moment, she looked very like his father.

"Oh!" she said, hearing her voice drop at the end of the interjection with a note of vague disapproval and uneasiness.

"I've seen you," continued Win, "once at *The Trumpet* office, when you were there with Mrs. Willers. I don't think you saw me. I was back in the corner, near the table where Jack—that's the boy—sits."

Mariposa murmured:

"No, I didn't see you."

She hardly knew what he said or what she responded. What did *this* mean? What was going to happen now?

"You must excuse my coming this way, without an introduction or anything, but as you knew my father and mother, I—I—thought you wouldn't mind."

He glanced at her again, anxiously, she thought, and she said suddenly, with her habitual directness:

"Did you come from your mother?"

"No, I came on—on—my own hook. I wanted"—he looked vaguely about and then laid his hat on a table near him—"I wanted to see you on business of my own."

The nervousness from which he was evidently suffering began to communicate itself to Mariposa. The Shackleton family had come to mean everything that was painful and agitating to her, and here was a new one wanting to talk to her about business that she knew, past a doubt, was of some unusual character.

"If you've come to talk to me about going to Europe," she said desperately, "I may as well tell you, there's no use. I won't go to Paris now, as I once said I would, and there's no good trying to make me change my mind. Your mother and Mrs. Willers have both tried to, and it's very kind of them, but I— can't."

She had an expression at once of fright and determination. The subject was becoming a nightmare to her, and she saw herself attacked again from a strange quarter, and with, she imagined, a new set of arguments.

"It's nothing to do with going to Europe," he said. "It's—it's"—he put up one of the long, bony hands, and with the two first fingers pressed his glasses back against his eyes, then dropped the hand and stared at Mariposa, the eyes looking strangely pale and prominent behind the powerful lenses.

"It's something that's just between you and me," he said.

She surveyed him without answering, her brows drawn, her mind concentrated on him and on what he could mean.

"Do you want me to teach somebody music?" she said, wondering if this could be the pleasant solution of the enigma.

"No. The—er—the business I've come to talk to you about ought to do away altogether with the necessity of your giving lessons."

They looked at each other silently for a moment. Win was conscious that his hands were trembling, and that his mouth was dry. He rose from his chair and mechanically reached for his hat. When he had started on his difficult errand he had been certain that she knew her relationship to his father. Now the dreadful thought entered his mind that perhaps she did not. And even if she did, it was evident that she was not going to give him the least help.

"What *is* the business you've come to see me about?" she asked.

"It's a question of money," he answered.

"Money!" ejaculated Mariposa, in baffled amaze. "What money? Why?"

He glanced desperately into his hat and then back at her. She saw the hat trembling in his hand and suddenly realized that this man was trying to say something that was agitating him to the marrow of his being.

"Mr. Shackleton," she said, rising to her feet, "tell me what you mean. I don't understand. I'm completely at sea. How can there be any question of money between us when I've never seen you or met you before? Explain it all."

He dropped the hat to his side and said slowly, looking her straight in the face:

"I want to give you a share of the estate left me by my father. I look upon it as yours."

There was a pause. He saw her paling under his gaze, and realized that, whatever she might pretend, she knew. His heart bled for her.

"As mine!" she said in a low, uncertain voice. "Why?"

"Because you have a right to it."

There was another pause. He moved close to her and said, in a voice full of a man's deep kindness:

"I can't explain any more. Don't ask it. Don't let's bother about anything in the background. It's just the present that's our affair."

He suddenly dropped his hat and took her hand. It was as cold now as his had been. He pressed it, and Mariposa, looking dazedly at him, saw a gleam like tears behind the glasses.

"It's hateful to have you living here like this, while we—that is, while other people—have everything. I can't stand it. It's too mean and unfair. I want you to share with me."

She shook her head, looking down, a hundred thoughts bursting in upon her brain. What did he know? How had he found it out? In his grasp, her hand trembled pitifully.

"Don't shake your head," he pleaded, "it's so hard to say it. Don't turn it down before you've heard me out."

"And it's hard to hear it," she murmured.

"No one knows anything of this but me," he continued, "and I promise you that no other ever shall. It'll be just between us as between"—he paused and then added with a voice that was husky—"as between brother and sister."

She shook her head again, feeling for the moment too upset to speak, and tried to draw away from him. But he put his other hand on her shoulder and held her.

"I'll go halves with you. I can have it all arranged so that no one will ever find out. I can't make the regular partition of the property until the end of the year. But, until then, I'll send you what would be your interest, monthly, and you can live where, or how, you like. I—I—can't go on, knowing things, and thinking of you living in this sort of way and teaching music."

"I can't do it," she said, in a strangled undertone, and pulling her hand out of his grasp. "I can't. It's not possible. I can't take money that was your father's."

"But it's not his—it's mine now. Don't let what's dead and buried come up and interfere."

She backed away from him, still shaking her head. She made an effort toward a cold composure, but her pain seemed to show more clearly through it. He looked at her, vexed, irresolute, wrung with pity, that he knew she would not permit him to express.

It was impossible for them to understand each other. She, with her secret knowledge of her mother's lawful claim and her own legitimacy—he regarding her as the wronged child of his father's sin. In her dazed distress she only half-grasped what he thought. The strongest feeling she had was once again to escape the toils that these terrible people, who had so wronged her mother, were spreading for her. They wanted to pay her to redeem the stain on their past.

"Money can't set right what was wrong," she said. "Money can't square things between your family and mine."

"Money can't square anything—I don't want it to. I'm not trying to square things; I've not thought about it that way at all. I just wanted you to have it because it seemed all wrong for you not to. You had a right, just as I had, and Maud had. I don't think I've thought much about it, anyway. It just came to me that you ought to have what was yours. I wouldn't make you feel bad for the world."

"Then remember, once and forever, that I take nothing from you or your people. I'd rather beg than take money that came from your father."

"But he has nothing to do with it. It's mine now. I've done you no injury, and it's I that want you to take it. Won't you take it from me?"

He spoke simply, almost wistfully, like a little boy. Mariposa answered:

"No—oh, Mr. Shackleton, why don't you and your people let me alone? I won't tell. I'll keep it all a secret. But your mother torments me to go to Europe —and now you come! If I were starving, I wouldn't —I couldn't—take anything from any of you. I think *you're* kind. I think you've just come to-day because you were sorry. But don't talk about it any more. Let me be. Let me go along teaching here where I belong. Forget me. Forget that you ever saw me. Forget the miserable tie of blood there is between us."

"That's the thing I can't forget. That's the thing that worries me. It's not the past. I've nothing to do with that. It's the present that's my affair. I can't have everything while you have nothing. It don't seem to me it's like a man to act that way. It goes against me, anyhow. I don't offer you this because of anything in the past; that's my father's affair. I don't know anything about it. I offer it because I—I—I"— he stammered over the unfamiliar words and finally jerked out—"because I want to give back what belongs to you. That's all there is to it. Please take it."

She looked directly into his eyes and said, gravely:

"No. I'm sorry if it's a disappointment, but I can't."

Then she suddenly looked down, her face began to quiver, and she said in a broken undertone:

"Don't talk about it any more; it hurts me so."

Win turned quickly away from her and picked up his hat. He was confused and disappointed, and relieved, too, for he had done the most difficult piece of work of his life. But, at the moment, his most engrossing feeling was sympathy for this girl, so bravely drawing her pride together over the bleeding of her heart.

She murmured a response in a steadier voice and he turned toward her. Had any of his society friends been by they would hardly have known him. The foolish manner behind which he sheltered his shy and sensitive nature was gone. He was grave and looked very much of a man.

"Well, of course, it's for you to say what you want. But there's one thing I'd like you to promise."

"To promise?" she said uneasily.

"Yes, and to keep it, too. And that is, if you ever want anything—help in any way; if you get blue in your spirits, or some one's not doing the straight thing by you, or gone back on you—to come to me. I'm not much in some ways, but I guess I could be of use. And, anyway, it's good for a girl to have some friend that she can count on, who's a man. And"—he paused with the door-handle in his hand—"and now you know me, anyway, and that's something. Will you promise?"

"Yes, I'll promise that," said Mariposa, and moving toward him she gave him her hand.

He pressed it, dropped it, and opened the door. A moment later Mariposa heard the hall door bang behind him. She sat down in the chair from which she had risen, her hands lying idle in her lap, her eyes on a rose in the carpet, trying to think, to understand what it meant.

She did not hear the door open or notice Benito's entrance, which was accomplished with some disturbance, as he was astride a cane. His spirited course round the room, the end of the cane coming in violent contact with the pieces of furniture that impeded his route, was of so boisterous a nature that it roused her. She looked absently at him, and saw him wreathed in smiles. Having gained her attention, he brought his steed toward her with some ornamental prancings. She noticed that he held a pair of gloves in his hands.

"That man what came to see you," he said, "left this cane. It was in the hat-rack, and I came out first, so I swiped it. I took these for Miguel"—he flourished the gloves—"but the cane's mine all right. Come in to supper."

And he wheeled away with a bridling step, the end of his cane rasping on the worn ribs of the carpet. Mariposa, mechanically following him, heard his triumphant cries as he entered the dining-room and then his sudden wails of wrath as Miguel expressed his disapprobation of the division of the spoils in the vigorous manner of innocent childhood.

CHAPTER XVIII

WITH ME TO HELP

"Look in my face, my name is—Might Have Been!
I am also called, No More, Too Late, Farewell."
—ROSETTI.

Had Essex realized that Mrs. Willers was an adverse agent in his suit of Mariposa, he would not have greeted her with the urbane courteousness that marked their meetings. He was a man of many manners, and he never would have wasted one of his best on the newspaper woman, to him essentially uninteresting and unattractive, unless he had intended thereby to further his own ends. Mrs. Willers he knew to be a friend of Mariposa's, and he thought it a wise policy to keep in her good graces. He made that mistake, so often the undoing of those who are unscrupulous and clever, of not crediting Mrs. Willers with her full amount of brains. He had seen her foolish side, and he knew that she was a good journalist of the hustling, energetic, unintellectual type, but he saw no deeper.

Since their meeting in the park and her unequivocal rejection of him his feeling for Mariposa had augmented in force and fire until it had full possession of him. He was of the order of men whom easy conquests cool. Now added to the girl's own change of front was the overwhelming inducement of the wealth she represented. His original idea of Mariposa as a handsome mistress that he would take to France and there put on the operatic stage, of whom he would be the proud owner, while they toured Europe together, her voice and beauty charming kings, had been abandoned since the night of his talk with Harney. He would marry her, and, with her completely under his dominion, he would turn upon the Shackleton estate and make her claim. He supposed her to be in entire ignorance of her parentage, and his first idea had been to marry her and not lighten this ignorance till she was safely in his power. He had a fear of her shrinking before the hazards of the enterprise, but he was confident that, once his, all scruples, timidity and will would give way before him.

But her refusal of him had upset these calculations, and her coldness and repugnance had been as oil to the flame of his passion. He was enraged with himself and with her. He thought of the night in the cottage and cursed himself for his precipitation, and his gods for the ill luck that, too late, had revealed to him her relationship to the dead millionaire. At first he had thought the offer of marriage would obliterate all unpleasant memories. But her manner that day in the park had frightened him. It was not the haughty manner, adopted to conceal hidden fires, of the woman who still loves. There had been a chill poise about her that suggested complete withdrawal from his influence.

Since then he had cogitated much. He foresaw

that it was going to be very difficult to see and have speech of her. An occasional walk up Third Street to Sutter with Mrs. Willers kept him informed of her movements and doings. Had he guessed that Mrs. Willers, with her rouge higher up on one cheek than the other, the black curls of her bang sprawlingly pressed against her brow by a spotted veil, was quite conversant with his pretensions and their non-success, he would have been more guarded in his exhibition of interest. As it was, Mrs. Willers wrote to Mariposa after one of these walks in which Essex's questions had been carelessly numerous and frank, and told her that he was still "camped on her trail, and for goodness' sake not to weaken." Mariposa tore up the letter with an angry ejaculation.

"Not to weaken!" she said to herself. If she had only dared to tell Mrs. Willers the whole instead of half the truth!

The difficulty of seeing Mariposa was further intensified by the fullness of his own days. He had little time to spare. The new proprietor worked his people for all there was in them and paid them well. Several times on the regular weekly holiday the superior men on *The Trumpet* were given, he loitered along streets where she had been wont to pass. But he never saw her. The chance that had favored him that once in the park was not repeated. Mrs. Willers said she was very busy. Essex began to wonder if she suspected him of lying in wait for her and was taking her walks along unfrequented byways.

Finally, after Christmas had passed and he had still not caught a glimpse of her, he determined to see her in the only way that seemed possible. He had inherited certain traditions of good breeding from his mother, and it offended this streak of delicacy and decency that was still faintly discernible in his character to intrude upon a lady who had so obviously shown a distaste for his society. But there was nothing else for it. Interests that were vital were at stake. Moreover, his desire, for love's sake, to see her again was overmastering. Her face came between him and his work. There were nights when he stood opposite the Garcia house watching for her shadow on the blind.

He timed his visit at an hour when, according to the information extracted from Mrs. Willers, Mariposa's last pupil for the day should have left. He loitered about at the corner of the street and saw the pupil—one of the grown-up ones in a sealskin sack and a black Gainsborough hat—open the gate and sweep majestically down the street. Then he strode from his coign of vantage, stepped lightly up the stairs, and rang the bell.

It was after school hours, and Benito opened the door. Essex, in his silk hat and long, dark overcoat, tall and distinguished, was so much more impressive a figure than Win that the little boy stared at him in overawed surprise, and only found his breath when the stranger demanded Miss Moreau.

"Yes, she's in," said Benito, backing away toward the stairs; "I'll call her. She has quite a lot of callers sometimes," he hazarded pleasantly.

The door near by opened a crack, and a female

voice issued therefrom in a suppressed tone of irritation.

"Benito, why don't you show the gentleman into the parlor?"

"He'll go in if he wants," said Benito, who evidently had decided that the stranger knew how to take care of himself; "that's the door; just open it and go in."

Essex, who was conscious that the eye which pertained to the voice was surveying him intently through the crack, did as he was bidden and found himself in the close, musty parlor. It was late in the afternoon, and the long lace curtains draped over the windows obscured the light. He wanted to see Mariposa plainly and he looped the curtains back against the brass hooks. His heart was beating hard with expectation. As he turned round to look at the door he noticed that the key was in the lock, and resolved, with a sense of grim determination, that if she tried to go when she saw who it was, he could be before her and turn the key.

Upstairs Benito had found Mariposa sitting in front of the fire. She had been giving lessons most of the day and was tired. She stretched herself like a sleepy cat as he came in, and put her hand up to her hair, pushing in the loosened hairpins.

"It's some one about lessons, I guess," she said, rising and giving a hasty look in the glass. "At this rate, Ben, I'll soon be rich."

"What'll we do then?" said Benito, clattering to the stairhead beside her.

"We'll buy a steam yacht, just you and I, and travel round the world. And we'll stop in all sorts of strange countries and ride on elephants and buy parrots, and shoot tigers and go up in balloons and do everything that's dangerous and interesting."

She was in good spirits at the prospect of a new pupil, and, with her hand on the door-knob, threw Benito a farewell smile, which was still on her lips as she entered.

It remained there for a moment, for at the first glance she did not recognize Essex, who was standing with his back to the panes of the unveiled windows; then he moved toward her and she saw who it was.

She gave a smothered exclamation and drew back.

"Mr. Essex!" she said; "why do you come here?"

He had intended to meet her with his customary half impudent, half cajoling suavity, but found that he could not. The sight of her filled him with fiery agitation.

"I came because I couldn't keep away," he said, advancing with his hand out.

"No," she said, glancing at the hand and turning her head aside with an impatient movement; "there can't be any pretenses at friendship between us. I don't want to shake hands with you. I don't want to see you. What did you come for?"

"To see you. I had to see you."

His eyes, fixed on her as she stood in the light of the window, seemed to italicize the words of the sentence.

"There's no use beginning that subject again," she

said hurriedly; "there's no use talking about those things."

"What things? What are you referring to?"

For a moment she felt the old helpless feeling coming over her, but she forced it aside and said, looking steadily at him:

"The things we talked about in the park the last time we met."

She saw his dark face flush. He was too much in earnest now to be able to assert his supremacy by teasing equivocations.

"Nevertheless, I've come to-day to repeat those things."

"Don't—don't," she said quickly; "there's no use. I won't listen to them. It's not polite to intrude into a lady's house and try to talk about subjects she detests."

"The time has passed for us to be polite or impolite," he answered hotly; "we're not the man and woman as society and the world has made them. We're the man and woman as they are and have always been from the beginning. We're not speaking to each other through the veils of conventionality; we're speaking face to face. We have hearts and souls and passions. We've loved each other."

"Never," she said; "never for a moment."

"You have a bad memory," he answered slowly; "is it natural or cultivated?"

He had the satisfaction of seeing her color rise. The sight sent a thrill of hope through him. He moved nearer to her and said in a voice that vibrated with feeling:

"You loved me once."

"No, never, never. It was never that."

"Then why," he answered, his lips trying to twist themselves into a sardonic smile, while rage possessed him, "why did you—let us say—encourage me so that night in the cottage on Pine Street?"

Though her color burned deeper, her eyes did not drop. He had never seen her dominating her own girlish impulses like this. It seemed to remove her thousands of miles from the circle of his power.

"I'll tell you," she answered; "I was lonely and miserable, and you seemed the only creature that I had to care for. I thought you were fond of me, and I thought it was wonderful that any one as clever as you could really care for me. That you regarded me as you did I could no more have imagined than I could have suspected you of picking my pocket or murdering me. And that night in the cottage, when in my loneliness and distress I seemed to be holding out my arms to you, asking you to protect and comfort me, you laughed at me and struck me a blow in the face. It was the end of my dream. I wakened then and saw the reality. But you—you as you are—as I know you now—I never loved, I never could have loved."

Her words inflamed his rage, not alone against her, but against himself, who had had her in this pliant mood in his very arms and had lost her.

"And was it only a desire for consolation and sympathy that made you behave toward me in what was hardly—a—" he paused as if hesitating for a word that would in a seemly manner express his thought, in reality racking his brains for the one that would hurt her most—"hardly a maidenly way considering your lack of interest in me?"

The word he had chosen told. Her color sank suddenly away, leaving her very pale. Her face seemed to stiffen and lose its youthful curves.

"I don't think," she said slowly, "that it's necessary to continue this conversation. It doesn't seem to me to be very profitable to anybody."

She looked at him, but he made no movement.

"You will have to excuse me, Mr. Essex," she said, moving toward the door, "but if you won't go I must."

The expected had happened. He sprang before her and locked the door. Leaning his back against it, he stared at her. Both were now very pale.

"No," he said, hearing his own voice shaken by his rapid breathing, "you're not going. I've not said half I came to say. I've not come to-day to plead and sue like a beggar for the love that you're ready to give one day and take back the next. I've other things to talk about."

"Open the door," she commanded; "open the door and let me out. I want to hear nothing that you have to say."

"Don't you want to hear who you are?" he asked.

The words passed through Mariposa like a current of electricity. Every nerve in her body seemed to tighten. She looked at him, staring and repeating:

"Hear who I am?"

"Yes," he said, leaning toward her while one hand still gripped the door-handle; "hear what your real name is, and who you are? Hear who your father was and where you were born?"

Her face blanched under his eyes. The sight pleased him, suggesting as it did weakness and fear that would give him back his old ascendancy. Horror invaded her. He, of all people on earth, to know! She could say nothing; could hardly think; only seemed a thing of ears to hear.

"Hear who my father was!" she repeated, this time almost in a whisper.

"Yes; I can tell you all that, and more, too. I've got a wonderfully interesting story for you. You'll not want to go when I begin. Sit down."

"What do you know? Tell me quickly."

"Don't be impatient. It's a long story. It begins on the Nevada desert. That's where you were born; not in the cabin in Eldorado County, as I heard you telling Jake Shackleton that day at Mrs. Willers'."

He was watching her like a tiger, still standing with his back against the door. Her eyes were on him, wild and intent. Each word fell like a drop of vitriol on her brain. She saw that he knew everything.

"Your mother was Lucy Fraser, but your father was not Dan Moreau. He was a very different man, and you were his eldest child, his eldest and only legitimate child. Do you know what his name was?"

"Yes," said Mariposa in a low voice; "Jake Shackleton."

It was Essex's turn to be amazed. He stared at her, speechless, completely staggered.

"DON'T YOU WANT TO HEAR WHO YOU ARE?"

"You know it?" he cried, starting forward toward her; "you know it?"

"Yes," she answered; "I know it."

He stood glaring, trying to collect his senses and grasp in one whirling moment what difference her knowledge would make to him.

"How—how—did you know it?" he stammered.

"That's not of any consequence. I know that I am Jake Shackleton's eldest living child; that my mother was married twice; that I was born in the desert instead of in Eldorado County. I know it all. And what is there so odd about that?" She threw her head up and looked with baffling coldness into his eyes. "Why shouldn't I know my own parentage and birthplace?"

"And—and—" he continued to speak with eager unsteadiness—"you've done nothing yet?"

"Done nothing yet," she repeated; "what should I do?"

"That's all right," he said hastily, evidently relieved; "you couldn't do anything alone. There must be some one to help you."

"Help me do what?"

Both had forgotten the quarrel, the locked door, the fever pitch of ten minutes earlier. All other thoughts had been crowded out of Mariposa's mind by the horrible discovery of Essex's knowledge, and by the apprehensions that were cold in her heart. She shrank from him more than ever, but had no desire now to leave the room. Instead, she persisted in her remark:

"Help me do what? I don't know what you mean."

"Help you in establishing your claim. And fate has put into my hands the very person, the one person who can do that. You know there was a man who was in the cabin with Moreau—a partner. Did you ever hear of him?"

She nodded, swallowing dryly. Her sense of apprehension strengthened with his every word.

"Well, I have that man under my hand. He and Mrs. Shackleton are the only living witnesses of the transaction whereby your mother and you passed into Moreau's keeping. And I have him. I've got him here." He made a gesture with his thumb as though pressing the ball of it down on something. Then he looked at Mariposa with eyes full of an eager cupidity.

She did not respond with the show of interest he had expected, but stood looking down, pale and motionless. Her brain was in an appalled chaos from which stood out only a few facts. This terrible man knew her secret—the secret of her mother's life and honor—that she would have died to hide in the sacredness of her love for the dead man and woman who could no longer defend themselves.

"It seems as if fate had sent me to help you," he went on; "you couldn't do it alone."

"Do what?" she asked without moving.

"Establish your claim as the real heir. Of course you're the chief heir. I've been looking it up. The others will get a share as acknowledged children. But you ought to get the bulk of the fortune as the only legitimate child."

"Establish my claim?" she repeated. "Do you mean, prove that I'm Jake Shackleton's daughter?"

"Yes. And there's a tremendously important point. Did your mother have papers or letters showing that she had been Shackleton's wife?"

"She left her marriage certificate," she said dully, hardly conscious of her words. "I have it."

"Here?—by you?" with quick curiosity.

"Yes; upstairs—in my little desk."

"Ah," he said, with almost a laugh of relief. "That settles it. You with the certificate and I with Harney! Why, we've got them."

"We?" she said, looking up as though waking. "We?"

"Yes; we," he answered.

He had come close to her and, standing at her side, bent his head in order to look more directly into her face.

"This ought to put an end, dear, to your objections," he said gently; "you can't do it alone. No woman could, much less one like you—young, inexperienced, ignorant of the world. You've got no idea what a big contest like this means. There must be a man to help you, and I must be that man, Mariposa. We can marry quietly as soon as you are ready. It would be better not to make any move until after that, as it would be much easier for me to conduct the campaign as your husband than as your fiancé. I'd take the whole thing off your shoulders. You'd have almost nothing to do, except be certain of your memories and dates, and I'd see to it that you were letter perfect in that when the time came. I'd stand between you and everything that was disagreeable."

He took her hand, which for the moment was passive in his.

"When will it be?" he said, giving it a gentle squeeze; "when, sweetheart?"

She tore her hand away.

"Why, you're crazy," she cried. "There'll never be any of it. Never be any claim made or contest, or anything that you talk of. You want me to make money out of my mother's story that was a tragedy—that I can hardly think of myself! Oh!—" She turned around, speechless, and put her hand to her mouth.

She thought of her dying mother, and grief for that smitten soul, so deeply loved, so tenderly loving, rent her with a throe of pity, poignant as bodily pain.

"Your mother is dead," he said, understanding her and feeling some real sympathy for her. "It can't hurt her now."

"Drag it all out into the light," she went on. "Fight in a court with those horrible Shackletons! Have it in the papers and all the mean, low people in California, who couldn't for one moment understand anything that was pure and noble, jeering and talking over my father and mother! That's what you call establishing my claim, isn't it?"

"That's not all of it," he stammered, taken aback by her violence. "And, anyway, it's all true."

"Well, then, I'll lie and say it was false. If it came to fighting I'd say it was false. That I was not Jake Shackleton's daughter, and that my mother never knew him, or saw him, or heard of him. I'd burn that certificate and say there never was such a thing, and that anybody who suggested it was a liar or a madman. And when it comes to you, there's just one thing to say: I wouldn't marry you if forty fortunes hung on it. I'd rather beg or steal than be your wife if you owned all the Comstock mines. That's the future you think is going to tempt me—you for a husband and a fortune for us both, made by proving that my mother was never really married to the man I called my father!"

"But—but," he said, not heeding her anger in his bewildered amazement, "you intended it sooner or later yourself?"

"I?—I?—Betray my parents for money? *I* do that?"

She stared at him, with eyes of wild indignation. He began to have a cold comprehension of what she felt, and it shook him as violently as his passion for her had ever done.

"But you don't understand," he cried. "This is not a matter of thousands; it's millions, and it's yours by right. It's a colossal fortune here in your hand— yours almost for the asking."

"It will never be mine. I wouldn't have it. Oh, let me go! This is too horrible."

"Wait—just one moment. If it came to an actual suit it might be painful and trying for you. But how if I can arrange a compromise with Mrs. Shackleton? I think I can. When she knows that you have the proofs of the marriage she'll be glad enough to settle. She doesn't want these things to come out any more than you do. She's a smart woman, and she'll know that your silence is the most valuable thing she can buy. Do you understand?"

"I understand just one thing."

"What's that?"

"You."

For the second time they looked at each other for a motionless, deep-breathing moment. There was nothing in their faces or attitudes that suggested lovers. They looked like a pair of antagonists at pause in their struggle—on the alert for a continuance of battle.

"Yes, I understand you now," she said in a low voice; "you've made me understand you."

"I only want to make you understand one thing—how much I love you."

She drew back with a movement of violent repugnance. He suddenly stretched out his arms and came toward her.

She ran toward the door, for the moment forgetting it was locked. Then, as it resisted, memory awoke. He was beside her and tried to take her in his arms, but she turned and struck him, with all her force, a blow on the face. She saw the skin redden under it.

"Open the door!" she gasped; "open the door!"

For the moment the blow so stunned and enraged him that he drew back from her, his hand instinctively rising to the smarting skin. An oath burst from his compressed mouth.

"I'd like to kill you for that," he said.

"Open the door," she almost shrieked, rattling the handle.

"I'll pay you for this. You seem to forget that I know all the disreputable secrets of your beginnings. I can tell all the world how your mother was sold to Dan Moreau, and how—"

Mariposa heard the click of the gate and a step on the outside stairs. She drowned the sound of Essex's voice in a sudden furious pounding on the door, while she cried with the full force of her lungs:

"Benito! Miguel! Mrs. Garcia!—Come and open this door! Come and let me out! I'm locked in! Come!"

Essex was at the door in an instant, the key in the lock. As he turned it he gave her a murderous look.

"You fool!" he said under his breath.

As the portal swung open and he passed into the hall, the front door was violently pushed inward, and Barron almost fell against him in the hurry of his entrance.

The new-comer drew back from the departing stranger with an apologetic start.

"Beg your pardon," he said bruskly, "but I thought I heard some one scream in here."

"Scream?" said Essex, languidly selecting his hat from the disreputable collection on the rack; "I didn't notice it, and I've been sitting in there for nearly an hour with Miss Moreau. I fancy you've made a mistake."

"I guess I must have. It's odd."

The hall door slammed behind Essex, and the other man turned into the parlor, where the light was now very dim. In his exit from the room Essex had flung the door open with violence, and Mariposa, who had backed against the wall, was still standing behind it. As Barron pushed it to he saw her, a vague black figure with white hands and face, in the dark.

"What on earth are you doing there?" he said; "standing behind the door like a child in the corner."

She thanked heaven for the friendly dark and answered hurriedly:

"I—I—I—didn't want you to catch me. I'm so—so—untidy."

"Untidy? I never saw you untidy, and don't believe you ever were. I met a man in the hall, who said he'd been here for an hour. You must have been playing puss in the corner with him."

"Yes; his name's Essex, and he's a friend of Mrs. Willers' that I know. He was here, and I thought he'd come about music lessons, so I came down looking rather untidy. That was how it happened."

"And he stayed an hour talking about music lessons?"

"No—oh, no; other things."

They turned into the hall, Barron, in his character of general guardian of the Garcia fortunes, shutting the door of the state apartment. He had the appearance of taking no notice of Mariposa, but as soon as he got into the light of the hall gas he sent a lightning-like glance over her face.

"It was funny," he said, "but as I came up the steps I thought I heard some one calling out. I dashed in and fell into the arms of your music-lesson man, who said no cries of any kind had disturbed the joy of his hour in your society."

Mariposa had begun to ascend the stairs.

"Cries?" she said over her shoulder; "I don't think there were any cries. Why should any one cry out here?"

"That's exactly what I wanted to know," he said, watching her ascending back.

She turned and passed out of sight at the top of the stairs. Barron stood below under the hall gas, his head drooped. He was puzzled, for, say what they might, he was certain he had heard cries.

CHAPTER XIX

NOT MADE IN HEAVEN

"Women are like tricks by sleight of hand
Which to admire we should not understand."
—Congreve.

At *The Trumpet* office the next morning Essex found a letter awaiting him. It was from Mrs. Shackleton, asking him to dinner on a certain evening that week—"very informally, Mr. Essex would understand, as the family was in such deep mourning."

Essex turned the letter over, smiling to himself. It was an admirable testimony to Bessie's capability. Her monogram, gilded richly, adorned the top of the sheet of cream-laid paper, and beneath it, in a fine running hand, were the few carefully-worded sentences, and then the signature—Bessie A. Shackleton. It was a remarkable letter, considering all things; wonderful testimony to that adaptive cleverness which is the birthright of Bessie's countrywomen. In her case this care of externals had not been a haphazard acquirement. She was not the woman to be slipshod or trust to the tutoring of experience. When her husband's star had begun to rise with such dazzling effulgence she had hired teachers for herself, as well as those for Maud, and there were many books of etiquette on the shelves in her boudoir.

The letter contained more for Essex than a simple invitation to dinner. It was the first move of the Shackleton faction in the direction he desired to see them take. Bessie had evidently heard something that had made her realize he, too, might be more than a pawn in the game. He answered the note with a sentence of acceptance and a well-turned phrase, expressing his pleasure at the thought of meeting her again.

He was not in an agreeable frame of mind. His interview with Mariposa had roused the sleeping devil within him, which, of late, had only been drowsy. His worst side—ugly traits inherited from his rascally father—was developing with overmastering force. Lessons learned in those obscure and unchronicled years when he had swung between London and Paris were beginning to bear fruit. At the blow from Mariposa a crop of red-veined passions had burst into life and grown with the speed of Jack's beanstalk. His face burned with the memory of that blow. When he recalled its stinging impact, he did not know whether he loved or hated Mariposa most. But his determination to force her to marry him strengthened with her openly expressed abhorrence. The memory of her face as she struck at him was constantly before his mental vision, and his fury seethed to the point of a still, level-brimming tensity, when he recalled the fear and hatred in it.

The dinner at Mrs. Shackleton's was a small and informal one. The company of six—for, besides himself, the only guests were the Count de Lamolle and

Pussy Thurston—looked an exceedingly meager array in the vast drawing-room, whose stately proportions were rendered even larger by mirrors which rose from the floor to the cornice, elongating the room by many shadowy reflections. A small fire burned at each end, under mantels of Mexican onyx, and these two little palpitating hearts of heat were the brightest spots in the spacious apartment where even Miss Thurston's dress of pale-blue gauze seemed to melt into the effacing shadows.

The Count de Lamolle gave Essex a quick glance, and, as they stood together in front of one of the fires —the two girls and Win having moved away to look at a painting of Bouguereau's on an easel—addressed a casual remark to him in French. The count had already met the newspaper man, and set him down, without illusion or hesitation, as a clever adventurer. He overcame his surprise at meeting him in the house of the bonanza widow, by the reflection that this was the United States where all men are equal, and women with money free to be wooed by any of them.

The count was in an uncertain and almost uncomfortable state of mind. The letter he had received from Mrs. Shackleton, bidding him to the feast, was the second from her since Maud's rejection of him. The first had been of a consolatory and encouraging nature. Mrs. Shackleton told him that Maud was young, and that many women said no, when they meant yes. The count knew both these things as well as Mrs. Shackleton; the latter, even better. But it seemed to him that Maud, young though she was, had not meant yes, and the handsome Frenchman was not the man to force his attentions on any woman. He watched her without appearing to notice her. She had been greatly embarrassed at sight of him, and only for the briefest moment let her cold fingers touch his palm. Under the flood of light from the dining-room chandelier she looked plainer than ever; her lack of color and stolid absence of animation being even more noticeable than usual in contrast with the brilliant pink and white prettiness of Pussy Thurston, who chattered gaily with everybody, and attempted a little French with De Lamolle.

Maud sat beside Essex, and even that easily fluent gentleman found her difficult to interest. She appeared dull and unresponsive. Looking at her with slightly narrowed eyes, he wondered how the count, of whose name and exploits he had often heard in Paris, could contemplate so brave an act as marrying her.

The count, who, having more heart, could see deeper, asked himself if the girl was really unhappy. As he listened to Miss Thurston's marvelous French he wondered, with a little expanding heat of irritation, if the mother was trying to force the marriage against the daughter's wish. He had broken hearts in his day, but it was not a pastime he found agreeable. He was too gallant a gentleman to woo where his courtship was unwelcome.

When the gentlemen entered the drawing-room from their after-dinner wine and cigars, they found the ladies seated by one of the fires below the Mexican onyx mantels. Bessie rose as they approached and, turning to Essex, asked him if he had seen the Bouguereau on the easel, and steered him toward it.

"It was one of Mr. Shackleton's last purchases," she said; "he was very anxious to have a fine collection. He had great taste."

Her companion, looking at the plump, pearly-skinned nymph and her attendant cupids, thought of Harney's description of Shackleton in the days when he had first entered California, and said, with conviction:

"What a remarkably versatile man your husband was! I had no idea he was interested in art."

"Oh, he loved it," said Bessie, "and knew a great deal about it. We were in Europe two years ago for six months, and Mr. Shackleton and I visited a great many studios. That is a Meissonier over there, and that one we bought from Rosa Bonheur. She's an interesting woman, looked just like a man. Then in the Moorish room there's a Gérôme. Would you like to see it? It's considered a very fine example."

He expressed his desire to see the Gérôme, and followed Bessie's rustling wake into the Moorish room. The little room was warm, with its handful of fire, and softly lit with chased and perforated lanterns of bronze and brass. The heat had drawn the perfume from the bowls full of roses and violets that stood about and the air was impregnated with their sweetness. The Gérôme, a scene in the interior of a harem, with a woman dancing, stood on an easel in one corner.

"That's it," said Bessie, drawing to one side that he might see it better. "One on the same sort of subject was in the studio when we first went there, but Mr. Shackleton thought it was too small, and this was painted to order."

"Superb," murmured Essex; "Gérôme at his best."

"We hoped," continued Bessie, sinking into a seat, "to have a fine collection, and build a gallery for them out in the garden. There was plenty of room, and they would have shown off better all together that way, rather than scattered about like this. But I've no ambition to do it now, and they'll stay as they are."

"Why don't you go on with the collection?" said the young man, taking a seat on a square stool of carved teak wood. "It would be a most interesting thing to do, and you could go abroad every year or two, and go to the studios and buy direct from the artists. It's much the best way."

"Oh, I couldn't," she said, with a little shrug; "I don't know enough about it. I only know what I like, and I generally like the wrong thing. I'm not versatile like my husband. When I first came to California I didn't know a chromo from an oil painting. In fact," she said, looking at him frankly and laughing a little, "I don't think I'd ever seen an oil painting."

Essex returned the laugh and murmured a word or two of complimentary disbelief. He was wondering when she would get to the real subject of conversation which had led them to the Gérôme and the Moorish room. She was nearer than he thought.

"It would be a temptation to go to Paris every year or two," she said. "That's the most delightful place in the world. It's your home, isn't it? So, of course, you agree with me."

"Yes, I was born there, and have lived there off and on ever since. To me, there is only one Paris."

"And can you fancy any one having the chance to go there, and live and study, with no trouble about money, refusing?"

Essex looked into the fire, and responded in a tone that suggested polite indifference:

"No, that's quite beyond my powers of imagination."

"I have a sort of—I think you call it protégée—isn't that the word?—yes"—in answer to his nod—"whom I want to send to Paris. She's a young girl with a fine voice. Mr. Shackleton was very much interested in her. He knew her father in the mining days of the early fifties and wanted to pay off some old scores by helping the daughter. And now the daughter seems to dislike being helped."

"There are such people," said Essex in the same tone. "Does she dislike the idea of going to Paris, too?"

"That seems to be it. We both wanted to send her there, have her voice trained, and put her in the way of becoming a singer. Lepine, when he was here, heard her and thought she had the making of a prima donna. But," she suddenly looked at him with a half-puzzled expression of inquiry, "I think you know her—Miss Moreau?"

Essex looked back at her for a moment with bafflingly expressionless eyes.

"Yes, I know her. She's a friend of Mrs. Willers's, one of the Sunday edition people on *The Trumpet*. A very handsome and charming girl."

"That's the girl," said Bessie, mentally admiring

his perfect aplomb. "She's a very fine girl, and, as you say, handsome. But I don't think she's got much common sense. Girls don't, as a rule, have more than enough to get along on. But when they're poor, and so alone in the world, they ought to pick up a little."

"Certainly, to refuse an offer such as you speak of, argues a lack of something. Have you any idea of her reason for refusing?"

He looked at Bessie as he propounded the question, his eyelids lowered slightly. She, in her turn, let her keen gray glance rest on him. The thought flashed through her mind that it was only another evidence of Mariposa's peculiarity of disposition that she should have refused so handsome and attractive a man.

"No—" she said with unruffled placidity, "I don't understand it. She's a proud girl and objects to being under obligations. But then this wouldn't be an obligation. Apart from everything else, there's no question about obligations where singers and artists and people like that are concerned. It's all a matter of art."

"Art levels all things," said the young man glibly.

"That's what I always thought. But Miss Moreau doesn't seem to agree with me. The most curious part of it all is that she was willing to go in the beginning. That was before her mother died; then she suddenly changed her mind, wouldn't hear of it, and said she'd prefer staying here in San Francisco, teaching music at fifty cents a lesson. I must say I was annoyed. I had her here and talked to her quite severely, but it didn't seem to make any impression. I was puzzled to death to understand it. But after thinking for a while, and wondering what could make a girl prefer San Francisco and teaching music at fifty cents a lesson, to Paris and being a prima donna, I came to the conclusion there was only one thing could influence a woman to that extent—there was a man in the case."

She saw Essex, whose eyes were on the fire, raise his brows by way of a polite commentary on her words.

"That sounds a very plausible solution of the problem," he said. "Love's a deadly enemy to common sense."

"That's the way it seemed to me. She had fallen in love, and evidently the man had not enough money to marry on, or was in a poor position, or something. When I thought of that I was certain I'd found the clue. The silly girl was going to give up everything for love. I suppose I ought to have felt touched. But I really felt sort of mad with her at first. Afterward, thinking it over, I decided it was not so foolish, and now I've veered round so far that I'm inclined to encourage it."

"On general principles you think domesticity is better for a woman than the glare of the footlights?"

"No, not that way. I think a gift like Mariposa Moreau's should be cultivated and given to the public. I never had any sympathy with that man in the Bible who buried his talent in the ground. I think talents were made to be used. What I thought, was, why shouldn't Mariposa marry the man she cared for and go with him to Paris. It would be a much better arrangement all round. She isn't very smart or capable, and she's young and childish for her years. Don't you think she is, Mr. Essex?"

Essex again raised his eyebrows and looked into the fire.

"Yes," he said in a dubious tone. "Yes, I suppose she is. She is certainly not a sophisticated or worldly person."

"That's just it. She's green—green about everything. Some way or other I didn't like the thought of sending her off there by herself, where she didn't know a soul. And then she's so handsome. If she was ugly it wouldn't matter so much. But she's very good-looking, and when you add that to her being so inexperienced and green about everything you begin to realize the responsibility of sending her alone to a strange country, especially Paris."

"Paris is not a city," commented her companion, "where young, beautiful and unprotected females are objects of public protection and solicitude."

"That's the reason why I want, now, to encourage this marriage. With a husband that she loves to take care of her, everything would be smooth sailing. She'd be happy and not homesick or strange. He'd be there with her, to watch over her and probably help her with her studies. Perhaps he could get some position, just to occupy his time. Because, so far as money went, I'd see to it that they were well provided for during the time she was preparing. Lepine said that he thought two or three years would be sufficient for her to study. Well, I'd give them fifteen thousand dollars to start on. And if that wasn't enough, or she was not ready to appear at the expected time, there would be more. There'd be no question about means of living, anyway. They could just put that out of their heads."

"I have always heard that Mrs. Shackleton was generous," said Essex, looking at her with a slight smile.

"Oh, generous!" she said, with a little movement of impatience, which was genuine. "This is no question of generosity; I want the girl to go and be a singer, and I don't want her to go alone. Now, I've found out a way for her to go that will be agreeable to her and to me, and, I take for granted, to the man."

She looked at Essex with a smile that almost said she knew him to be that favored person.

"Of course," she continued, "it would be better for him to get some work. It's bad for man or woman to be idle. If he knows how to write, it would be an easy matter to make him Paris correspondent of *The Trumpet*. It was my husband's intention to have a correspondent, and he had some idea of offering it to Mrs. Willers. But it's not the work for her, nor she the woman for it. It ought to be a man, and a man that's conversant with the country and the language. There'll be a good salary to go with it. Win was talking about it only the other evening."

"What a showering of good fortune on one person," said Essex—"a position ready-made, a small fortune and a beautiful wife! He must be a favorite of the gods."

"You can call it what you like, Mr. Essex," said Bessie. "It's been my experience that the gods take for their favorites men and women who've got some hustle. Everybody has a chance some time or other. Miss Moreau and her young man have theirs now."

She rose to her feet, for at that moment, Pussy Thurston appeared in the doorway to say good night.

The pretty creature had cast more than one covertly admiring look at Essex, during the dinner, and now, as she held out her hand to him in farewell, she said after the informal Western fashion:

"Won't you come to see me, Mr. Essex? I'm always at home on Sunday afternoon. If you're bashful, Win will bring you. He comes sometimes when he's got nowhere else in the world to go to."

Win, who was just behind her, expressed his willingness to act as escort, and laughing and jesting, the party passed through the doorway into the drawing-room. The little fires were burning low. By the light of one, Maud and Count de Lamolle were looking at a book of photographs of Swiss views. The count's expression was enigmatic, and as Bessie approached them she heard Maud say:

"Oh, that's a mountain. What's the name of it, now? I can't remember. It's very high and pointed, and people are always climbing it and falling into holes."

"The Matterhorn, perhaps," suggested the count, politely.

To which Maud gave a relieved assent. Her words were commonplace enough, but there was a quality of light-heartedness, of suppressed elation, in her voice, that her mother's quick ear instantly caught. As the girl looked up at their approaching figures her face showed the same newly-acquired sparkle that was almost joyous.

It had, in fact, been a critical evening for Maud, and so miserable did she feel her situation to be, that she had taken her courage in both hands and struck one desperate blow for freedom.

When her mother and Essex had begun their pictorial migrations she had felt the cold dread of a tête-à-tête with the count creeping over her heart. For a space she had tried to remain attached to Win and Pussy Thornton, but neither Win nor Pussy, who were old friends and had many subjects of mutual interest to discuss, encouraged her society. Maud was not the person to develop diplomatic genius under the most favorable circumstances. Half an hour after the men had entered the drawing-room, she found herself alone with the count, in front of the fire, Win and Pussy having strayed away to the Bouguereau.

The count had tried various subjects of conversation, but they had drooped and died after a few minutes of languishing existence. He stood with his back to the mantelpiece, looking curiously at Maud, who sat on the edge of an armchair just within reach of the fluctuating light. Her hands were clasped on her knee and she was looking down so that he could not see her face.

Suddenly she rose to her feet and faced him. She was pale and her eyes looked miserable and terrified.

"Count de Lamolle," she breathed in a tremulous voice.

"Mademoiselle," he said, moving toward her, very much surprised by her appearance.

"I've got to say something to you. It may sound queer, but I've got to say it."

"Dear Miss," said the Frenchman, really concerned by her tragic demeanor, "say whatever pleases you. I am only here to listen."

"You don't really care for me. Oh, if you'd only tell the truth!"

"That is a strange remark," he said, completely taken by surprise, and wondering what this extraordinary girl was going to say next.

"If I thought you really cared it would be different. Perhaps I couldn't say it. I hate making people miserable, and yet so many people make me miserable."

"Who makes you miserable, dear young lady?" he said, honestly touched.

"You," she almost whispered. "You do. You don't mean to, I know, for I think you're kinder than lots of other men. But—but— Oh please, don't keep on asking me to marry you. Don't do it any more; that makes me miserable. Because I can't do it. Truly, I can't."

Count de Lamolle became very grave. He drew himself up with an odd, stiff air, like a soldier.

"If a lady speaks this way to a man," he said, "the man can only obey."

Maud hung on his words. When she grasped their import, she suddenly moved toward him. There was something pathetic in her eagerness of gratitude.

"Oh, thanks! thanks! I knew you'd do it. It's not

you I object to. I like you better than any of the others. But"—she glanced over her shoulder into the lantern-lit brilliance of the Moorish room and dropped her voice—"there's some one I like more."

"Oh," said the count, and his dark eyes turned from her face, which had become very red.

"He's going to marry me some day. He's just Jack Latimer, the stenographer in the office. But I like him, and that's all there is to it. But mommer's terribly set on you. And she's so determined. Oh, Count de Lamolle, it's very hard to make determined people see things differently to what they want. So please, don't want to marry me any more, for if you don't want to, that will have to end it."

She stopped, her lips trembling. The count took her hand, cold and clammy, and lifting it pressed his lips lightly on the back. Then, dropping it, he said, quietly:

"All is understood. You have honored me highly, Mademoiselle, by giving me your confidence."

They stood silent for a moment. The kiss on her hand, the something friendly and kind—so different from the cold looks of unadmiring criticism she was accustomed to—in the man's eyes brought her uncomfortably close to tears. Few people had been kind to Maud Shackleton in the midst of her riches and splendor.

The count saw her emotion and turned toward the fire. He felt more drawn to her than he had ever been during his courtship. From the tail of his eye he saw her little handkerchief whisk out and then into her pocket. As it disappeared he said:

"I see, Miss Shackleton, that you have some albums of views on the table. Might we not look at them together?"

Thus it was that Bessie and Essex found them. They had worked through two volumes of Northern Italy, and were in Switzerland. And over the stiffened pages with their photographs, not one-half of which Maud could remember though she had been to all the places on her trip abroad, they had come nearer being friends than ever before.

CHAPTER XX

THE WOMAN TALKS

"My heart was hot within me, while I was musing the fire burned; then I spake with my tongue."—PSALMS.

The morning after her interview with Essex Mariposa had appeared at breakfast white-cheeked and apathetic. She had eaten nothing, and when questioned as to her state of health had replied that she had passed a sleepless night and had a headache. Mrs. Garcia, the younger, in a dingy cotton wrapper belted by a white apron, shook her head over the coffee-pot and began to tell how the late Juan Garcia had been the victim of headaches due to green wall-paper.

"But," said Mrs. Garcia, looking up from under the lambrequin of blond curls that adorned her brow, "there's nothing green in your wall-paper. It's white, with gold wheat-ears on it. So I don't see what gives you headaches."

"Headaches *do* come from other things besides green wall-paper," said Pierpont; "I've had them from overwork. I'd advise Miss Moreau to give her pupils a week's holiday. And then she can come down some afternoon and sing for me."

This was an old subject of discourse at the Garcia

THE WOMAN TALKS

table, Mariposa continually refusing the young man's invitations to let him hear and pass judgment upon her voice. Since he had met her he had heard further details of the recital at the opera-house and the opinion of Lepine, and was openly ambitious to have Mariposa for a pupil. Now she looked up at him with a sudden spark of animation in her eyes.

"I will some day. I'll come in some afternoon and sing for you—some afternoon when I have no headache," she added hastily, seeing the prospect of urging in his eyes.

Barron, sitting opposite, had been watching her covertly through the meal. He saw that she ate nothing, and guessed that the headache she pleaded was the result of a wakeful night. The evening before, when he had gone in to see the little boys in bed, he had casually asked them if they had been playing games that afternoon in which shouting had been a prominent feature.

"Indians?" Benito had suggested, sitting up in his cot and scratching the back of his neck; "that's a hollering game."

"Any game with screams. When I came in I thought I heard shouts coming from somewhere."

"That wasn't us," said Miguel from his larger bed in the corner. "We was playing burying soldiers in the back yard, and that's a game where you bury soldiers, cut out of the papers, in the sandy place. There's no sorter hollering in it. Sometimes we play we're crying, but that's quiet."

"P'raps," said Benito sleepily, "it was Miss Moreau's gentleman in the parlor. I let him in. They might have been singing. Now tell us the story about the Indians and the pony express."

This was all the satisfaction he got from the boys. After the story was told he did not go downstairs, but went into his own room and sat by his littered table, thinking. The details of his entrance into the house a few hours before were engraved on his mind's eye. By the uncertain gaslight he saw the dark face of the stranger, with its slightly insolent droop of eyelid and non-committal line of clean-shaven lip. It was to his idea a disagreeable face. The simple man in him read through its shield of reserve to the complexities beneath. The healthily frank American saw in it the intricate sophistication of older civilizations, of vast communities where "God hath made man upright; but they have sought out many inventions."

On his ear again fell the cold politeness of the voice. Gamaliel Barron was too lacking in any form of self-consciousness, was too indifferently confident of himself as a Westerner, the equal of any and all human creatures, to experience that sensation of *mauvaise honte* that men of smaller fiber are apt to feel in the presence of beings of superior polish. Polish was nothing to him. The man everything. And it seemed to him he had seen the man, deep down, in that one startled moment of encounter in the hall. Thoughtfully smoking and tilting back in his chair, he mentally summed him up in the two words, "bad egg." He would keep his eye on him, and to do so would put off the trip to the mines he was to take in the course of the next two weeks.

The next morning Mariposa's appearance at the

breakfast table roused the uneasiness he felt to poignant anxiety. With the keenness of growing love, he realized that it was the mind that was disturbed more than the body. He came home to lunch—an unusual deviation, as he almost invariably lunched down town at the Lick House—and found her at the table as pale and distrait as ever. After the meal was over he followed her into the hall. She was slowly ascending the stairs, one hand on the balustrade, her long, black dress sliding upward from stair to stair.

He followed her noiselessly, and at the top of the flight, turning to go to her room, she saw him and paused, her hand still touching the rail.

"Miss Moreau," he said, "you're tired out—too tired to teach. Let me go and put off your pupils. I've a lot of spare time this afternoon."

"How kind of you," she said, looking faintly surprised; "I haven't any this afternoon, luckily. I don't work every day; that's the point I'm trying to work up to; that's my highest ambition."

She looked down at his upturned face and gave a slight smile.

"*Is* it overwork that kept you awake last night and makes you look so pale to-day?" he queried in a lowered voice.

"Oh, I don't know,"—she turned away her face rather impatiently,—"I'm worried, I suppose. Everybody has to be worried, don't they?"

"I can't bear to have you worried. There isn't one wild, crazy thing in the world I wouldn't do to prevent it."

He was looking up at her with his soul in his eyes.

Barron was not the man to hide or juggle with his love. It possessed him now and shone on his face. Mariposa's eyes turned from it as from the scrutiny of something at once painful and holy. He laid his hand on hers on the rail.

"You know that," he said, his deep voice shaken.

Her eyes dropped to the hands and she mechanically noticed how white her fingers looked between his large, brown ones. She drew them softly away, feeling his glance keen, impassioned and unwavering on her face.

"Something's troubling you," he continued in the same voice. "Why won't you let me help you? You needn't tell me what it is, but you might let me help you. What am I here for but to take care of you, and fight for you, and protect you?"

The words were indescribably sweet to the lonely girl. All the previous night she had tossed on her pillow haunted by terror of Essex and what he intended to do. She had felt herself completely helpless, and her uncertainty at what step he meant to take was torturing. For one moment of weakness she thought of pouring it all out to the man beside her, whose strong hand on her own had seemed symbolic of the grip, firm and fearless, he could take on the situation that was threatening her. Then she realized the impossibility of such a thing and drew back from the railing.

"You can't help me," she said; "no one can."

He mounted a step and stretched his hand over the railing to try to detain her.

"But I can do one thing: I can always be here, here close to you, ready to come when you call me, either in trouble or for advice. If ever you want help, help of any kind, I'll be here. And if you had need of me I think I'd know it, and no matter where I was, I'd come. Remember that."

She had half turned away toward her door as he spoke, and now stood in profile, a tall figure, with her throat and wrists looking white as milk against the hard black line of her dress. She seemed a picture painted in few colors, her hair a coppery bronze, and her lips a clear, pale red, being the brightest tones in the composition.

"Will you remember?" he said.

"Yes," she murmured.

"And when you want help come to me, or call for me, and if I were at the ends of the world I'd hear you and come."

She turned completely away without answering and, opening her door, vanished into her room.

For the next three or four days she looked much the same. Mrs. Garcia, junior, talked about the green wall-paper, and Mrs. Garcia, senior, cooked her Mexican dainties, which were so hot with chilli peppers that only a seasoned throat could swallow them. Mariposa tried to eat and to talk, but both efforts were failures. She was secretly distracted by apprehensions of Essex's next move. She thought of his face as he had raised his hand to his smitten cheek, and shuddered at the memory. She lived in daily dread of his reappearance. The interview had shattered her nerves, never fully restored from the series of miserable events that had preceded and followed her mother's death. When she heard the bell ring her heart sprang from her breast to her throat, and a desire to fly and hide from her persecutor seized her and held her quivering and alert.

Barron's anxiety about her, though not again openly expressed, continued. He was certain that some blow to her peace of mind had been delivered by the man he had seen in the hall. He did not like to question her, or attempt an intrusion into her confidence, but he remembered the few words she had dropped that evening. The man's name was Essex, and he was a friend of Mrs. Willers'. Barron had known Mrs. Willers for years. He had been a guest in the house during the period of her tenancy, and though he did not see her frequently, had retained an agreeable memory of her and her daughter.

It was therefore with great relief that, a few days after his meeting with Essex, he encountered her in the heart of a gray afternoon crossing Union Square Plaza.

Mrs. Willers was hastening down to *The Trumpet* office after a morning's work in her own rooms. Her rouge had been applied with the usual haste, and she was conscious that three buttons on one of her boots were hardly sufficient to retain that necessary article in place. But she felt brisk and light-hearted, confident that the article in her hand was smart and spicy and would lend brightness to her column in *The Trumpet*.

She greeted Barron with a friendly hail, and they paused for a moment's chat in the middle of the plaza.

"You're looking fresh as a summer morning," said the mining man, whose life, spent searching for the mineral secrets of the Sierra, had not made him conversant with those of complexions like Mrs. Willers'.

"Oh, get out!" said she, greatly pleased; "I'm too old for that sort of taffy. It's almost Edna's turn now."

"I'll be afraid to see Edna soon. She's going to be such a beauty that the only safety's in flight."

The mother was even more pleased at this.

"You're right," she said, nodding at him with a grave eye; "Edna's a beauty. Where she gets it from is what stumps me. My glass tells me it's not from her mommer, and my memory tells me it's not from her popper."

"There's a man on your paper called Essex," said Barron, who was not one to beat about the bush; "what sort of a fellow is he, Mrs. Willers?"

"A bad sort, I'm inclined to think. Why do you ask?"

"He was at the house the other afternoon, calling on Miss Moreau. I met him in the hall. I didn't cotton to him at all. She told me he was a friend of yours and a writer on *The Trumpet*."

He looked at her inquiringly, hardly liking to go farther till she gave him some encouragement. He noticed that her expression had changed and that she was eying him with a hard, considering attention.

"Why didn't you like his looks?" she said.

"Well, I've seen men like that before—at the mines. Good-looking chaps, who are sort of imitation gentlemen, and try to make you take the imitation for the real thing by putting on dog. I didn't like his style, anyhow, and I don't think she does, either."

"You're right about that," said Mrs. Willers; "do you know what he was there for?"

"Something about music lessons, she said. I didn't like to ask her."

"Music lessons!" exclaimed Mrs. Willers, with a strong inflection of surprise.

"Yes," said Barron, uneasy at her tone and the strange look of almost agitated astonishment on her face; "and I'm under the impression he said something to her that frightened her. As I was coming up the steps that afternoon I heard distinctly some one call out in the drawing-room. I burst in on the full jump, for I was certain it was a woman's voice, and that man came out of the drawing-room as I opened the door. He was smooth as a summer sea; said he hadn't heard a sound, and went out smirking. Then I went into the drawing-room to see who had been in there and found Miss Moreau, leaning against the wall and white as my cuffs."

He looked frowningly at Mrs. Willers. She had listened without moving, her face rigidly attentive.

"Mariposa didn't tell you what they'd been talking about?" she asked.

"No; she told me nothing. And when I asked her about the screams she said I'd been mistaken. But I hadn't, Mrs. Willers. That man had scared her some way, and she'd screamed. She called for Benito and Mrs. Garcia. I heard her. And she's looked pale and miserable ever since. What does that blackguard come to see her for, anyway? What's he after?"

"Her," said Mrs. Willers, solemnly; "he wants to marry her."

"Wants to marry her! That foreign spider! Well, he's got a gall. Humph!—"

Words of sufficient scorn seemed to fail him. That he should be similarly aspiring did not at that moment strike him as reason for moderation in his censure of a rival.

"And is he trying to scare her into marrying him? I wish I'd known that. I'd have broken his neck in the hall."

"Don't you go round breaking people's necks," said Mrs. Willers, "but I'm glad you're in that house. If Barry Essex is going to try to make her marry him by bullying and bulldozing her, I'm glad there's a man there to keep him in his place. That's no way to win a woman, Mr. Barron. I know, for that's the way Willers courted me. Wouldn't hear of my saying no; said he'd shoot himself. I knew even then he wouldn't, but I didn't know but what he'd try to wound himself somewhere where it didn't hurt, leaving a letter for me that would be published in the morning paper. So I married him to get rid of him, and then I had to get the law in to get rid of him a second time. A man that badgers a woman into marrying him is no good. You can bank on that."

"Well," said Barron, "I'm glad you've told me this. I'll keep my eye on Mr. Essex. I was going to the mines next week, but guess I'll put it off."

"Do. But don't you let on to Mariposa what I've told you. She wouldn't like it. She's a proud girl. But I'll tell you, Mr. Barron, she's a good one, too; one of the best kind, and I love her nearly as much as my own girl. But look!" glancing at an adjacent clock with a start, "I must be traveling. This stuff's got to go in at once."

"Good by," said Barron, holding out his hand; "it's a good thing we had this minute of talk."

"Good by," she answered, returning the pressure with a grip almost as manly; "it's been awfully good to see you again. I must get a move on. So long."

And they parted, Barron turning his face toward the Garcia house, where he had an engagement to take the boys to the beach at the foot of Hyde Street, and Mrs. Willers to *The Trumpet* office.

Her walk did not occupy more than fifteen minutes, and during that time the anger roused by the mining man's words grew apace. From smothered indignation it passed to a state of simmering passion. Her conscience heated it still further, for it was she who had introduced Essex to Mariposa, and in the first stages of their acquaintance had in a careless way encouraged the friendship, thinking it would be cheerful for the solitary girl to have the occasional companionship of this clever and interesting man of the world. She had thoughtlessly kindled a fire that might burn far past her power of control and lead to irreparable disaster.

She inferred from Barron's story that Essex was evidently attempting to frighten Mariposa into smiling on his suit. The cowardice of the action enraged her, for, though Mrs. Willers had known many men of many faults, she had counted no cowards among her friends. Her point of view was Western. A man might do many things that offend Eastern conventions and retain her consideration. But, as she expressed it to herself in the walk down Third Street, "He's got to know that in this country they don't drag women shrieking to the altar."

She ran up the stairs of *The Trumpet* building with the lightness of a girl of sixteen. Ire gave wings to her feet, and it was ire as much as the speed of her ascent that made her catch her breath quickly at the top of the fourth flight. Still, even then, she might have held her indignation in check,—years of training in expedient self-control being a powerful force in the energetic business woman,—had she not caught a glimpse of Essex in his den as she passed the open door.

He was sitting at his desk, leaning languidly back in his chair, evidently thinking. His face, turned toward her, looked worn and hard, the lids drooping with their air of faintly bored insolence. Hearing the rustle of her dress, he looked up and saw her making a momentary pause by the doorway. He did not look pleased at the sight of her.

"Ah, Mrs. Willers," he said, leaning forward to pick up his pen and speaking with the crisp clearness of utterance certain people employ when irritated, "what is it that you want to see me about?"

"Nothing," said Mrs. Willers abruptly and with battle in her tone; "why should I?"

"I have not the least idea," he answered, looking at his pen, and then, dipping it in the ink, "unless perhaps you want a few hints for your forthcoming article, 'The Kind of Shoestrings Worn by the Crowned Heads of Europe.'"

Essex was out of temper himself. When Mrs. Willers interrupted him he had been thinking over the situation with Mariposa, and it had seemed to him very cheerless. His remark was well calculated to enrage the leading spirit of the woman's page, who was as proud of her weekly contributions as though they had been inspired by the genius of George Eliot.

"Well," she said, and her rouge became quite unnecessary in the flood of natural color that rose to her face, "if I was going to tackle that subject I think you'd be about the best person to come to for information. For if you ever have had anything to do with crowned heads it's been as their bootblack."

Essex was startled by the stinging malice revealed in this remark. He swung round on his swivel chair and sat facing his antagonist, making no attempt to rise, although she entered the room. As he saw her face in the light of the window he realized that, for the first time, he saw the woman stirred out of her carefully acquired professional calm.

As she entered she pushed the door to behind her, and, taking the chair beside the desk, sat down.

"Mr. Essex," she said, "I want a word with you."

"Any number," he answered with ironical politeness. "Do you wish the history of my connection with the crowned heads as court bootblack?"

"No," she said. "I want to know what business you've got to go to Mrs. Garcia's boarding-house and frighten one of the ladies living there?"

An instantaneous change passed over Essex's face. His eyes seemed suddenly to grow veiled as they narrowed to a cold, non-committal slit. His mouth hardened. Mrs. Willers saw the muscles of his cheeks tighten.

"Really," he said, "this sudden interest in me is quite flattering. I hardly know what to say."

He spoke to gain time, for he was amazed and enraged. Mariposa had evidently made a confidante of Mrs. Willers, and he knew that Mrs. Willers was high in favor with Winslow Shackleton and his mother.

"In this country, Mr. Essex," Mrs. Willers went on, clenching her hands in her lap, for they trembled with her indignation, "men don't scare and browbeat young women who don't happen to have the good taste to favor them. When a man gets the mitten he knows enough to get out."

"Very clever of him, no doubt," he murmured with unshaken suavity.

"If you're going to live here you've got to live by our laws. You've got to do as the Romans do. And take my word for it, young man, the Romans don't approve of nagging and scaring a woman into marriage."

"No?" he answered with a blandly questioning inflection, "these are interesting facts in local manners and customs. I'm sure they'd be of value to some one who was making a special study of the subject. Personally I am not deeply interested in the California aborigines. Even the original and charming specimen now before me would oblige me greatly by withdrawing. It is now"—looking at the clock that stood on the side of the desk—"half-past two, and my time is valuable, my dear Mrs. Willers."

Mrs. Willers rose to her feet, burning with rage.

"Put me off any way you like," she said, "and be as fresh and smart as you know how. But I tell you, young man, this has got to stop. That girl's got no one belonging to her here. But don't imagine from that you can have the field to yourself and go on persecuting her. No—this is not France nor Spain, nor any other old monarchy, where a woman didn't have any more to say about herself than a mule, or a pet parrot. No, sir. You've run up against the wrong proposition if you think you can scare a woman into marrying you in California in the nineteenth century."

Essex rose from his chair. He was pale.

"Look here," he said in a low voice, "I've had enough of this. By what right, I'd like to know, do you dare to dictate to me or interfere in my acquaintance with another lady?"

"I'd dare more than that, Barry Essex," said Mrs. Willers, with her rouge standing out red on her white face, "to save that girl from a man like you. I don't know what I wouldn't dare. But I'm a good fighter when my blood's up, and I'll fight you on this point till one or the other of us drops."

She saw Essex's nostrils fan softly in and out. His cheek-bones looked prominent.

"Will you kindly leave this room?" he said in a suppressed voice.

"Yes," she answered, "I'm going now. But understand that I'm making no idle threats. And if this persecution goes on I'll tell Winslow Shackleton of the way you're acting to a friend of his and a protégée of his mother's."

She was at the door and had the handle in her hand. Essex turned on her a face of livid malignity.

"Really, Mrs. Willers," he said, "I had no idea you were entitled to speak for Winslow Shackleton. I congratulate you."

For a moment of blind rage Mrs. Willers neither spoke nor moved. Then she felt the door-handle turn under her hand and the door push inward. She mechanically stepped to one side, as it opened, and the office boy intruded his head.

"I knocked here twict, and y'aint answered," he said apologetically. "There's a man to see you, Mr. Essex, what says he's got something to say about a new kind of balloon."

"Show him in," said Essex, "and—oh—ah—Jack, show Mrs. Willers out."

Jack gaped at this curious order. Mrs. Willers brushed past him and walked up the hall to her own cubby-hole. She was compassed in a lurid mist of fury, and through this she felt dimly that she had done no good.

"Did getting into a rage ever do any good?" she thought desperately, as she sank into her desk chair.

Her article lay unnoticed and forgotten by her side, while she sat staring at her scattered papers, trying to decide through the storm that still shook her whether she had not done well in throwing down her gage in defense of her friend.

CHAPTER XXI

THE MEETING IN THE RAIN

"A time to love and a time to hate."
—ECCLESIASTES.

It was the afternoon of Edna Willers' music lesson. Over a week had elapsed since Mariposa's interview with Essex, yet to-day, as she stood at her window looking out at the threatening sky, her fears of him were as active as ever. Though he had made no further sign, her woman's intuitions warned her that this was but a temporary lull in his campaign. She was living under an exhausting tension. She went out with the fear of meeting him driving her into unfrequented side streets, and returned, her eyes straining through the foliage of the pepper-tree to watch for a light in the parlor windows.

This afternoon, standing at the window drumming on the pane with her finger-tips, she looked at the dun, low-hanging clouds, and thought with shrinking of her walk to Sutter Street, at any turn of which she might meet him.

"Well, and if I do?" she said to herself, trying to whip up her dwindling courage, "he can't do any more than threaten me with telling all he knows. He can't make a scene on the street proposing to me."

She felt somewhat cheered by these assurances and

THE MEETING IN THE RAIN

began putting on her outdoor things. The day was darkening curiously early, she thought, for, though it was not yet four, the long mirror, with its top-heavy gold ornaments, gave back but a dim reflection of her. There had been fine weather for two weeks, and now rain was coming. She put on her long cloak, the enveloping "circular" of the mode which fastened at the throat with a metal clasp, and took her umbrella, a black cotton one, which seemed to her quite elegant enough for a humble teacher of music. A small black bonnet, trimmed with loops of ribbon, crowned her head and showed her rich hair, rippling loosely back from her forehead.

The air on the outside was warm and at the same time was softly and stilly humid. There was not a breath of wind, and in this motionless, tepid atmosphere the gardens exhaled moist earth-odors as if breathing out their strength in panting expectation of the rain. From the high places of the city one could see the bay, flat and oily, with its surrounding hills and its circular sweep of houses, a picture in shaded grays. The smoke, trailing lazily upward, was the palest tint in this study in monochrome, while the pall of the sky, leaden and lowering, was the darkest. A faint light diffused itself from the rim of sky, visible round the edges of the pall, and cast an unearthly yellowish gleam on people's faces.

Mariposa walked rapidly downward from street to street. She kept a furtive lookout for the well-known figure in its long overcoat and high hat, but saw no one, and her troubled heart-beats began to moderate. The damp air on her face refreshed her. She had been keeping in the house too much of late, and did not realize that this was still further irritating her already jangled nerves. The angle of the building in which Mrs. Willers housed herself broke on her view just as the first sullen drops of rain began to spot the pavement—slow, reluctant drops, falling far apart.

The music lesson had hardly begun when the rain was lashing the window and pouring down the panes in fury. Darkness fell with it. The night seemed to drop on the city in an instant, coming with a whirling rush of wind and falling waters. The housewifely little Edna drew the curtains and lit the gas, saying as she settled back on her music-stool:

"You'd better stay to dinner with me, Mariposa. Mommer won't be home till late because it's Wednesday and the back part of the woman's page goes to press."

"Oh, I couldn't stay to-night," said Mariposa hurriedly, affrighted by the thought of the walk home alone at ten o'clock, which she had often before taken without a tremor; "I must go quite soon. I forgot it was the day when the back sheet goes to press. Go on, Edna, it will be like the middle of the night by the time we finish."

This was indeed the case. When the lesson was over, the evening outside was shrouded in a midnight darkness to an accompaniment of roaring rain. It was a torrential downpour. The two girls, peering out into the street, could see by the blurred rays of the lamps a swimming highway, down which a car dashed at intervals, spattering the blackness with the broken lights of its windows. Despite the child's urgings to remain, Mariposa insisted on going. She was well prepared for wet she said, folding her circular about her and removing the elastic band that held together her disreputable umbrella.

But she did not realize the force of the storm till she found herself in the street. By keeping in the lee of the houses on the right-hand side, she could escape the full fury of the wind, and she began slowly making her way upward.

She had gone some distance when the roll of music she carried slipped from under her arm and fell into water and darkness. She groped for it, clutched its saturated cover, and brought it up dripping. The music was of value to her, and she moved forward to where the light of an uncurtained window cut the darkness, revealing the top of a wall. Here she rested the roll and tried to wipe it dry with her handkerchief. Her face, down-bent and earnest, was distinctly visible in the shaft of light. A man, standing opposite, who had been patrolling these streets for the past hour, saw it, gave a smothered exclamation, and crossed the street. He was at her side before she saw him.

Several hours earlier Essex had been passing down a thoroughfare in that neighborhood, when he had met Benito, slowly wending his way homeward from school. The child recognized him and smiled, and with the smile, Essex recollected the face and saw that fate was still on his side.

Pressing a quarter into Benito's readily extended palm, he had inquired if the boy knew where Miss Moreau was.

"Mariposa?" said Benito, with easy familiarity; "she's at Mrs. Willers' giving Edna her lesson. This is Wednesday, ain't it? Well, Edna gets her lesson on Wednesday from half-past four till half-past five, and so that's where Mariposa is. But she's generally late 'cause she stays and talks to Mrs. Willers."

At five o'clock, sheltered by the dripping dark, Essex began his furtive watch of the streets along which she might pass. He knew that every day was precious to him now, with Mrs. Willers among his enemies and ready to enlist Winslow Shackleton against him. Here was an opportunity to see the girl, better than the parlor of the Garcia house offered, with its officious boarders. There was absolute seclusion in these black and rain-swept streets.

He had been prowling about for an hour when he finally saw her. A dozen times he had cursed under his breath fearing she had escaped him; now his relief was such that he ran toward her, and with a rough hand swept aside her umbrella. In the clear light of the uncurtained pane she saw his face, and shrank back against the wall as if she had been struck. Then a second impulse seized her and she tried to dash past him. He seemed prepared for this and caught her by the arm through her cloak, swinging her violently back to her place against the wall.

Keeping his grip on her he said, trying to smile:

"What are you afraid of? Don't you know me?"

"Let me go," she said, struggling, "you're hurting me."

"I don't want to hurt you," he answered, "but I

mean to keep you for a moment. I want to talk to you. And I'm going to talk to you."

"I won't listen to you. Let me go at once. How cowardly to hold me in this way against my will!"

She tried again to wrench her arm out of his grasp, but he held her like a vise. Her resistance of him and the repugnance in face and voice maddened him. He felt for a moment that he would like to batter her against the wall.

"There's no use trying to get away, and telling me how much you hate me. I've got you here at last. I'll not let you go till I've had my say."

He put his face down under the tent of her umbrella and gazed at her with menacing eyes and tight lips. In the light of the window and against the inky blackness around them the two faces were distinct as cameos hung on a velvet background. He saw the whiteness of her chin on the bow beneath it, and her mouth, with the lips that all the anger in the world could not make hard or unlovely.

"You've got to listen to me," he said, shaking her arm as if trying to shake some passion into the set antagonism of her face; "you've got to be my wife."

She suddenly seized her umbrella and, turning it toward him, pressed it down between them. The action was so quick and unexpected that the man did not move back, and the ferrule striking him on the cheek, furrowed a long scratch on the smooth skin. A drop of blood rose to the surface.

With an oath he seized the umbrella and, tearing it from her grasp, sent it flying into the street. Here the wind snatched it, and its inverted shape, like a large black mushroom, went sweeping forward, tilted and already half full of water, before the angry gusts.

Essex tried to keep his own over her, still retaining his hold on her arm.

"Come, be reasonable," he said; "there's no use angering me for nothing. This is a wet place for lovers to have meetings. Give me my answer, and I swear I'll not detain you. When will you marry me?"

"What's the good of talking that way? You know perfectly what I'll say. It will always be the same."

"I'm not so sure of that. I've got something to say that may make you change your mind."

He pushed the umbrella back that the light might fall directly on her. It fell on him also. She saw his face under the brim of his soaked hat, shining with rain, pallidly sinister, the trickle of blood on one cheek.

"Nothing that you can say will ever make me change my mind. Mr. Essex, I am wet and tired; won't you, please, let me go?"

She tried to eliminate dislike and fear from her voice and spoke with a gentleness that she hoped would soften him. He heard it with a thrill; but it had an exactly contrary effect to what she had desired.

"I would like never to let you go. Just to hold you here and look at you. Mariposa, you don't know what this love is I have for you. It grows with absence, and then when I see you it grows again with the sight of you. It's eating into me like a poison. I can't get away from it. You loved me once, why have you changed? What has come over you to take all that out of you? Is it because I made a foolish mistake?

THE MEETING IN THE RAIN

I'm ready to do anything you suggest—crawl in the dust, kneel now in the rain, and ask you to forgive it. Don't be hard and revengeful. It's not like you. Be kind, be merciful to a man who, if he said what hurt you, has repented it with all his soul ever since. I am ready to give you my whole life to make amends. Say you forgive me. Say you love me."

He was speaking the truth. Passion had outrun cupidity. Mariposa, poor or rich, had become the end and aim of his existence.

"It's not a question of forgiveness," she answered, seeing he still persisted in the thought that she was hiding her love from wounded pride; "it's not a question of love. I—I—don't like you. Can't you understand that? I don't like you."

"It's not true—it's not true," he vociferated. "You love me—say you do."

He shook her by the arm as though to shake the words out of her reluctant lips. The brutal roughness of the action spurred her from fear to indignation.

"It's not love. It's not even hate. It's just repulsion and dislike. I can't bear to look at you, or have you come near me, and to have you hold me, as you're doing now, is as if some horrible thing, like a spider or a snake, was crawling on me."

Amid the rustling and the splashing of the rain they again looked at each other for a fierce, pallid moment. Another drop of blood on his cheek detached itself and ran down. He had no free hand with which to wipe it off.

"Yet you're going to marry me," he said softly.

"I've heard enough of this," she cried. "I'm not going to stand here talking to a madman. It's early yet and these houses are full of people. If I give one cry every window will go up. I don't want to make a scene here on the street, but if you detain me any longer talking in this crazy way, that's what I'll have to do."

"Just wait one moment before you take such desperate measures. I want to ask a question before you call out the neighborhood to protect you. How do you think the story of your mother's and father's early history will look on the front page of *The Era?*"

In the light of the window that fell across them both he had the satisfaction of seeing her face freeze into horrified amazement.

"It will be the greatest scoop *The Era's* had since *The Trumpet* became Shackleton's property. There's not a soul here that even suspects it. It will be a bombshell to the city, involving people of the highest position, like the Shackletons, and people of the most unquestioned respectability, like the Moreaus. Oh—it will be good reading!"

Her eyes, fastened on him, were full of anguish, but it had not bewildered her. In the stress of the moment her mind remained clear and active.

"Is the world interested in stories of the dead?" she heard herself saying in a cold voice.

"Everybody's interested in scandals. And what a scandal it is! How people will smack their lips over it! Shackleton a Mormon, and you his only legitimate child. Your mother and father, that all the world honored, common free-lovers. Your mother sold to your father for a pair of horses, and living with him in a cabin in the Sierra for six months before they even attempted to straighten things out by a bogus marriage ceremony. Why, it's a splendid story! *The Era's* had nothing with as much ginger as that for months!"

"And who'd believe you? Who are you, to know about the early histories of the pioneer families? Who'd believe the words of a man who comes from nobody knows where, whose very name people doubt? If Mrs. Shackleton and I deny the truth of your story, who'd believe you then?"

"You forget that I have under my hand the man who was witness of the transaction whereby Moreau bought your mother from Shackleton for a pair of horses."

"A drunken thief! He stole all my father had and ran away. Can his word carry the same weight as mine to whose interest it would be to prove myself Shackleton's daughter? No. The only real proof in existence is the marriage certificate. And I have that. And so long as I have that any story you choose to publish I can get up and deny."

He knew she was right. Even with Harney his story would be discredited, unbacked by the one piece of genuine evidence of the first marriage—the certificate which she possessed. Her unexpected recognition of the point staggered him. He had thought to break her resistance by threats which even to him seemed shameful, and only excusable because of the stress he found himself in. Now he saw her as defiantly unconquered as ever. In his rage he pushed her back against the wall, crying at her:

"Deny, deny all you like! Whether you deny or not,

the thing will have been said. Next Sunday the whole city, the whole state will be reading it—how you're Shackleton's daughter and your mother was Dan Moreau's mistress. But say one word—one little word to me, and not a syllable will be written, not a whisper spoken. On one side there's happiness and luxury and love, and on the other disgrace and poverty—not your disgrace alone, but your father's, your mother's—"

With a cry of rage and despair Mariposa tried to tear herself from him. Nature aided her, for at the same moment a savage gust of wind seized the umbrella and wrenched it this way and that. Instinctively he loosened his hold on her to grasp it, and in that one moment she tore herself away from him. He gripped at the flapping wing of her cloak, and caught it. But the strain was too much for the cheap metal clasp, which broke, and Mariposa slipped out of it and flew into the fury of the rain, leaving the cloak in his hand.

The roar of many waters and the shouting of the wind obliterated the sound of her flying feet. The darkness, shot through with the blurred faces of lamps or the long rays from an occasional uncurtained pane, in a moment absorbed her black figure. Essex stood motionless, stunned at the suddenness of her escape, the sodden cloak trailing from his hand. Then shaken out of all reason by rage, not knowing what he intended doing, he started in pursuit.

She feared this and her burst of bravery was exhausted. As she ran up the steep street having only the darkness to hide her, her heart seemed shriveled with the fear of him.

Suddenly she heard the thud of his feet behind her. An agony of fright seized her. The Garcia house was at least two blocks farther on, and she knew he would overtake her before then. A black doorway with a huddle of little trees, formless and dark now, loomed close by, and toward this she darted, crouching down among the small wet trunks of the shrubs and parting their foliage with shaking hands.

There was a lamp not far off and in its rays she saw him running up, still holding the cloak in a black bunch over his arm. He stopped, just beyond where she cowered, and looked irresolutely up and down. The lamplight fell on his face, and in certain angles she saw it plainly, pale and glistening with moisture, all keen and alert with a look of attentive cunning. He moved his head this way and that, evidently trusting more to hearing than to sight. His eyes, no longer half veiled in cold indifference, swept her hiding-place with the preoccupation of one who listens intently. He looked to her like some thwarted animal harkening for the steps of his prey. Her terror grew with the sight of him. She thought if he had approached the bushes she would have swooned before he reached them.

Presently he turned and went down the hill. In the pause his reason had reasserted itself, and he felt that to hound her down with more threats and reproaches was useless folly.

But, with her, reason and judgment were hopelessly submerged by terror. She crept out from among the shrubs with white face and trembling limbs, and fled up the hill in a wild, breathless race, hearing Essex in every sound. The rain had dripped on her through the bushes, and these last two blocks under its unrestrained fury soaked her to the skin.

Her haunting terror did not leave her till she had rushed up the stairs and opened the door of the glass porch. She was fumbling in her pocket for the latch-key, when the inner door was opened and Barron stood in the aperture, the lighted hall behind him.

"What on earth has delayed you?" he said sharply. "They're all at supper. I was just going down to Mrs. Willers' to see what was keeping you."

She stumbled in at the door, and stood in the revealing light of the hall, for the moment unable to answer, panting and drenched.

"What's the matter?" he said suddenly in a different tone; and quickly stepping back he shut the door into the dining-room. "Has anything happened?"

"I'm—only—only—frightened," she gasped between broken breaths. "Something frightened me."

She reeled and caught against the door-post.

"I'm all wet," she whispered with white lips; "don't let them know. I don't want any dinner."

He put his arm round her and drew her toward the stairs. He could feel her trembling like a person with an ague and her saturated clothes left rillets along the stairs.

When they were half way up he said:

"How did you get so wet? Have you been out in this storm without an umbrella?"

"I lost it," she whispered.

"Lost it?" he replied. "Where's your cloak?"

THE MEETING IN THE RAIN

"Somewhere," she said vaguely; "somewhere in the street. I lost that, too."

They were at the top of the stairs. She suddenly turned toward him and pressed her face into his shoulder, trembling like a terrified animal.

"I'm frightened," she whispered. "Don't tell them downstairs. I'll tell you to-morrow. Don't ask me anything to-night."

He took her into her room and placed her in an armchair by the fireplace. He lit the gas and drew the curtains, and then knelt by the hearth to kindle the fire, saying nothing and apparently taking little notice of her. She sat dully watching him, her hands in her lap, the water running off her skirts along the carpet.

When he had lit the fire he said:

"Now, I'll go, and you take off your things. I'll bring you up your supper in half an hour. Be quick, you're soaking. I'll tell them downstairs you're too tired to come down."

He went out, softly closing the door. She sat on in her wet clothes, feeling the growing warmth of the flames on her face and hands. She seemed to fall into a lethargy of exhaustion and sat thus motionless, the water running unheeded on the carpet, *frissons* of cold occasionally shaking her, till a knock at the door roused her. Then she suddenly remembered Barron and his command to take off her wet clothes. She had them on still and he would be angry.

"Put it down on the chair outside," she called through the door; "I'm not ready."

"Won't you open the door and take this whisky and drink it at once?" came his answer.

She opened the door a crack and, putting her hand through the aperture, took the glass with the whisky.

"Are you warm and dry?" he said; all she could see of him was his big hand clasped round the glass.

"Yes, quite," she answered, though she felt her skin quivering with cold against the damp garments that seemed glued to it.

"Well, drink this now, right off. And listen—" as the door began to close—"if you get nervous or anything just come to your door and call me. I'll leave mine open, and I'm a very light sleeper."

Then before she could answer she felt the door-handle pulled from the outside and the door was shut.

She hastily took off her things and put on dry ones, and then shrugged herself into the thick wrapper of black and white that had been her mother's. Even her hair was wet, she found out as she undressed, and she mechanically undid it and shook the damp locks loose on her shoulders. She felt penetrated with cold, and still overmastered by fear. Every gust that made the long limb of the pepper-tree grate against the balcony roof caused her heart to leap. When she opened the door to get her supper, the glow of light that fell from Barron's room, across the hallway, came to her with a hail of friendship and life. She stood listening, and heard the creak of his rocking-chair, then smelt the whiff of a cigar. He was close to her. She shut the door, feeling her terrors allayed.

She picked at her supper, but soon set the tray on the center-table and took the easy-chair before the fire. The sense of physical cold was passing off, but the indescribable oppression and apprehension remained.

She did not know exactly what she dreaded, but she felt in some vague way that she would be safer sitting thus clad and wakeful before the fire than sleeping in her bed. Once or twice, as the hours passed and her fears strengthened in the silence and mystery of the night, she crept to her door, and opening it, looked up the hall. The square of light was still there, the scent of the cigar pungent on the air. She shut the door softly, each time feeling soothed as by the pressure of a strong, loving hand.

Sometime toward the middle of the night the heaviness of sleep came on her, and though she fought against it, feeling that the safety she was struggling to maintain against mysterious menace was only to be preserved by wakefulness, Nature overcame her. Curled in her chair before the crumbling fire, she finally slept—the deep, motionless sleep of physical and mental exhaustion.

CHAPTER XXII

A NIGHT'S WORK

"Have is have, however men may catch."
—SHAKESPEARE.

Under cover of the darkness Essex hurried down the street toward where the city passed from a place of homes to a business mart. He had at first no fixed idea of a goal, but after a few moments' rapid march, realized that habit was taking him in the direction of Bertrand's. An illumined clock face shining on him over the roofs told him it was some time past his dinner hour. He obeyed his instinct and bent his steps toward the restaurant, throwing the cloak over the fence of a vacant lot and wiping the trickle of blood from his cheek with his handkerchief.

He was cool and master of himself once more. His brain was cleared, as a sky by storm, and he knew that to-night's interview must be one of the last he would have with the woman who had come to stand to him for love, wealth, success and happiness. He must win or lose all within the next few days.

Bertrand's looked invitingly bright after the tempestuous blackness of the streets. Many of the white draped tables were unoccupied. His accustomed eye noted that the lady in the blue silk dress and black hat, and her companion with the bald head and cross-eye, who always sat at the right-hand corner table, were absent. He had fallen into the habit of bowing to them, and had more than once idly wondered what their relations were.

"Monsieur Esseex" to-night ate little and drank much. Etienne, the waiter, a black-haired, pink-cheeked garçon from Marseilles, noticed this and afterward remarked upon it to Madame Bertrand. To the few other habitués of the place, the thin-faced, handsome man with an ugly furrow down his cheek, and his hair tumbled on his forehead by the pressure of his hat, presented the same suavely imperturbable demeanor as usual. But Madame Bertrand, as a woman whose business it was to observe people and faces, noticed that monsieur was pale, and that when she spoke to him on the way in he had given a distrait answer, not the usual phrase of debonair, Gallic greeting she had grown to expect.

She looked at him from her cashier's desk and reflected. As Etienne afterward repeated, he ate little and drank much. And how pale he looked, with the lamp on the wall above him throwing out the high lights on his face and deepening the shadows!

"He is in love," thought the sentimental Madame Bertrand, "and to-night for the first time he knows that she does not respond."

He sat longer than he had ever done before over his dinner, blowing clouds of cigarette smoke about his head, and watching the thin blue flame of the burning lump of sugar in the spoon balanced on his coffee-cup.

Everybody had left, and he still sat smoking, leaning

back against the wall, his eyes fixed on space in immovable, concentrated thought. Bertrand came out of his corner, and in his cap and apron stood cooling himself in the open door watching the rain. Etienne and Henri, the two waiters apportioned to that part of the room, hung about restless and tired, eagerly watching for the first symptoms of his departure. Even Madame Bertrand began to burrow under the cashier's desk for her rubbers, and to struggle into them with much creaking of corset bones and subdued French ejaculations. It was after nine when the last guest finally pushed back his chair. Etienne rushed to help him on with his coat, and Madame Bertrand bobbed up from her rubbers to give him a parting smile.

A half-hour later he was lighting the gas in his own room in Bush Street. The damp air of the night entered through a crack of opened window, introducing a breath of sweet, moist freshness into the smoke-saturated chamber. He threw off his coat and lit the fire. As soon as it had caught satisfactorily he left the room, crossed the hall noiselessly, and with a slight preliminary knock, opened Harney's door. The man was sitting there in a broken rocking-chair, reading the evening paper by the light of a flaming gas-jet. He had the air of one who was waiting, and as Essex's head was advanced round the edge of the door, he looked up with alert, expectant eyes.

"Come into my room," said the younger man; "there's work for you to-night."

Harney threw down his paper and followed him across the hall. It was evident that he was sober, and beyond this some new sense of importance and power had taken from his manner its old deprecation. They were equals now, pals and partners. The drunken typesetter and one-time thief was still under Barry Essex's thumb, but he was also deep in his confidence.

He sat down in his old seat by the fire, his eyes on Essex.

"What's up?" he said; "what work have you got for me such a night as this?"

"Big work, and with big money behind it," said the younger man; "and when it's done we each get our share and go our ways, George Harney."

He drew his chair to the other side of the fire and began to talk—his voice low and quiet at first, growing urgent and authoritative, as Harney shrank before the dangers of the work expected of him. The moments ticked by, the fire growing hotter and brighter, the roaring of the storm sounding above the voices of the master and his tool. The night was half spent before Harney was conquered and instructed.

Then the men, waiting for the hour of deepest sleep and darkness, continued to sit, occasionally speaking, the light of the leaping flames catching and losing their anxious faces as the firelight in another room was touching the face of the sleeping girl of whom they talked.

It was nearly three when a movement of life stirred the blackness of the Garcia garden. The rushing of the rain beat down all sound; in the moist soddenness of the earth no trace lingered. The pepper-tree bent and cracked to the gusts as it did to the additional weight of the creeping figure in its boughs.

This was merely a shapeless bulk of blackness amid

the fine and broken blackness of the swaying foliage. It stole forward with noiseless caution, though it might have shouted and all sound been lost in the angry turmoil of the night. Creeping upward along the great limb that stretched to the balcony roof, a perpendicular knife-edge of light that gleamed from between the curtains of a window, now and then crossed its face, sometimes dividing it clearly in two, sometimes illuminating one attentive eye, a small shining point of life in the dead murk around it, one eye, aglow with purpose, gleaming startlingly from blackness.

The loud drumming of the rain on the balcony roof drowned the crackle of the tin under a feeling foot. To slide there from the limb only occupied a moment. The branch had grown well up over the roof, grating now and then against it when the wind was high. The thin streak of light from between the curtains made the man wary. Why was she burning a light at this hour unless she was sleepless and up?

Pressed close to the pane he applied his eye to the crack which was the widest near the sill. He saw a portion of the room, looking curiously vivid and distinct in the narrow concentration of his view. It seemed flooded with unsteady, warmly yellow light. Straight before him he saw a table with a rifled tea-tray on it, and back of that another table. The one eye pressed to the crack grew absorbed as it focused itself on the second table. Among a litter of books, ornaments and feminine trifles, stood a small desk of dark wood. It was as if it had been placed there to catch his attention—the goal of his line of vision.

Shifting his position he pressed his cheek against the glass and squinted in sidewise to where a deepening and quivering of the light spoke of a fire. Then he saw the figure of the sleeping woman, lying in an attitude of complete repose in the armchair. He gazed at her striving to gage the depth of her sleep. One of her hands hung over the arm of the chair, with the gleam of the fire flickering on the white skin. The same light touched a strand of loosened hair. Her face was in profile toward him, the chin pressed down on the shoulder. It looked like a picture in its suggestion of profound unconsciousness.

He pushed fearfully on the cross-bar of the pane, and the window rose a hair's-breadth. Then again, and it was high enough up for him to insert his hand. He did so, and drew forward the curtain of heavy rep so as to hide from the sleeper the gradual stages of his entrance. By degrees he raised it to a height sufficient to permit the passage of his body. The curtain shielded the girl from the current of cold air that entered the room. He crept in softly on his hands and knees, then rose to his feet.

For a moment he made no further movement, but stood, his gaze riveted on the sleeper, watching for a symptom of roused consciousness. She slept on peacefully, the light sound of her breathing faintly audible.

The silence of the hushed house seemed weirdly terrifying after the tumult of the night outside. The thief stole forward to the desk, his eye continually turned toward her. When he reached the table she was so far behind him that he could only see the sweep of her wrapper on the floor, her shoulder, and the top of her head over the chair back.

He tried the desk with an unsteady hand. It was locked, but the insertion of a steel file he carried broke the frail clasp. It gave with a sharp click and he stood, his hair stirring, watching the top of her head. It did not move, the silence resettled, he could again hear her light, even breathing.

There were many papers in the desk, bundles of letters, souvenirs of old days of affluence. He tossed them aside with tremulous quickness until, underneath all, he came on a long, dirty envelope and a little chamois leather bag. He lifted the latter. It was heavy and emitted a faint chink. The old thief's instincts rose in him. But he first opened the envelope, and softly drew out the two certificates, took the one he wanted, and put the other back. Then he opened the mouth of the bag. The gleam of gold shone from the aperture. Stricken with temptation he stood hesitating.

At that moment the fire, a heap of red ruins, fell together with a small, clinking sound. It was no louder noise than he had made when opening the desk, but it contained some penetrating quality the former had lacked. Still hesitating, with the sack of money in his hand, he turned again to the chair. A face, white and wide-eyed, was staring at him round the side.

He gave a smothered oath and the sack dropped from his hand to the table. The money fell from it in a clattering heap and rolled about, in golden zigzags in every direction. The sound roused the still unawakened intelligence of the girl. She saw the paper in his hand, half-opened. Its familiarity broke through her dazed senses. She rose and rushed at him gasping:

"The certificate! the certificate!"

Harney made a dash for the open window, but she caught him by the shoulder and arm, and with the unimpaired strength of her healthy youth struggled with him hand to hand, reaching out for the paper he tried to keep out of her grasp. In the fury of the moment's conflict, neither made any sound, but fought like two enraged animals, rocking to and fro, panting and clutching at each other.

He finally wrenched his arm free and struck her a savage blow, aimed at her head but falling on her shoulder, which sent her down on her knees and then back against the fire. He thought he had stunned her, and raised his arm again when she sprang up, tore the paper out of his grasp and pressed it with her hand down into the coals beside her. As she did so, for the first time she raised her voice and shrieked:

"Mr. Barron! Mr. Barron! Come, come! Oh hurry!"

From the hall Harney heard a movement and an answering shout. With the cries echoing through the room he beat her down against the grate, and tore the paper, curling with fire on the edges, from her hand. With it, he dashed through the open sash, a shiver of glass following him.

Almost simultaneously, Barron burst into the room. He had been reading and had fallen asleep to be waked by the shrieks of the girl's voice, which were still in his ears. The falling of broken glass and a rush of cold air from the opened window greeted him. Piled on the table and scattered about the floor were gold pieces. Mariposa was kneeling on the rug.

"He's got it!" she cried wildly, and struggling to her feet rushed to the window. "He's got it! Oh go after him! Stop him!"

"Got what?" he said. "No, he hasn't got the money. It's all there."

He seized her by the arm, for she seemed as if intending to go through the broken window.

"Not the money—not the money," she shrieked, wringing her hands; "the paper—the certificate! He's got it and gone, this way, through the window."

Barron grasped the fact that she had been robbed of something other than the money, the loss of which seemed to render her half distracted. With a hasty word of reassurance, he turned and ran from the room, springing down the stairs and across the hall. In the instant's pause by the window he had heard the sound of feet on the steps below and judged that he could get down more quickly by the stairs than by the limb of the tree.

But the few minutes' start and the darkness of the night were on the side of the thief. The roar of the rain drowned his footsteps. Barron ran this way and that, but neither sight nor sound of his quarry was vouchsafed to him. The man had got away with his booty, whatever it was.

In fifteen minutes Barron was back and found the Garcia ladies in Mariposa's room, ministering to the

"WITH THE STRENGTH OF HER HEALTHY YOUTH SHE STRUGGLED WITH HIM"

girl who lay in a heavy swoon, stark and white on the hearth-rug.

The old lady, in some wondrous and intimate déshabille, greeted him eagerly in Spanish, demanding what had happened. He told her all he knew and knelt down beside the younger Mrs. Garcia, who was attempting with a shaking hand to pour brandy between Mariposa's set teeth.

"We heard the most awful shrieks, and we rushed up, and here she was standing and screaming: 'He's got it! He's got it!' And then she fell flat, quite suddenly, and has lain here this way ever since."

"It was a robber," said the old woman, looking at the scattered gold, "but he didn't get her money. What was it he took, I wonder?"

"Some papers, I think," said Barron, "that were evidently of value to her. I'll lift her up and put her on the bed and then I'll go. As soon as she's conscious ask her what the man took and come and tell me, and I'll go right to the police station."

"Oh, don't leave us," implored Mrs. Garcia, junior —"if there are burglars anywhere round. Oh, please don't go. Pierpont's away and we'd have no man in the house. Don't go till morning. I'm just as scared as I can be!"

"There's nothing to be scared about. The man's got what he wanted, and he'll take precious good care not to come back."

"Oh, but don't go till it gets light. The window's broken and any one can come in who wants."

"All right, I'll wait till it gets light. I'll lift her up now, if you'll get the bed ready."

With the assistance of old Mrs. Garcia he lifted her and carried her to the bed. One of her arms fell limp against his shoulder as he laid her down, and the old lady uttered an exclamation. She lifted it up and showed him a curious red welt on the white wrist.

"It's a burn," she said. "How did she get that?"

"She must have fallen against the grate," he answered. His eyes grew dark as they encountered the scar. "As soon as she's conscious tell me."

A few minutes later, the young widow found him sitting on a chair under a lamp in the hall.

"Well," he said eagerly, "how is she?"

"She's come back to her senses all right. But she doesn't seem to want to tell what he took. She says it was a paper, and that's all, and that she never saw him before. Mother doesn't think we ought to worry her. She says she's got a fever, and she's going to give her medicine to make her sleep, and not to disturb her till she wakes up. She's all broken up and sort of limp and trembly."

"Well, I suppose the señora knows best. It'll be light soon now, and I'll go to the police station. The señora and you will stay with her?"

"O yes," said Mrs. Garcia, the younger. "My goodness, what a night it's been! It's lucky the man didn't get her money. There was quite a lot; about five hundred dollars, I should think. Oh, my curl papers! I forget them. Gracious, what a sight I must look!" and she shuffled down the stairs.

Barron sat on till the dawn broke gray through the

hall window. He was beginning to wonder if this girl was the central figure of some drama, secret, intricate and unsuspected, which was working out to its conclusion.

CHAPTER XXIII

THE LOST VOICE

"There may be heaven; there must be hell;
Meantime there is our earth here—well!"
—BROWNING.

The fears of Mrs. Garcia held Barron to the house till the morning light was fully established. This was late, even for the winter season, as the rain still fell heavily, retarding the coming of day with a leaden veil.

He made his report at the police station, and then went down town to his office where business detained him till noon. It was his habit to lunch at the Lick House, but to-day he hurried back to the Garcias', striding up the series of hills at top speed, urged on by his desire to hear news of Mariposa. He burst into the house to find it silent—the hall empty. As he was hanging his hat on the rack, young Mrs. Garcia appeared from the kitchen, her bang somewhat limp, though it was still early in the day, her face looking small and peaked after her exciting night's vigil.

Mariposa was still asleep, she said in answer to his query. The señora had given her a powerful sleeping draft and had said that the rest would be the best restorative after such a shock. If, when she waked, she

THE LOST VOICE

showed symptoms of suffering or prostration, they would send for the doctor.

"Have you found her paper?" she asked anxiously. "She seemed in such a way about it last night."

He muttered a preoccupied answer, mentioning his visit to the police station.

"What was it, anyway? Do *you* know?" inquired the young woman who was not exempt from the weaknesses of her sex.

"Some legal document, I think, but I don't know. The police can't do much till they know what it is."

"Perhaps it was a will," said the widow, whose sole literature was that furnished by the daily press; "though I should think if it was a will she'd have told about it by now and not kept it hid away up there. Anyway, she thought a lot of it, for when she came to I told her her money was all right, and she said she didn't care about the money, she wanted the paper."

"I'll see her when she wakes," said Barron, "and find out what it was. Our affair now is to see that she is not frightened again and gets well."

"Well, mother says to let her sleep. So that's what we're going to do. No one's going to disturb her, and Pierpont, who got back an hour ago, has promised not to give any lessons all afternoon."

The conversation was here interrupted by the appearance of the Chinaman, who loungingly issued from the kitchen, shouted an unintelligible phrase at his mistress, and disappeared into the dining-room. His words seemed to have meaning to her, for she pulled off her apron, saying briskly:

"There, dinner's ready and we're going to have enchilados. Don't you smell them? The boys will be crazy."

A cautious inspection made after dinner by young Mrs. Garcia, resulted in the information that Mariposa still slept. Barron, who was feverishly desirous to know how she progressed and also anxious to learn from her the nature of the lost document, was forced to leave without seeing her. A business engagement of the utmost importance claimed him at his office at two or he would have awaited her awakening.

It was nearly an hour later before this occurred. The drug the señora had administered was a heroic remedy, relic of the days when doctors were a rarity and the medicine chest of the hardy Spaniard contained few but powerful potions. The girl rose, feeling weak and dizzy. For some time she found it difficult to collect her thoughts and sat on the edge of her bed, eying the disordered room with uncomprehending glances. Bodily discomfort at first absorbed her mind. A fever burned through her, her head ached, her limbs felt leaden and stiff.

The sight of the opened desk gave the fillip to her befogged memory, and suddenly the events of the night rushed back on her with stunning force. She felt, at first, that it must be a dream. But the rifled desk, with the money which the Garcias had gathered up and laid in a glittering heap on the table, told her of its truth. The man's face, yellow and flabby, with the dark line of the shaven beard clearly marked on his jaws, and the frightened rat's eyes, came back to her as he had turned in the first paralyzed moment of fear. With hot, unsteady hands she searched through the scattered papers and then about the room, in the hope that he had dropped the paper in the struggle. But all search was fruitless. She remembered his tearing it from her grasp as Barron's shout had sounded in the passage. He had escaped with it. The irrefutable evidence of the marriage was in Essex's hands. He had her under his feet. It was the end.

She began to dress slowly and with constant pauses. Every movement seemed an effort; every stage of her toilet loomed colossal before her. The one horror of the situation kept revolving in her brain, and she found it impossible to detach her thoughts from it and fix them on anything else. At the same time she could think of no way to escape, or to fight against it.

Next Sunday it would all be in *The Era.* Those words seemed written in letters of fire on the walls, and repeated themselves in maddening revolution in her mind. It would all be there, sensationally displayed as other old scandals had been. She saw the tragic secret of the two lives that had sheltered hers, the love that had been so sacred a thing written of with all the defiling brutality of the common scribe and his common reader, for all the world of the low and ignoble to jeer at and spit upon.

She stopped in her dressing and pressed her hands to her face. How could she live till next Sunday, and then, when Sunday came, live through it? There were three days yet before Sunday. Might not something be done in three days? But she could think of nothing. Something had happened to her brain. If there was only some one to help her!

And with that came the thought of Barron. A flash of relief went through her. He would help her; he would do something. She had no idea what, but something, and, uplifted by the idea, she opened the door and looked up the hall. She felt a sudden drop of hope when she saw that his door was closed. But she stole up the passage, watching it, not knowing what she intended saying to him, only actuated by the desire to throw her responsibilities on him and ask for his help.

The door was ajar and she listened outside it. There was no sound from within and no scent of cigar-smoke. She tapped softly and receiving no answer pushed it open and peered fearfully in. The room was empty. The man's clothes were thrown about carelessly, his table littered with papers and books. From the crevice of the opened window came the smell and the sound of the rain, with a chill, bleak suggestion.

A sudden throttling sense of lonely helplessness overwhelmed her. She stood looking blankly about, at the ashes of cigars in a china saucer, at an old valise gaping open in a corner. The room seemed to her to have a vacated air, and she remembered hearing Barron, a few days before, speak of going to the mines again soon. Her mind leaped to the conclusion that he had gone. Her hopes suddenly fell around her in ruins, and in his looking-glass she saw a blanched face that she hardly recognized as her own.

Stealing back to her room she sat down on the bed again. The house was curiously quiet and in this silence her thoughts began once more to revolve round the one topic. Then suddenly they broke into a burst of rebellion. She could not bear it. She must go, somewhere, anywhere to escape. She would flee away like a hunted animal and hide, creeping into some dark distant place and cowering there. But where would she go, and what would she do? The world outside seemed one vast menace waiting to spring on her. If her head would stop aching and the fever that burned her body and clouded her brain would cease for a moment, she could think and come to some conclusion. But now—

And suddenly, as she thought, a whisper seemed to come to her, clear and distinct like a revelation—"You have your voice!"

It lifted her to her feet. For a moment the pain and confusion of developing illness left her, and she felt a thrill of returning energy. She had it still, the one great gift neither enemies nor misfortune could take from her—her voice!

The hope shook her out of the lethargy of fever, and her mind sprang into excited action like a loosened spring. She went to her desk and placed the gold back in its bag. The five hundred dollars that had seemed so meaningless had now a use. It would take her away to Europe. With the three hundred she still had in the bank, it would be enough to take her to Paris and leave her something to live on. Money went a long way over there, she had heard. She could study and sing and become famous.

It all seemed suddenly possible, almost easy. Only leaving would be hard—fearfully. She thought of the door up the passage and the voice that in those first days of her feebleness had called a greeting to her every morning; the man's deep voice with its strong, cheery note. And then like a peevish child, sick and unreasonable, she found herself saying:

"Why does he leave me now when I want him so?"

No—her voice was all she had. She would live for it and be famous, and the year of terror and anguish she had spent in San Francisco would become a dim memory upon which she could some day look back with calm. But before she went she would sing for Pierpont and hear what he said.

The thought had hardly formed in her mind when she was out in the hall and stealing noiselessly down the stairs of the silent house. It struck her as odd that the house should be so quiet, as these were the hours in which Pierpont's pupils usually made the welkin resound with their efforts. Perhaps he was out. But this was not so, for in the lower hall she met the girl with the fair hair and prominent blue eyes who possessed the fine soprano voice she had so often listened to, and who in response to her query told her that Mr. Pierpont was in, but not giving lessons this afternoon.

In answer to her knock she heard his "come in" and opened the door. He was sitting on a divan idly turning over some loose sheets of music. The large, sparsely furnished room—it was in reality the back drawing-room of the house—looked curiously gray and cold in the dreaı afternoon light. It was only slightly furnished—his bed and toilet articles being in a curtained alcove. In the center of its unadorned, occupied bareness, the grand piano, gleaming richly, stood open, the stool in front of it.

THE LOST VOICE

"Miss Moreau," he said, starting to his feet, "I thought you were sick in bed. How are you? You've had a dreadful experience. I've been sending away my pupils because I was told you were asleep."

"Oh, I'm quite well now," she said, "only my head aches a little. Yes, I was frightened last night—a burglar came in, crept up the bough of the pepper-tree. I was dreadfully frightened then, but I'm all right now. I've come to sing for you."

"To sing for me!" he exclaimed; "but you're not well enough to sing. You've had a bad fright and you look—excuse me"—he took her hand—"you're burning up with fever. Take my advice and go up-stairs, and as soon as Mrs. Garcia comes in we'll get a doctor."

"No—no!" she said almost violently; "I'm quite well now. My hand's hot and so is my head, but that's natural after the fright I had last night. I want to sing for you now and see what you say about my voice."

"But, you know, you can't do yourself justice and I can't form a fair opinion. Why do you want to sing this afternoon when you wouldn't all winter?"

"Well," she said, "I don't mind telling you. I'm going to Europe to study. I've just made up my mind."

"Going to Europe! Isn't that very sudden? But it will be splendid! When are you going?"

"Soon—in a day or two—as soon as I can get my things packed in my trunks."

He looked at her curiously. Her manner, which was usually calm and deliberate, was marked by tremulous restlessness. She spoke rapidly and like one laboring under suppressed excitement.

"Come," she said, going to the piano stool and pushing it nearer the keyboard, "I'll be very busy now and I don't want to waste any time."

He moved reluctantly to the piano and seated himself.

"Have you your music?" he asked.

"No, but I can sing what some of your pupils do. I can sing 'Knowest thou the land?' and Mrs. Burrell sings that. Where is it?"

Her feverish haste and nervousness impressed him more than ever as her hands tossed aside the sheets of piled-up music, throwing them about the piano and snatching at them as they slipped to the floor. From there he picked up the 'Mignon' aria which she had overlooked and spreading it on the rack struck the opening notes. She leaned over him to see the first line and he felt that she was trembling violently. He raised his hands and wheeled round on the stool.

"Miss Moreau," he said, "I truly don't think you're well enough to sing. Don't you think we'd better put it off till to-morrow?"

"No, no—I'm going to now. I'm ready. I'm anxious to. I must. Begin again, please."

He turned obediently and began again to play the chords of accompaniment. He had been for a long time intensely anxious to hear her voice, of which he had heard so much. It irritated him now to have her determined to sing when she was obviously ill and still suffering from the effects of her fright.

The accompaniment reached the point where the

THE LOST VOICE 419

voice joins it. He played softly, alert for the first rich notes. Mariposa's chest rose with an inflation of air and she began to sing.

A sound, harsh, veiled and thin, filled the room. There was no volume, nor resonance, nor beauty in it. It was the ghost of a voice.

The teacher was so shocked that for a moment he stumbled in the familiar accompaniment. Then he went on, bending his head low over the keys, fearful of her seeing his face. Sounds unmusical, rasping, and discordant came from her lips. Everything that had once made it rich and splendid was gone, the very volume of it had dwindled to a thin, muffled thread, the color had flown from every tone.

For a bar or two she went on, then she stopped. Pierpont dared not turn at first. But he heard her behind him say hoarsely:

"What—what—is it?"

Then he wheeled round and saw her with wild eyes and white lips.

For a moment he could say nothing. Her appearance struck him with alarm, and he sat dumb on the stool staring at her.

"What is it?" she cried. "What has happened to it? Where is my voice?"

'It's—it's—certainly not in good condition," he stammered.

"It's gone," she answered in a wail of agony; "it's gone. My voice has gone! What shall I do? It's gone!"

"Your fright of last night has affected it," he said, speaking as kindly as he could, "and you're not well.

I told you you were feverish and ought not to sing. Rest will probably restore it."

"Let me try it again," she said wildly. "It may be better. Play again."

He played over the opening bars again, and once more she drew the deep breath that in the past had always brought with it so much of exultation and began to sing. The same feeble sounds, obscured as though passing through a thick, muffling medium, hoarse, flat, unlovely, came with labor from her parted lips.

They broke suddenly into a wild animal cry of despair. Pierpont rose from the stool and went toward her where she stood with her arms drooping by her sides, pallid and terrible.

"Don't look like that," he said, taking her hand; "there's no doubt the voice has been injured. But rest does a great deal, and after a shock like last night—"

She tore herself away from him and ran to the door crying:

"Oh, my voice! My voice! It was all I had!"

He followed her into the hall, not knowing what to say in the face of such a calamity, only anxious to offer her some consolation. But she ran from him, up the stairs with a frantic speed. As he put his foot on the lower step he heard her door.

He turned round and went back slowly to his room. He was shocked and amazed, and a little relieved that he had failed to catch her for he had no words ready for such a misfortune. Her voice was completely gone. She was unquestionably ill and nervous—but—

He sat down on the divan, shaking his head. He had never heard a voice more utterly lost and wrecked.

Barron's business engagement detained him longer than he had expected. The heavy rain was shortening the already short February day with a premature dusk when he opened the gate of the Garcia house and mounted the steps.

He had made a cursory investigation of the ground under the pepper-tree when he went out in the early morning. Now, before the light died, he again stepped under its branches for a more thorough survey. The foliage was so thick that no grass grew where the tree's shadow fell, and the rain sifted through it in occasional dribbles or shaken showers. The bare stretch of ground was now an expanse of mud, interspersed with puddles. Here and there a footprint still remained, full of water. He moved about the base of the tree studying these, then looking up into the branch along which the burglar had crept to the balcony. What paper could the girl have possessed of sufficient value to lure a man to such risks?

With his mind full of this thought his glance dropped to the root of the trunk. A piece of burnt paper, half covered with the trampled mud, caught his eye, and he picked it up and absently glanced at it. He was about to throw it over the fence into the road, when he saw the name of Jacob Shackleton. The next moment his eyes were riveted on the printed lines here and there filled in with writing. He moved so that the full light fell on it through a break in the branches.

It was a minute or two before he grasped its real meaning. But he knew the name of Lucy Fraser, too. Mariposa had once told him it had been her mother's maiden name.

For a space he stood motionless under the tree, staring at the paper, focusing his mind on it, seizing on waifs and strays from the past that surged to the surface of his memory. It dazed him at first. Then he began to understand. The mysterious drama that environed the girl upstairs began to grow clear to him. This was the document that had been stolen from her last night, the loss of which had thrown her into a frenzy of despair—the record of a marriage between her mother and Jake Shackleton.

Without stopping to think further he thrust it into his pocket and ran to the house. As he mounted the porch steps the scene of his first meeting with Mariposa flashed suddenly like a magic-lantern picture across his mind. He heard her hysterical cry of—"He was my father!" Another veil of the mystery seemed lifted.

And now he shrank from penetrating further, for he began to see. If Mariposa had some sore secret to hide let her keep it shut in her own breast. All he had to do was to give the paper to her as soon as he could. In the moment's passage of the balcony and the pause while he inserted his latch-key in the door he tried to think how he could restore it to her without letting her think he had read it. The key turned and as the door gave he decided that it must be given her at once without wasting time or bothering about comforting lies.

He burst into the hall and then stood still, the door-handle in his hand. In the dim light, the two Garcia ladies and the two boys met his eyes, standing in a group at the foot of the stairs. There was something in their faces and attitudes that bespoke uneasiness and anxiety. Their four pairs of eyes were fastened on him with curious alarmed gravity.

He kicked the door shut and said:
"How's Miss Moreau?"
The question seemed to increase their disquietude.
"We don't know where she is," said young Mrs. Garcia.
"Isn't she in her room?" he demanded.
"No—that's what's so funny. I thought she was sleeping an awful long time and I just peeked in and she isn't there. And Benito's been all over the house and can't find her. It seems so crazy of her to go out in all this rain, but her outside things are not in the closet or anywhere."

They stood silent for a moment, eying one another with faces of disturbed query.

The opening of Pierpont's door roused them. The young man appeared in the aperture and then came slowly forward.

"Have you seen Miss Moreau?" he said to young Mrs. Garcia.
"No," said Barron hurriedly; "but have you?"
"Yes, she was down in my room this afternoon singing."
"Singing!" echoed the others in wide-eyed amazement.
"Yes, and I'm rather anxious about her. That's why I came out when I heard your voices. She's had

a pretty severe disappointment, I'm afraid. She seems to have lost her voice."

"Lost her voice!" ejaculated Mrs. Garcia in a low gasp of horror. "Good heavens!"

The boys looked from one to the other with the round eyes of growing fear and dread. The calamity, as announced by Pierpont, did not seem adequate for the consternation it caused, but an oppressive sense of apprehension was in the air.

"What made her want to sing?" said the widow; "she was too sick to sing."

"That's what I told her, but she insisted. She was determined to. She said she was going to Europe to study."

"Going to Europe!" It was Barron's deep voice that put the question this time, Mrs. Garcia being too astonished by this last piece of intelligence to have breath for speech. "When was she going to Europe?"

"In a day or two—as soon as she could pack her trunks, she said. I don't really think she was quite accountable for what she said. She was burning with a fever and she seemed in a tremendously wrought-up state. I think her fright of the night before had quite upset her. I tried to cheer her up, but she ran away as if she was frantic. Have any of you seen her?"

"No," said Mrs. Garcia, her voice curiously flat. "She's gone."

"Gone?" echoed Pierpont. "Gone where?"

"We don't any of us know. But she's not in the house anywhere. And now it's getting dark and—"

There was a pause, one of those pregnant pauses

of mute anxiety while each eyed the other with glances full of an alarmed surmise.

"Perhaps the robber came and took her away," said Benito in a voice of terror.

No one paid any attention. As if by common consent all present fastened questioning eyes on Barron. He stood looking down, his brows knit. The silence of dumb uneasiness was broken by the entrance of the Chinaman from the kitchen. With the expressionless phlegm of his race he lit the two hall gas-jets, gently but firmly moving the señora out of his way, and paying no attention to the silent group at the stair foot.

"Ching," said Barron suddenly, "have you seen Miss Moreau this afternoon?"

"Yes," returned the Celestial, carefully adjusting the tap of the second gas, "she go out hap-past four. She heap hurry. She look welly bad—heap sick I guess; no umblella; get awful wet."

With his noiseless tread he retreated up the passage to the kitchen.

"Well, I'll go," said Barron suddenly. "She's just possibly gone out to see some one and will be back soon. But no umbrella in this rain! Have her room warm and everything ready."

He turned round and in an instant was gone. The little group at the stairpost looked at one another with pale faces. It was possible that Mariposa had gone out to see some one. But the dread of disaster was at every heart.

CHAPTER XXIV

A BROKEN TOOL

"A plague o' both your houses!
They have made worms' meat of me."
—SHAKESPEARE.

It had been close upon half-past two when Harney had left the house in Bush Street. Essex at the window had heard the sound of his retreating feet soon lost in the rush of the rain, and had then returned to the fire. He had made a close calculation of the time Harney should take. To go and come ought not to occupy more than a half-hour. The theft, itself, if no mischances occurred, should be accomplished in ten or fifteen minutes.

As the hands of the clock on the table drew near three, the man rose from his post by the fire and began to move restlessly about the room. The house was wrapped in the dead stillness of sleep, round which the turmoil of the storm circled and upon which it seemed to press. Pausing to listen he could hear the creaks and groan of the old walls, as the wind buffeted them. Once, thinking he heard a furtive step, he went to the door, opened it and peered out into the blackness of the hall. The stairs still creaked as if to a light ascending foot, but his eyes encountered nothing but the impenetrable darkness, charged with the familiar smell of stale smoke.

Back in his room he went to the window and throwing it wide, leaned out listening. The rain fell with a continuous drumming rustle, through which the chinks and gurgles of water caught in small channels penetrated with a near-by clearness. Here and there the darkness broke away in splinters from a sputtering lamp, and where its light touched, everything gleamed and glistened. Gusts of wind rose and fell, tore the wet bushes in the garden below, and banged a shutter on an adjacent house.

Essex left the window, drawing the curtain to shut its light from the street. It was a quarter past three. If at four Harney had not returned he would go after him. The thief might easily have missed his footing in the tree and have fallen, and be lying beneath it, stunned, dead perhaps, the papers in his hand.

The clock hands moved on toward twenty—twenty-five minutes past. The creaking came from the stairs again, exactly, to the listening ear, like the soft sound of a cautiously-mounting step. From the cupboard came a curious loud tick and then a series of rending cracks. It made Essex start guiltily, and swearing under his breath, he again turned toward the window and, as he did so, caught the sound of hurrying feet. He drew the curtain and leaned out. Above the uproar of the night he heard the quick, regular thud of the feet of a runner, rushing onward through the storm, and then, across the gleam of a lamp, a dark figure shot, with head down, flying.

He dropped the curtain and waited, immense relief

at his heart. In a moment he heard the footsteps stop at the gate, furtively ascend the stairs of the two terraces, and then the stealthy grating of the door. He silently pushed his own door open that the light might guide the ascending man, and he heard Harney's loud breathing as he crept up.

The thief rose up out of the gulf of darkness like an apparition of terror. He dropped into a chair, his face gray, white and pinched, the sound of his rasping breaths, drawn with pain from the bottom of his lungs, filling the room. He was incapable of speech, and Essex, pouring him out whisky, was forced to take the glass from his shaking hand and hold it to his lips. From his soaked clothes and the cap that crowned his head, like a saturated woolen rag, water streamed. But the rain had not been able to efface from his coat a caking of mud that half-covered one arm and shoulder, and there was blood on one of his hands. He had evidently fallen.

"Have you got it?" said Essex, putting the glass down.

The other nodded and let his head sink on the chair-back.

"I'm dead," he gasped, "but I done it."

"Where is it? Give it to me."

The man made a faint movement of assent, but evidently had not force enough to produce the paper and lay limp in the chair, Essex watching him impatiently. Presently he put his feeble hand out for the glass and drank again. The rattling loudness of his breathing moderated. Without moving his head he turned his eyes on Essex and said:

A BROKEN TOOL

"I'm most killed—I'm all shook up. I fell coming down the tree, some way—I don't know how far—but I got it all right. She fought like a wildcat, tried to burn it—but I got it. Then she hollered and a man answered. I knew it was a man's voice, and I made a dash for the winder only jest in time. I'm cut somewheres—"

He raised the hand with the blood on it and fumbled at his coat-sleeve. The other hand was smeared with blood from the contact.

"Like a pig," he said in a low voice, and pulled out a rag of handkerchief which he tried to push up his sleeve; "I'm cut somewheres all right, but I don't know where."

"Give me the paper and take your things off. You're dripping all over everything," said Essex, extending his hand.

Harney sat up.

"I dunno how I done it," he said; "how I got down. The man was right on my heels. When I fell I saw him, pullin' her up on her feet—I saw that through the winder. Then I riz up and I went—God, how I went!"

He had stuffed his handkerchief up his sleeve by this time, and now put his bloody tremulous hand into the outer breast-pocket of his coat. As the hand fumbled about the opening he said:

"I didn't stop to look no more nor take no risks. I wanted to git away from thar and I tell you I lit out, and—"

He stopped, his jaw dropped, his nerveless figure stiffened, a look of animal terror came into his eyes.

"Where is it?" he almost yelled, staring at Essex.

"How the devil should I know! Where did you put it? Isn't it there?"

Essex himself had suddenly paled. He stood erect before the crouched and trembling figure of his partner, his eyes fiercely intense.

"It ain't here," cried Harney, his hand clawing about in the pocket. "It ain't there. Oh Lordy, Lordy! I've lost it! It's gone. It fell out when I came off the tree. I fell. I told you I fell. Didn't I tell you I fell?" he shouted, as if he had been contradicted.

He rose up, his face pasty white, wringing his hands like a woman. There was something grotesque and almost overdone in his terror, but his pallor and the fear in his eyes were real.

"Lost it!" cried Essex. "No more of those lies! Give me the paper, you dog."

"Don't you hear me say I ain't got it? Ain't I told you I fell? When I jumped for the tree I jest smashed it down into my pocket. I had to have both hands to climb. And I suppose I ain't pressed it in tight enough. God, man, it was ten years in San Quentin for me if I'd lost two minutes."

Essex drew closer, his mouth tight, his eyes fixed with a fiercely compelling gaze on the wretch before him.

"Don't think you can make anything by stealing that paper. Give it up; give it up now; I've got you here, and I'll know what you've done with it before you leave or you'll never leave at all."

"I lost it, and that's what I done with it. If you want it, come on with me now and look round under that tree. Ain't you understood I fell sideways from

A BROKEN TOOL

the branch to the ground? Look at my hand—" he held up his arm, pulling the muddy sleeve back from the blood-stained wrist.

"Where is it?" said Essex, without moving. "You were gone nearly an hour. Where have you hidden it?"

"Nowheres. It took time. I had to clim' up careful, 'cause she had a light burning, and I thought she was awake. Why can't you believe me? What can I do with it alone?"

"You can blackmail Mrs. Shackleton well enough alone. Give me that paper, or tell me where you put it, or, by God, I'll kill you!"

Fear of the man that owned him gave Harney the air of guilt. He backed away in an access of pallid terror, shouting:

"I ain't lying. Why can't yer believe me? It took time—it took time! Ain't I told you I fell? Look at the mud; and feel, feel in every pocket." He seized on them and tore the insides outward. "I'm tellin' you the whole truth. I ain't got it."

"Where is it, then? You'll tell me where you've hidden it, or—"

Essex made a sudden leap forward and caught the man by his neck-cloth and collar. In his blind alarm Harney was given fictitious strength, and he tore himself loose and rushed for the door. Essex's hat, coat and stick lay on the table. Without thought or premeditation their owner seized the cane—a heavy malacca—by the end, flew round the table, and as Harney turned the door-handle, brought the knob of the loaded cane down on the crown of his head.

It struck with a thud and sent the water squirting from the saturated cap. The thief, without cry or word, spun round, waving his hands in the air, and then fell heavily face downward. For a moment he quivered, and once or twice made a convulsive movement, then lay still, the water running from his clothes along the floor.

With the cane still in his hand, Essex came around the table and looked at him. For a space he stood staring, his hand resting on the edge of the table, his neck craned forward, his face set in a rigid intensity of observation. The sudden silence that had succeeded to the loud tones of Harney's voice was singularly deep and solemn. The room seemed held in a spell of stillness, almost awful in its suddenness and isolation.

"Get up," he said in a low voice. "Harney, get up."

There was no response, and he leaned forward and pushed at the motionless figure with the cane.

"Damn!" he said under his breath, "he's fainted."

And throwing the cane away, he approached the man and bent over him. There was no sound of breathing or pulse of life about the sodden figure with its hidden face. Drops formed on Essex's forehead as he turned it over. Then, as it confronted him, livid with fallen jaw and a gleam of white between the wrinkled eyelid, the drops ran down his face.

With a hand that shook as Harney's had a few moments before he felt the pulse and then tore the shirt open and tried the heart. His face was white as the man's on the floor as he poured whisky down the throat that refused to swallow. Finally, tearing off his coat, he knelt beside his victim and tried every means in his power to bring back life into the miserable body in which he had only recognized a tool of his own. But there was no response. The minutes ticked on, and there was no glimmer of intelligence in the cold indifference of the eyes, no warmth round the stilled heart, no flutter of breath at the slack, gray lips.

The night was still dark, the rain in his ears, when he rose to his feet. A horror unlike anything he had even imagined was on him. All the things in life he had struggled for seemed shriveled to nothing. The whole worth of his existence was contained in the unlovely body on the floor. To bring life back to it he would have given his dearest ambition—sacrificed love, money, happiness—all for which he had held life valuable, and thought himself blessed. What a few hours before were ends to struggle and sin for seemed now of no moment to him. Mariposa had faded to a dim, undesired shadow; the millions she stood for to dross he would have passed without a thought. How readily would he have given it all to bring back the breath to the creature he had held as a worm beneath his foot!

He seized the table-cloth and threw it over the face whose solemn, tragic calm filled him with a sick dread. Then with breathless haste he flung some clothes into a valise and made the fire burn high with the letters and papers he threw on it at intervals. The first carts of the morning had begun their rattling course through the stirred darkness when he crept out, a haggard, hunted man.

. He had to hide himself in unfrequented corners, cower beneath the shadow of trees on park benches till the light strengthened and morning shook the city into life. Then, as its reawakening tides began to surge round him, he made a furtive way—for the first time in his life fearful of his fellow men—to the railway station, and there took the earliest south-bound train for the Mexican border.

The fire had died down, the leaden light of coming day was filtering in through the crack between the half-drawn curtains, when the shrouded shape on the floor moved and a deep groan broke upon the stillness. Another followed it, groans of physical anguish beating on awakening consciousness. An early riser from the floor above heard them as he stole downward, stopped, listened, knocked, then receiving no reply, opened the door and peered fearfully in. In the dim room, cut with a sword of faint light, he saw the covered shape, and, as he stood terrified, heard the groan repeated and saw the drapery twitched. Shouting his fears over the balustrade, he rushed in, flung the curtains wide, tore off the table-cloth, and in the rush of pallid light, saw Harney, leaden eyed, withered to a waxen pallor, smeared with the blood of the cut wrist which he feebly moved, struggling back to existence.

CHAPTER XXV

HAVE YOU COME AT LAST

"Yesterday this day's madness did prepare."
—OMAR KHAYYAM.

At ten o'clock Barron returned to the Garcia house. His search for Mariposa in such accustomed haunts as the Mercantile Library, the shops on Kearney Street. and Mrs. Willers', had been fruitless. Mrs. Willers was again at *The Trumpet* office, where another and more important portion of the Woman's Page was going to press, but Edna was at home, and told Barron that neither she nor her mother had seen Mariposa since the lesson of the day before.

In returning to the house he had hopes of finding her there. From the first his anxiety had been keen. Now, as he put his key in the lock, it clutched his heart with a suffocating force. The house was silent as he entered, and then the sound of his step in the hall called the head of young Mrs. Garcia to the opened door of the kitchen. The first glimpse of her face told him Mariposa had not returned.

"Have you got her?" cried the young woman eagerly.

"No," he answered, his voice sounding colorless and flat. "I thought she might be back here."

Mrs. Garcia shook her head and withdrew it. He followed her into the kitchen, where she and the señora were sitting by the stove. A large fire was burning, the room was warm and bright—the trim, finically neat kitchen of a clean Chinaman. To the señora's quick phrase of inquiry, the younger woman answered with a sentence in Spanish. For a moment the silence of sick anxiety held the trio.

"Did you go to Mrs. Willers'?" said young Mrs. Garcia, trying to speak with some lightness of tone.

"Yes; she's not been there since yesterday. I've been everywhere I could think of where it was likely she would be. I couldn't find a trace of her."

"Then's she's gone to Europe, or is going to-morrow, as she told Pierpont. She took her money. We looked after you'd gone, and it wasn't there."

"It'll be too late to find out to-night if she's gone. The ticket offices are closed. I can't think she's done that—without a word to any one. It's not like her."

The señora here asked what they said. Barron, who spoke Spanish indifferently, signaled to the young woman to answer for him. She did so, the señora listening intently. At the end of her daughter-in-law's speech she shook her head.

"No, she has not gone," she said slowly in Spanish. "She could not take that journey. She was not able—she was sick."

"Sick, and out on such a night with all that money!" moaned her daughter-in-law.

Barron got up with a smothered ejaculation. He knew more than either of the women. The attempt at robbery the night before had failed. To-night the girl herself had disappeared. What might it all mean? He was afraid to think.

"I'm going out again," he said. "I'll be in probably in four or five hours to see if, by any chance, she's come back. You have everything ready—fires and warm clothes and things to eat in case I bring her with me. The rain's worse than ever. Ching says she had no umbrella."

Without more conversation he left, the two women bestirring themselves to make ready the supper he had ordered. At three o'clock he returned again to find the señora sitting alone, by the ruddy stove, Mrs. Garcia, the younger, being asleep on a sofa in the boys' room. The old lady persuaded him to drink a cup of coffee she had kept warm, and, as she gave it him, looked with silent compassion into his haggard face.

When day broke he had not again appeared. By this time the household was in a ferment of open alarm. The boys were retained from school, as it was felt they might be needed for messages. Pierpont undertook to visit all Mariposa's pupils, in the dim hope of finding through them some clue to her movements, though it was well known she was on intimate terms with none of them. Soon after breakfast Mrs. Willers appeared, uneasy, and by the time the now weeping Mrs. Garcia had told her all, pale and deeply disturbed.

She repaired to *The Trumpet* office without loss of time, and there acquainted her chief with the story of Miss Moreau's disappearance, not neglecting to mention the burglary of the night before, which even to the women, having no knowledge of its real import, seemed to indicate a sinister connection with subsequent events. Winslow did not disappoint Mrs. Willers by pooh-poohing the matter, as she had half imagined he would; a young lady's disappearance for twelve hours not being a subject for such tragic consternation. He seemed extremely worried—in fact, showed an anxiety that struck the head of the Woman's Page as almost odd. He assured her that if Miss Moreau was not heard from that day by mid-day he would offer secretly to the police department the largest reward ever given in San Francisco, for any trace or tidings of her.

Meantime Barron, having assured himself by visits to all the ticket offices that she had not left the city on any train, had finally taken his case to the police. It had been in their hands only an hour or two, when young Shackleton's offer of what, in even those extravagant days seemed an enormous reward, was communicated to the department. It put life into the somewhat dormant energies of the officers detailed on the case. Mariposa had not been missing twenty-four hours when the search for her was spreading over the face of the city, where she had been so insignificant a unit, in a thorough and secret network of investigation.

The day wore away with maddening slowness to the women in the house, whose duty it was to sit and wait. To Barron, whose anxiety had been intensified by the torture of his deeper knowledge of the girl's strange circumstances, existence seemed only bearable as it was directed to finding her. He did not dare now to pause or think. Without stopping to eat or rest he continued his search, now with the detectives, now alone. Several times in the course of the day he reappeared at the Garcia house, drawn thither by the hope that she might have returned. The señora, with the curious tranquillity of the very old which seems not to need the repairing processes of sleep or food, was always to be found sitting by the kitchen stove, upon which some dish or drink simmered for him. He rarely stopped to take either. But returning in the early dusk, he was grateful to find that she had a dry overcoat hanging before the fire for him. The rain still fell in torrents, and the long day spent at its mercy had soaked him.

It was between ten and eleven at night that the old lady and her daughter-in-law, sitting before the stove as they had done the evening before, again heard his step and his key. This time there was no pretense at expectation on either side. His first glance inside the room showed him the heavy dejection of the two faces turned toward him. They, on their part, saw him pale and drawn, as by a month's illness. They had heard nothing. No investigation of which they were aware had brought in a crumb of comfort. He had heard worse than nothing. There had been talk at the police station that evening of the finding of George Harney, suffering from concussion of the brain, and the sudden departure of Barry Essex, believed to be his assailant.

This information added the last straw to Barron's agony of apprehension. It seemed as if a plot had culminated in those two days, a plot dark and inexplicable, in which the woman he loved was in some mysterious way involved.

He was standing by the stove responding to the somber queries of the women, when the sound of feet on the porch steps suddenly transfixed them all. Young Mrs. Garcia screamed, while the old lady sat with head bent sidewise listening. Before Barron could get to the door a soft ring at the bell had drawn another scream from the younger woman, who, nevertheless, followed him and stood peeping into the hall, clinging to the doorpost.

The opened door sent a flood of light over three figures huddled in the glass porch—two men, a detective and policeman, Barron already knew, and a third, a stranger to him, whose face against the shadowy background looked fresh and boyish.

"Ah, Mr. Barron, we're lucky to strike you this way at the first shot," said the detective. "We think we've found the lady."

"Found her? Where? Have you got her there?"

"No; we're not certain yet if it's the right one."

The man, as he spoke, entered the hall, the policeman and the stranger following him. Under the flare of the two gas-jets they looked big, ungainly figures in their smoking rubber capes that ran rillets of water on the floor. The third, revealed in the full light, was a boy of some fourteen or fifteen years, well dressed and with the air of a gentleman.

"This gentleman came to the station a half hour ago," said the policeman, indicating the stranger, "with a story of finding a lady on his own grounds, and we thought from his description it was the one you're looking for."

Barron directed on the youth a glance that would have pried open the lips of the Sphinx.

"What does she look like? Where is she?"

"She's in our garden," said the boy, "under some trees. She looks tall and has on black clothes, and has dark red hair and a very white face."

Mrs. Garcia gave a loud cry from the background.

"It's Mariposa sure," she screamed. "Is she alive?"

"Alive!" echoed the youth. "Oh, yes, she's quite alive, but I don't know whether she's exactly in her right mind. She's sort of queer."

Barron had brushed past him into the streaming night.

"Come on," he shouted back. "Good Lord, come quick!"

At the foot of the zigzag stairs he saw the two gleaming lights of a hack. With the other men clattering at his heels, he dashed down the steps, and was in it, chafing and swearing, while they were fumbling for the latch of the gate.

As the boy, after giving the coachman an address, scrambled in beside him, he said peremptorily:

"When did you find her? Tell me everything."

"About two hours ago. My dog found her. I live, I and my mother, on the slope of Russian Hill. It's quite a big place with a lot of trees. I went down to get Jack (that's my dog) at the vet's, where he's been for a week, and I was bringing him home. When we got to the top of the steps he began sniffing round and barking, and then he ran to a place where there's a little sort of bunch of fir-trees and barked and jumped round, and went in among the trees. I followed him to see what was up, and all of a sudden I heard some one say from under the trees: 'Oh, it's only a dog.' I was scared and ran into the house and got a lamp, and when I came out with my mother, and we went in among the trees, there was a woman in there, who was lying on the ground. When she saw us she sort of sat up, as if she'd been asleep, and said: 'Is it Sunday yet?' We saw her distinctly; she was staring right at us. She didn't look as if she was crazy, but we both thought she was. She was terribly white. We knew she couldn't be drunk, because she was like a lady—she spoke that way."

"And then—and then," said Barron, "what did she do?"

"She said again, 'It isn't Sunday yet?' and mother said, 'No, not yet,' and we went away. I ran to the police office, but we left one of the Chinamen to watch so she wouldn't get away, 'cause we didn't know what was the matter with her. We'll be there in a minute now. It isn't far."

The hack, which had been rattling round corners at top speed, now began to ascend. Barron could see the gaunt flank of Russian Hill looming above them, with here and there a house hanging to a ridge or balanced on a slope. The lights of the town dropped away on their right in a series of sparkling terraces.

"Do you guess it's the lady you're hunting?" said the policeman politely.

"I'm almost certain it is," answered Barron. "Can't you make this man go faster?"

"The hill's pretty steep here," said the guardian of the city's peace. "I don't seem to think he could do it."

"We're almost there," said the boy; "it's just that house where the aloe is—there on the top of that high wall."

Barron looked in the direction, and saw high above them, on the top of a wall like the rampart of a fortress, the faint outline of a house and the black masses of trees etched against the only slightly paler sky.

"I don't see any aloe," he growled; "is that the house you mean?"

"That's it," said the boy. "I guess it's too dark for the aloe to-night."

With a scrambling and jolting the horses began what appeared an even steeper climb than that of the block before. The beasts seemed to dig their hoofs into the crevices between the cobbles and to clamber perilously up. With an oath Barron kicked open the door and sprang out.

"Come on, boy," he shouted. "I can't stand this snail of a carriage any longer." And he set out running up the hill.

The boy, who was light of foot and young, kept up with him, but the two heavier men, who had followed, were left behind, puffing and blowing in the darkness.

Suddenly the great wall, at the base of which they ran, was crossed by a flight of stairs that made two oblique stripes across its face.

"Up the stairs," said the boy.

And Barron, without reply, turned and began the ascent at the same breakneck speed.

"You may as well let me go first," gasped his conductor from behind him. "You don't know the way, and you might scare the Chinaman. He said he had a gun."

Barron stood aside for him to pass and then followed the nimble figure as it darted up the second flight. The boy was evidently nearing the top, when he sang out:

"Ah, there, Lee! It's me coming back."

There was an unmistakable Chinese guttural from somewhere, and then Barron himself rose above the stair-top. A black mass of garden lay before him, with the bulk of a large house a short distance back. Many windows were lit, and in one he saw a woman standing. Their light fell out over the garden, barring it with long rectangular stripes of brilliance. The wild bark of the dog rose from the house and on the unseen walk the Chinaman's footsteps could be heard crunching the pebbles.

"Is she there yet, Lee?" said the boy in a hissing whisper.

The Chinaman's affirmative grunt rose from the darkness of massed trees, into which his footsteps continued to retreat.

"This way," said his conductor to Barron. "But hang it all, it's so dark we can't see.

"Where is she?" said Barron. "Never mind the light. Show me where she is. Mariposa!" he said suddenly, in a voice which, though low, had a quality so thrilling it might have penetrated the ear of death.

The garden, rain-swept and rustling, grew quiet.

The sound of the Chinaman's footsteps ceased, even the panting breath of the boy was suddenly suspended.

In this moment of pause, when nature seemed to quell her riot to listen, a woman's voice, sweet and soft, rose out of impenetrable darkness:

"Who called me?"

The sound broke the agony that had congealed Barron's heart. With a shout he answered:

"It's I, dearest. Where are you? Come to me."

The voice rose again, faint, but with joy in it.

"Oh, have you come—have you come, at last!"

He made a rush forward into the blackness before him. At the same moment the two men rose, spent and breathless, from the stairs. The boy was behind Barron, and they behind the boy.

"Where are you? Where are you?" they heard him cry, as he crashed forward through shrubs and flower beds.

Then suddenly the policeman drew the small lantern he had carried from beneath his cape and shot the slide. A cube of clear, steady light cut through the inky wall in front of them. For a second they all stopped, the man sending the cylinder of radiance over the shrubs and trees in swift sweeps. In one of these it crossed a white face, quivered and rested on it. Barron gave a wild cry and rushed forward.

She was, as the boy described, crouched under a clump of small fir-trees, the lower limbs of which had been removed. The place was sheltered from observation from the house and the intrusion of the elements. As the light fell on her she was kneeling, evidently having been drawn to that posture by Barron's voice. The light revealed her as hatless, with loosened hair, her face pinched, her eyes large and wild.

As she saw Barron she shrieked and tried to move forward, but was unable to and held out her arms. He was at her side in a moment, his arms about her, straining her to him, his lips, between frantic kisses, saying words only for him and for her.

The policeman, with a soft ejaculation, turned the lantern, and its cube of light fell into the heart of a bed of petunias; then the two men and the boy stood looking at it silently for a space.

Presently they heard Barron say: "Come, we must go. I must take you home at once. Turn the light this way, please."

The light came back upon her. She was on her feet, holding to him.

"Is it Sunday yet?" she said, looking at them with an affrighted air.

"That's what she keeps asking all the time," said the boy in a whisper.

"No," said Barron, "it's Friday. What do you expect on Sunday?"

"Only Friday," she said, hanging back. "I thought I'd hide here till Sunday was over."

Without answering, he put his arm about her and drew her forward. At the steps she hesitated again, and he lifted her and carried her down, the policeman preceding with the lantern. The men helped him into the carriage, not saying much, while the boy stood with his now liberated dog at the top of the steps and shouted, "Good night." Barron hardly spoke to any of them. A vague thought crossed his mind that he would go to see the boy some day and thank him.

She lay with her head on his shoulder, and as the carriage passed the first lamp of the route he leaned forward eagerly to scan her face. It was haggard, white and thin, as by a long illness. He could not speak for a moment, could only hold her in his arms as if thus to wind her round with the symbol of his love.

Presently she groaned, and he said:

"Are you suffering?"

"Yes," she murmured; "always now. I am sick. I don't breathe well any more. It hurts in my chest all the time."

"Why did you hide under those trees?" he asked.

"I was too sick to go any farther. I wanted to hide somewhere, to get away from it all, and anyway, till Sunday was over. It was all to be published on Sunday, you know. Everything was ruined. My voice was gone, too. I saw those steps in the dark and climbed up and crept under the trees. I was terribly tired, and it was very quiet up there. I don't remember much more."

As the light of another lamp flashed through the window he could not bear to look at her, but tightened his arms about her and bowed his face on her wet head.

"Oh God, dearest," he whispered, "there can't be any hell worse than what I've been in for the last two days."

She made no response, but lay passively against him.

When the carriage stopped at the Garcia gate, and he told her they were home, she made no attempt to move, and he saw she was unconscious.

He lifted her out and carried her up the steps. The door opened as he ascended and revealed the Garcia family in the aperture.

"Is she dead?" screamed young Mrs. Garcia, as she saw the limp figure in his arms.

"No, but sick. You must get a doctor at once."

"Oh, how awful she looks!" cried the young woman as she caught sight of the white face against his shoulder. "What are you going to do with her?"

"Take her upstairs now, and then get a doctor and get her cured, and when she's well, marry her."

EPILOGUE

CHAPTER I

THE PRIMA DONNA

"And thou
Beside me singing in the wilderness."
—OMAR KHAYYAM.

The plant of the Silver Star Mine lay scattered along the edge of a mountain river on the site of one of the camps of forty-nine. Where the pioneers had scratched the surface with their picks, their successors had torn wounds in the Sierra's mighty flank. Where once the miners' shouts had broken the quiet harmonies of stirred pine boughs, and singing river, the throb of engines now beat on the air, thick with the dust, noisy with the strife of toiling men.

It was a morning in the end of May. The mountain wall was dark against the rising sun; tall fir and giant pine stood along its crest in inky silhouette thrown out by a background of gold leaf. Here and there, far and aërial in the clear, cool dawn, a white peak of the high Sierra floated above the shadows, a rosy pinnacle. The air was chill and faintly touched with woodland odors. The expectant hush of Nature awaiting the miracle of sunrise, held this world of huge, primordial forms, grouped in colossal indifference round the swarm of men who delved in its rock-ribbed breast.

In the stillness the camp's awakening movements rose upon the morning air with curious distinctness. Through the blue shadows in which it swam the tall chimneys soared aloft, sending their feathers of smoke up to the new day. It lay in its hollow like a picture, all transparent washes of amethyst and gray, overlaid by clear mountain shadows. The world was in this waiting stage of flushed sky and shaded earth when the superintendent's wife pushed open the door of her house and with the cautious tread of one who fears to wake a sleeper, stepped out on the balcony.

With her hand on the rail she stood, deeply inhaling the freshness of the hour. The superintendent's house, a one-story cottage, painted white, and skirted by a broad balcony, stood on an eminence above the camp. From its front steps she looked down on the slant of many roofs, the car tracks, and the red wagon roads that wound along the slopes. Raising her eyes, they swept the ramparts of the everlasting hills, and looking higher still, her face met the radiance of the dawn.

She stepped off the balcony with the same cautious tread, and along the beaten footpath that led through the patch of garden in front of the house. Beyond this the path wound through a growth of chaparral to where the pines ascended the slopes in climbing files. As she approached she saw the sky barred with their trunks, arrow-straight and bare of branches to a great height. Farther on she could see the long dim aisles, held in the cloistral silence of the California forest, shot through with the golden glimmer of sunrise.

The joy of the morning was in her heart, and she walked forward with a light step, humming to herself.

Two months before she had come here, a bride from San Francisco, weak from illness, pale, hollow-eyed, a shadow of her former self. She had only crept about at first, swung for hours on the balcony in her hammock, or sat under the trees looking down on the hive of men, where her husband worked among his laborers. As her mother had grown back to the fullness of life in the healing breath of the mountains, so Mariposa slowly regained her old beauty, with an added touch of subtlety, and found her old beliefs returned to her with a new significance.

To-day she had awakened with the first glimmer of dawn, and stirred by a sudden desire for the air of the morning on her face and in her lungs, had stolen up and out. Breathing in the resinous atmosphere a new influx of life seemed to run like sap along her limbs, and lend her step the buoyancy of a wood-nymph's. Her eye lingered with a look that was a caress on flower and tree and shrub. The song she had been humming passed from tune to words, and she sang softly as she brushed through the chaparral, snipping off a leaf, bending to pluck a wild flower, pausing to admire the glossy green of a manzanita bush. Under the shadow of the pines she halted by a rugged trunk, a point of vantage she had early discovered, and leaning her hand on the bark, surveyed the wild prospect.

The sense of expectancy in the air seemed intensified. The quivering radiance of pink and gold pulsed up the sky from a point of concentration which every moment brightened. The blue shadows in the camp grew thinner, the little wisps of mist that hung over the river more threadlike and phantasmal. A throwback to unremembered days came suddenly upon her with a mysterious sense of familiarity. She seemed to be repeating a dear, long dead experience. The vision and the dream of days of exquisite well-being, carefree, cherished, were with her again. Faint recurring glimpses of such mornings, strong of balsam of pine and fir, musical with the sleepy murmur of a river, serene and sweet with an enfolding passion of love in which she rested secure, rose out of the dim places of memory. The perfect content of her childhood spoke to her across the gulf of years, finding itself repeated in her womanhood. The old joy in living, the old thrill of wonder and mystery, the old sense of safety in a surrounding, watchful love, were hers once more.

The song on her lips passed from its absent undertone to notes gradually full and fuller. It was the aria from "Mignon," and, as she stood, her hand on the tree trunk, looking down into the swimming shadows of the camp, it swelled outward in tones strong and rich, vibrating with their lost force.

Pervaded by a sense of dreamy happiness, she at first failed to notice the unexpected volume of sound. Then, as note rose upon note, welling from her chest with the old-time, vibrant facility, as she felt once again the uplifting sense of triumph possess her, she realized what it meant. Dropping her hand from the tree trunk she stood upright, and facing the dawn, with squared shoulders and raised chin, let her voice roll out into the void before her.

The song swelled triumphant like a hymn of some pagan goddess to the rising sun. In the stillness of the dawn-hush, with the columns of the monumental pines behind her, the mountain wall and the glowing sky in front, she might have been the spirit of youth and love chanting her joy in a primeval world.

When the last note had died away she stood for a moment staring before her. Then suddenly she wheeled, and, catching up her skirts with one hand, ran back toward the house, brushing between the tree trunks and through the chaparral with breathless haste. As she emerged from the thicket, she saw her husband, in his rough mining clothes, standing on the top step of the balcony.

"Gam," she cried, "Gam!"

He started, saw her, and then waited smiling as she came running up the garden path toward him, the blaze of the sky behind her, her face alight with life and color.

"Why, dearest, I didn't know what had happened to you," he cried. "Where did you go?"

Her unslackened speed carried her up the stairs and into his arms. Standing on the step below him she flung hers round his shoulders, and holding him tight, said breathlessly:

"What do you think has happened?"

"You met a bear in the wood."

"My voice has come back."

The two pairs of eyes, the woman's looking up, the man's down, gazed deeply into each other. There was a moment of silence, the silence of people who are still unused to and a little overawed by their happiness.

"I heard you," he said.

"You did? From here?"

"Yes. I heard some one singing and stood here listening, watching the light coming up."

"Was it good?" she asked, anxiously.

"Very. I had never heard you sing before. You're a prima donna."

"That's what I was going to be. You remember hearing us talking about it at the Garcias'?"

He nodded, looking down at the face where health was coming back in delicate degrees of coral to lips and cheeks.

"And it really did sound good?" she queried again.

"Lovely."

"Quite soft and full, not harsh and with all the sound of music gone out of it?"

"Not a bit. It was fine."

She continued to hold him around the shoulders, but her eyes dropped away from his, which regarded her with immovable earnestness, touched by a slight, tender humor. She appeared to become suddenly thoughtful.

"You can be a prima donna still," he said.

"Yes," she answered, nodding slightly. "I suppose I can."

"And it's a great career."

"Yes, a splendid career."

"You travel everywhere and make a fortune."

"If you're a success."

"Oh, you'd be a success all right."

She drew away from him, letting one hand rest on his shoulder. Her face had grown serious. She looked disappointed.

"Well, do you *want* me to be a prima donna?" she asked, looking at her hand.

He continued to regard her without answering, the gleam of amusement dying out of his eyes.

"Of course," she added in a small voice, "if you've set your heart on it, I will."

"What do you think about it yourself?" he asked.

She gave him a swift, side look, just a raising and dropping of the lashes.

"Say what you think first," she coaxed.

"Well, then, I will."

He put his two hands suddenly on her shoulders, big, bronzed hands, hard and muscular, that seemed to seize upon her delicate flesh with a master's grip.

"Look at me," he commanded.

She obeyed. The gray eyes held hers like a magnet.

"I think no. You don't belong to the public, you belong to me."

The color ran up into her face to the edge of her hair.

"Oh, Gam," she whispered on a rising breath, "I'm so relieved."

He dropped his hands from her shoulders and drew her close to him. With his cheek against hers he said softly:

"You didn't think I was that kind of a fool, did you?"

The sun had risen as they talked, at first slowly peering with a radiant eye over the mountain's shoulder, then shaking itself free of tree-top and rock-point, and swimming up into the blue. The top of the range stood all glowing and golden, with here and there a white peak, snowily enameled. The rows of pines were overlaid with a rosy brilliance, their long shadows slanting down the slopes as if scurrying away from the flood of heat and light. The clear blues and amethysts that veiled the hollow of the camp were dispersed; the films of mist melted; a quivering silvery sparkle played over the river shallows.

In the clearing beams the life of the hive below seemed to swarm and fill the air with the clamor of its awakening. The man and woman, looking down, saw the toiling world turning to its day's work—the red dust rising beneath grinding hoof and wheel, the cars sliding swiftly on their narrow tracks, heard the shouts of men, the hum of machinery, and through all and over all, the regular throb of the engines like the heart which animated this isolated world of labor.

Barron looked at his domain for an attentive moment.

"There," he said, pointing down, "is where I belong. That's my life,—to work in wild places with men. And yours is with me, my prima donna. We go together, side by side, I working and you singing by the way."